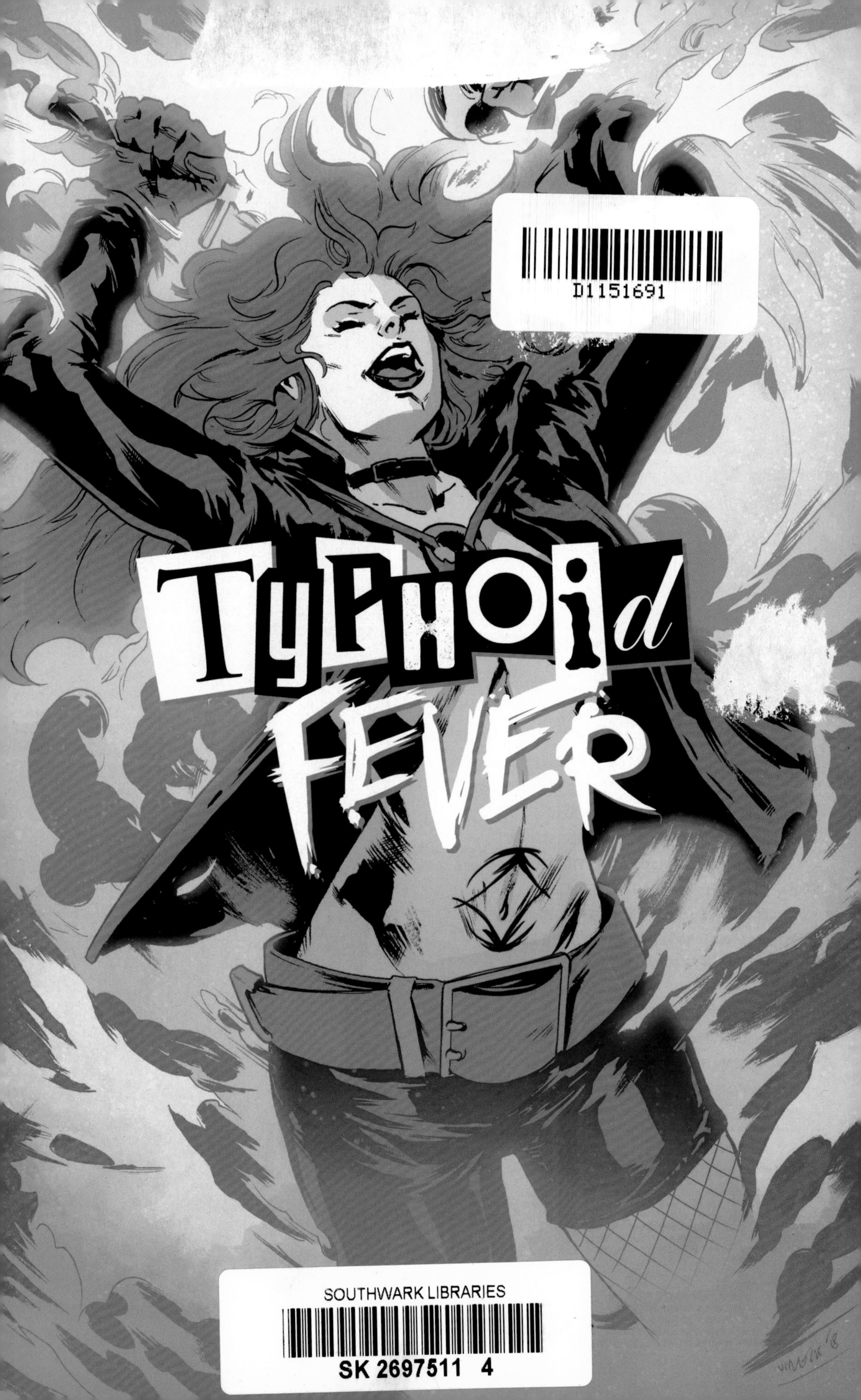
TYPHOID
FEVER

Collection Editor: **JENNIFER GRÜNWALD**

Assistant Editor: **CAITLIN O'CONNELL**

Associate Managing Editor: **KATERI WOODY**

Editor, Special Projects: **MARK D. BEAZLEY**

VP Production & Special Projects: **JEFF YOUNGQUIST**

SVP Print, Sales & Marketing: **DAVID GABRIEL**

Book Designer: **JEFF POWELL**

Editor in Chief: **C.B. CEBULSKI**

Chief Creative Officer: **JOE QUESADA**

President: **DAN BUCKLEY**

Executive Producer: **ALAN FINE**

TYPHOID FEVER. Contains material originally published in magazine form as TYPHOID FEVER: SPIDER-MAN #1, X-MEN #1 and IRON FIST #1. First printing 2019. ISBN 978-1-302-91526-1. Published by MARVEL WORLDWIDE, INC., a subsidiary of MARVEL ENTERTAINMENT, LLC. OFFICE OF PUBLICATION: 135 West 50th Street, New York, NY 10020. Copyright © 2019 MARVEL No similarity between any of the names, characters, persons, and/or institutions in this magazine with those of any living or dead person or institution is intended, and any such similarity which may exist is purely coincidental. **Printed in Canada.** DAN BUCKLEY, President, Marvel Entertainment; JOHN NEE, Publisher; JOE QUESADA, Chief Creative Officer; TOM BREVOORT, SVP of Publishing; DAVID BOGART, SVP of Business Affairs & Operations, Publishing & Partnership; DAVID GABRIEL, SVP of Sales & Marketing, Publishing; JEFF YOUNGQUIST, VP of Production & Special Projects; DAN CARR, Executive Director of Publishing Technology; ALEX MORALES, Director of Publishing Operations; DAN EDINGTON, Managing Editor; SUSAN CRESPI, Production Manager; STAN LEE, Chairman Emeritus. For information regarding advertising in Marvel Comics or on Marvel.com, please contact Vit DeBellis, Custom Solutions & Integrated Advertising Manager, at vdebellis@marvel.com. For Marvel subscription inquiries, please call 888-511-5480. **Manufactured between 1/4/2019 and 2/5/2019 by SOLISCO PRINTERS, SCOTT, QC, CANADA.**

10 9 8 7 6 5 4 3 2 1

TYPHOID FEVER

WRITER
CLAY McLEOD CHAPMAN

ARTISTS
STEFANO LANDINI *(SPIDER-MAN)*
WILL ROBSON & DANILO S. BEYRUTH *(X-MEN)*
PAOLO VILLANELLI *(IRON FIST)*

COLOR ARTISTS
RACHELLE ROSENBERG WITH
DONO SÁNCHEZ-ALMARA *(X-MEN)*

LETTERER
VC'S TRAVIS LANHAM

COVER ART
R.B. SILVA &
CHRIS SOTOMAYOR

ASSISTANT EDITOR
LAUREN AMARO

EDITOR
DEVIN LEWIS

EXECUTIVE EDITOR
NICK LOWE

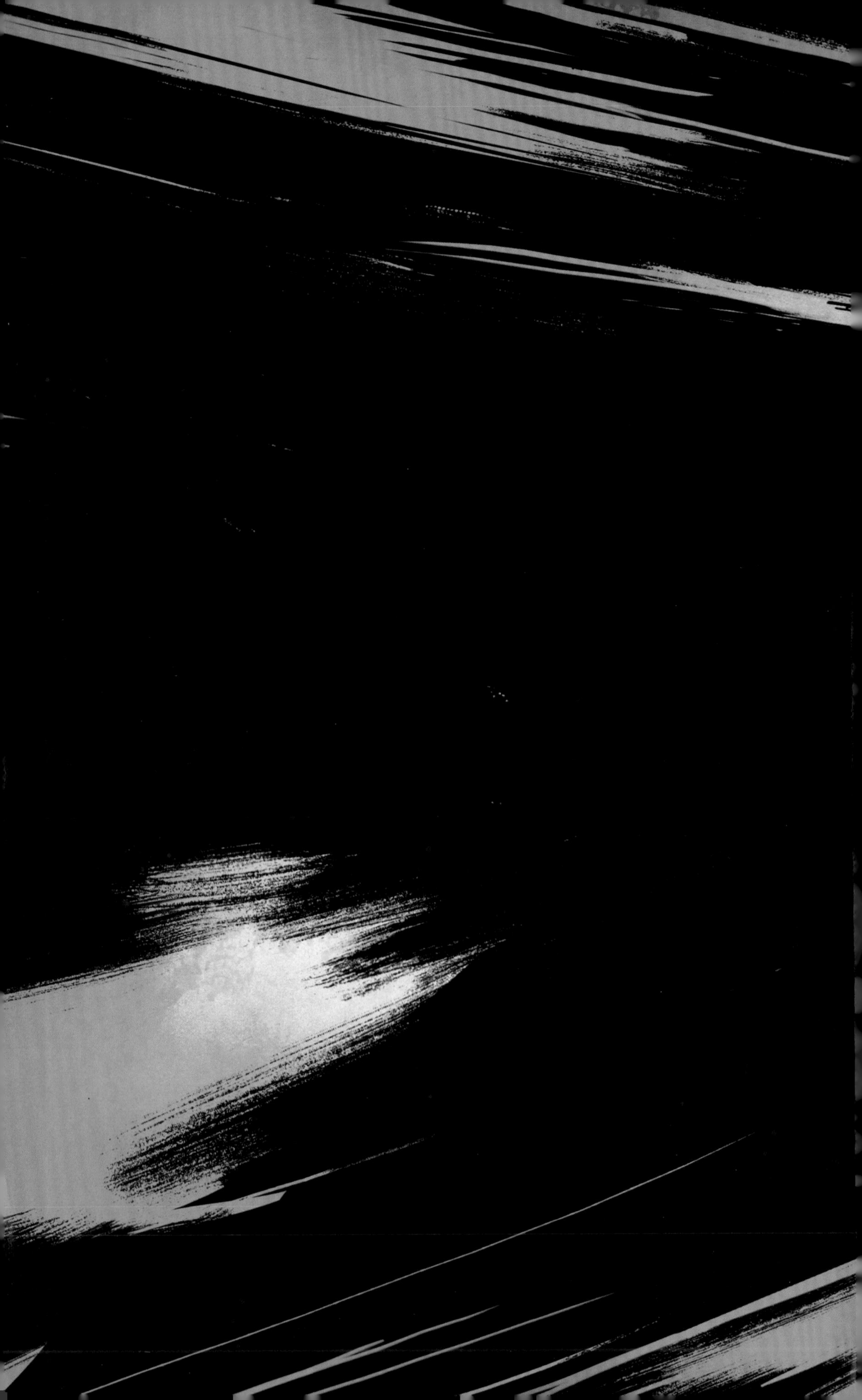

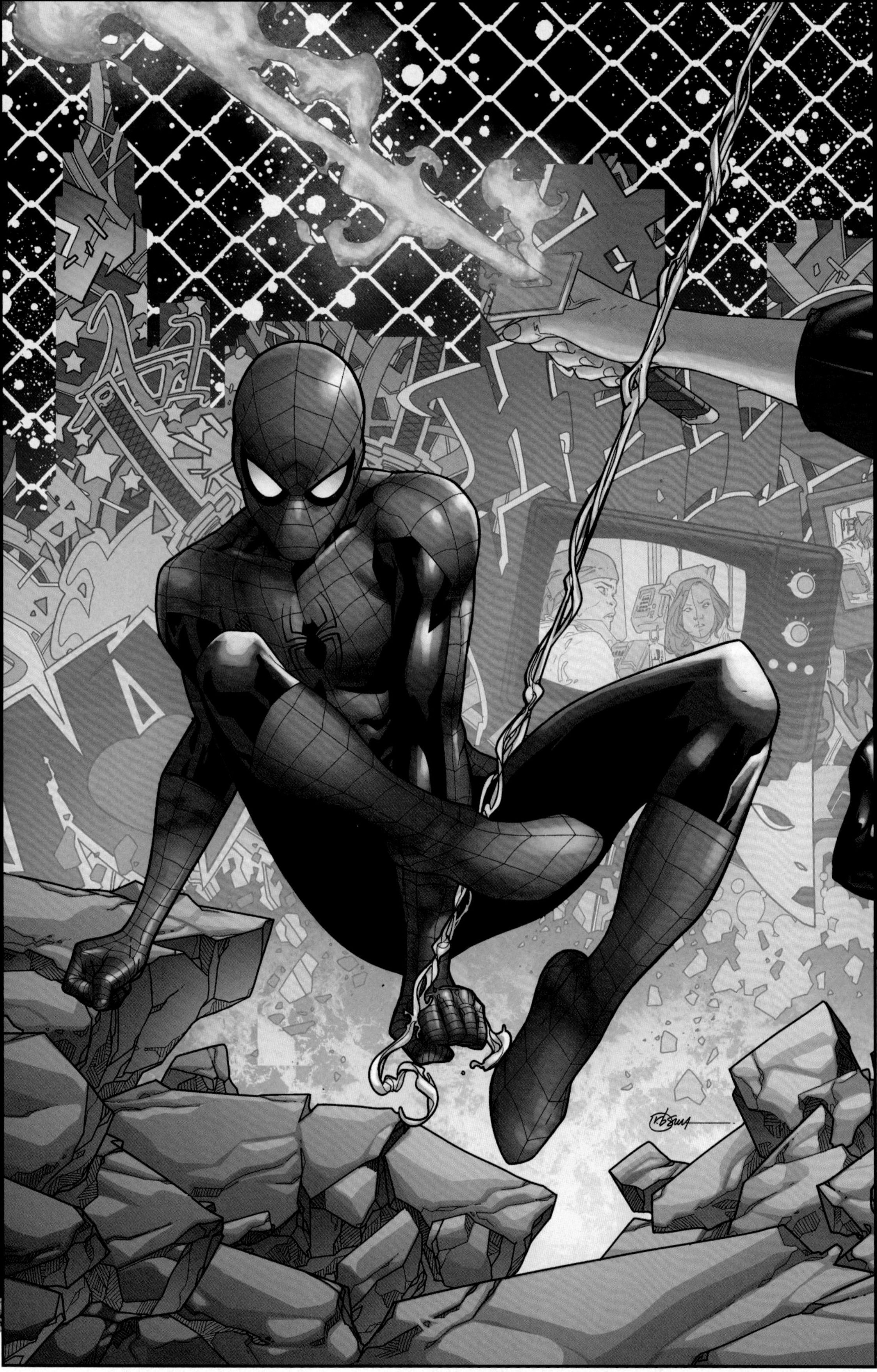

TYPHOID FEVER: SPIDER-MAN

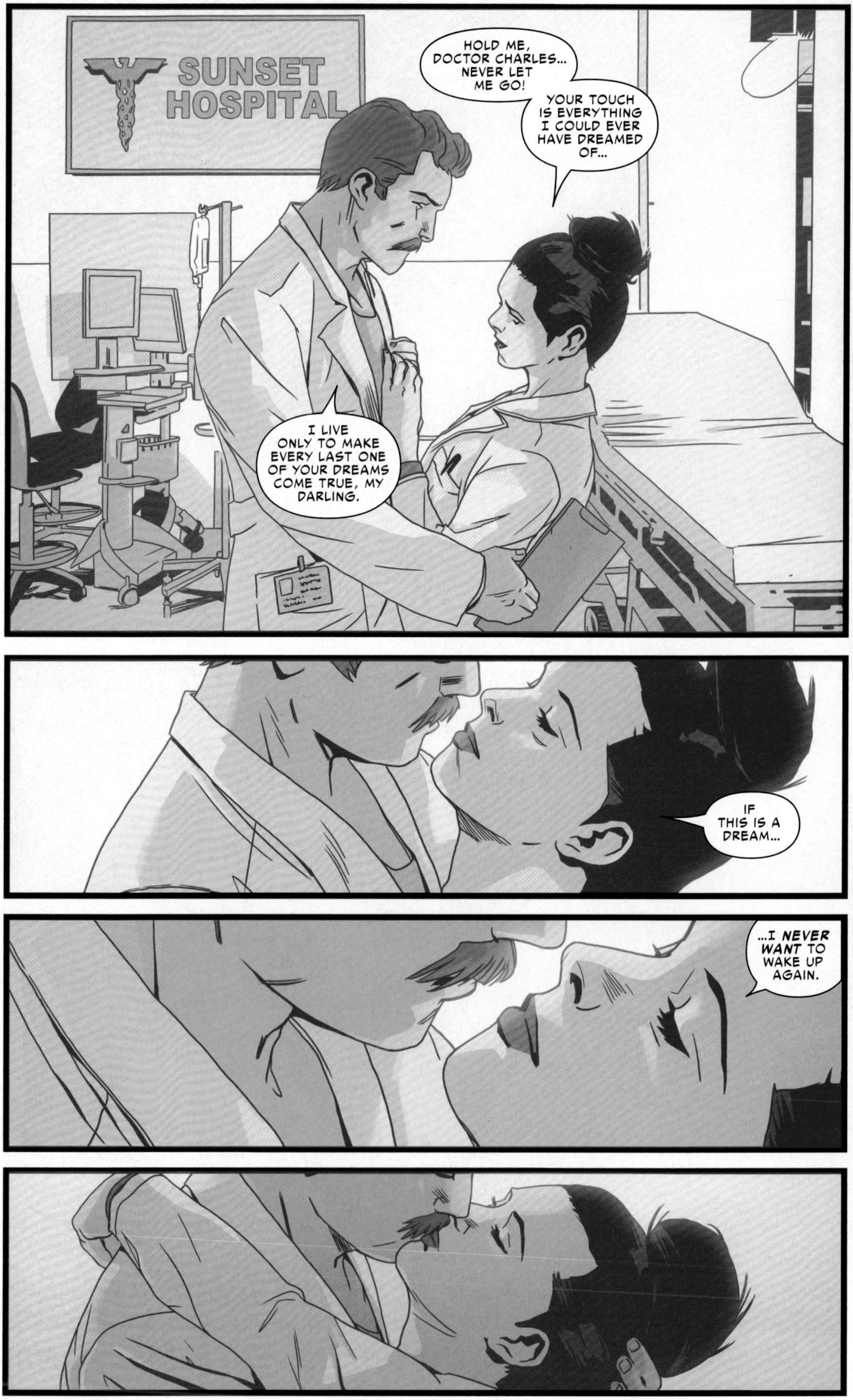
SUNSET HOSPITAL
HOLD ME, DOCTOR CHARLES... NEVER LET ME GO!
YOUR TOUCH IS EVERYTHING I COULD EVER HAVE DREAMED OF...
I LIVE ONLY TO MAKE EVERY LAST ONE OF YOUR DREAMS COME TRUE, MY DARLING.
IF THIS IS A DREAM...
...I *NEVER WANT* TO WAKE UP AGAIN.

MRRF! N-N--

NO! I... I CAN'T!

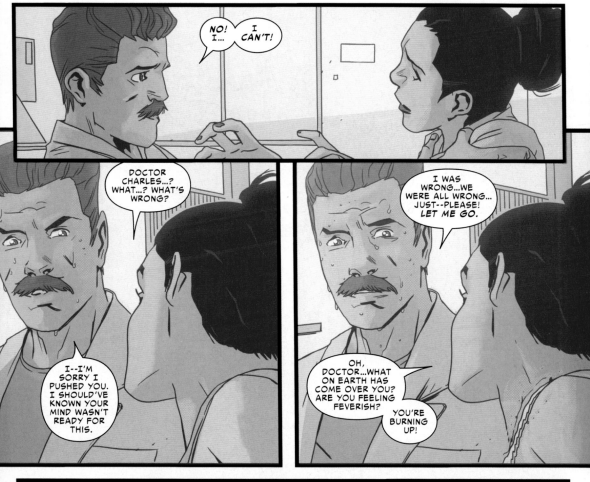

DOCTOR CHARLES...? WHAT...? WHAT'S WRONG?

I--I'M SORRY I PUSHED YOU. I SHOULD'VE KNOWN YOUR MIND WASN'T READY FOR THIS.

I WAS WRONG...WE WERE ALL WRONG... JUST--PLEASE! LET ME GO.

OH, DOCTOR...WHAT ON EARTH HAS COME OVER YOU? ARE YOU FEELING FEVERISH? YOU'RE BURNING UP!

OH...OH GOD...PLEASE NO. PLEASE DON'T...

BUT DON'T YOU SEE, MY DARLING?

PLEASE DON'T PLEASE DON'T PLEEEEEEEASE

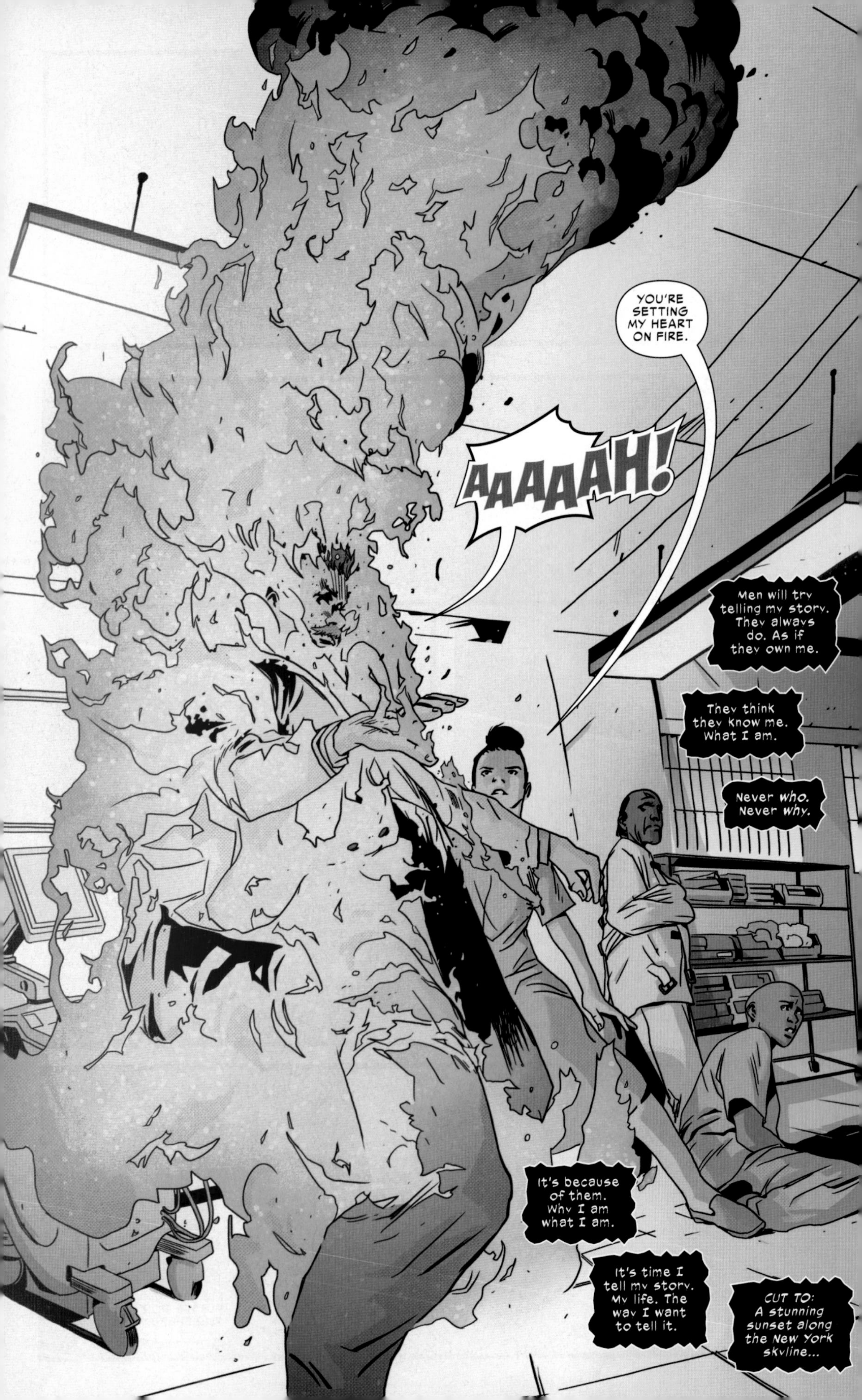

YOU'RE SETTING MY HEART ON FIRE.
AAAAAH!
Men will try telling my story. They always do. As if they own me.
They think they know me. What I am.
Never who. Never why.
It's because of them. Why I am what I am.
It's time I tell my story. My life. The way I want to tell it.
CUT TO: A stunning sunset along the New York skyline...

NEW YORK CITY.
HELL'S KITCHEN.

KRSH

EEEEEEE--

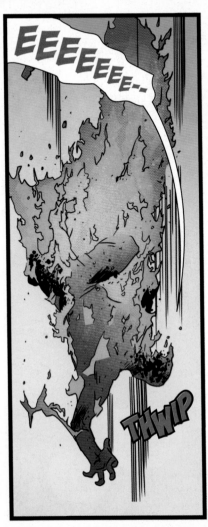

EEEEEEE--

THWIP

WUMP

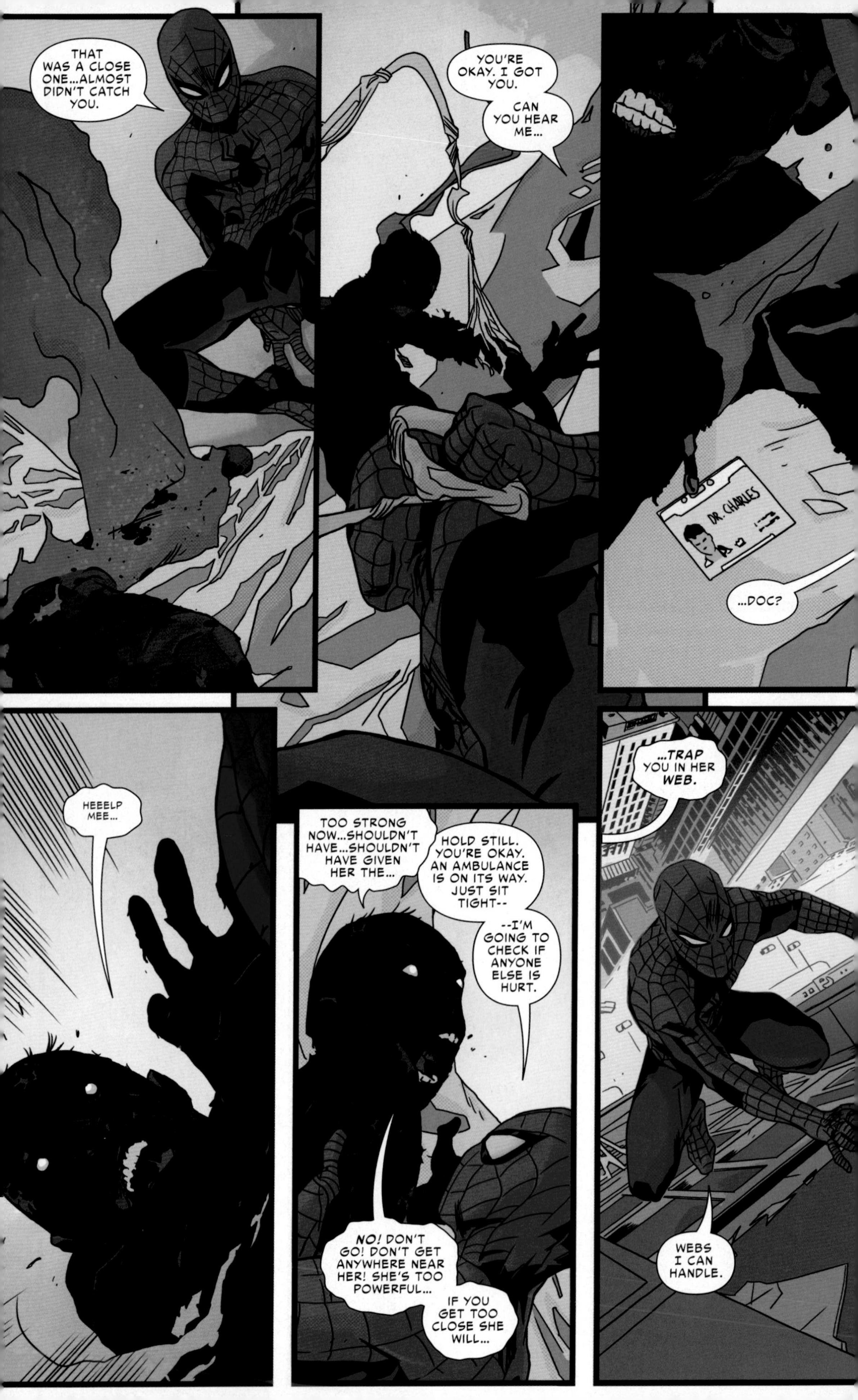
THAT WAS A CLOSE ONE...ALMOST DIDN'T CATCH YOU.
YOU'RE OKAY. I GOT YOU.
CAN YOU HEAR ME...
DR. CHARLES
...DOC?
HEEELP MEE...
TOO STRONG NOW...SHOULDN'T HAVE...SHOULDN'T HAVE GIVEN HER THE...
HOLD STILL. YOU'RE OKAY. AN AMBULANCE IS ON ITS WAY. JUST SIT TIGHT--
--I'M GOING TO CHECK IF ANYONE ELSE IS HURT.
NO! DON'T GO! DON'T GET ANYWHERE NEAR HER! SHE'S TOO POWERFUL...
IF YOU GET TOO CLOSE SHE WILL...
...TRAP YOU IN HER WEB.
WEBS I CAN HANDLE.

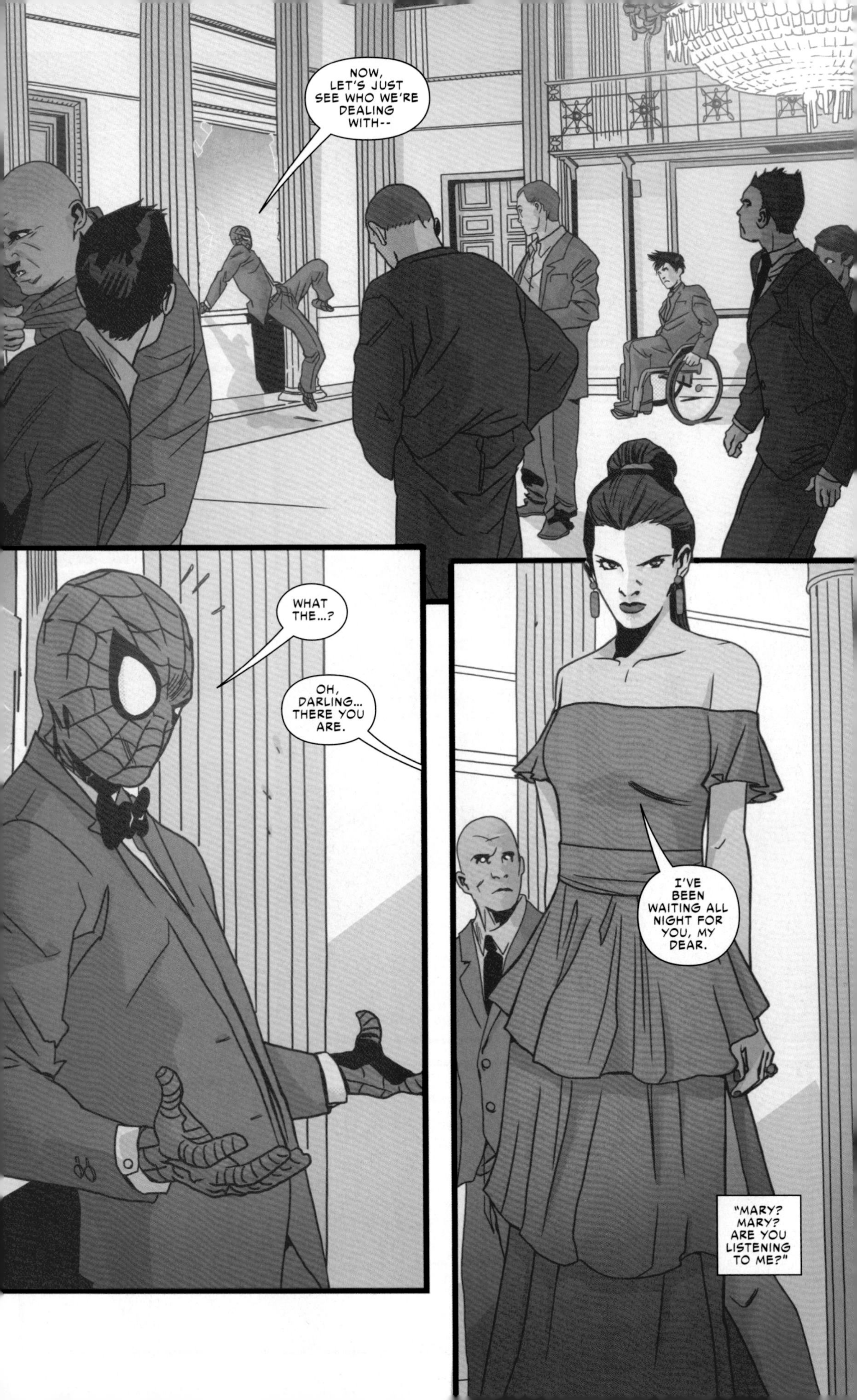
NOW, LET'S JUST SEE WHO WE'RE DEALING WITH--
WHAT THE...?
OH, DARLING... THERE YOU ARE.
I'VE BEEN WAITING ALL NIGHT FOR YOU, MY DEAR.
"MARY? MARY? ARE YOU LISTENING TO ME?"

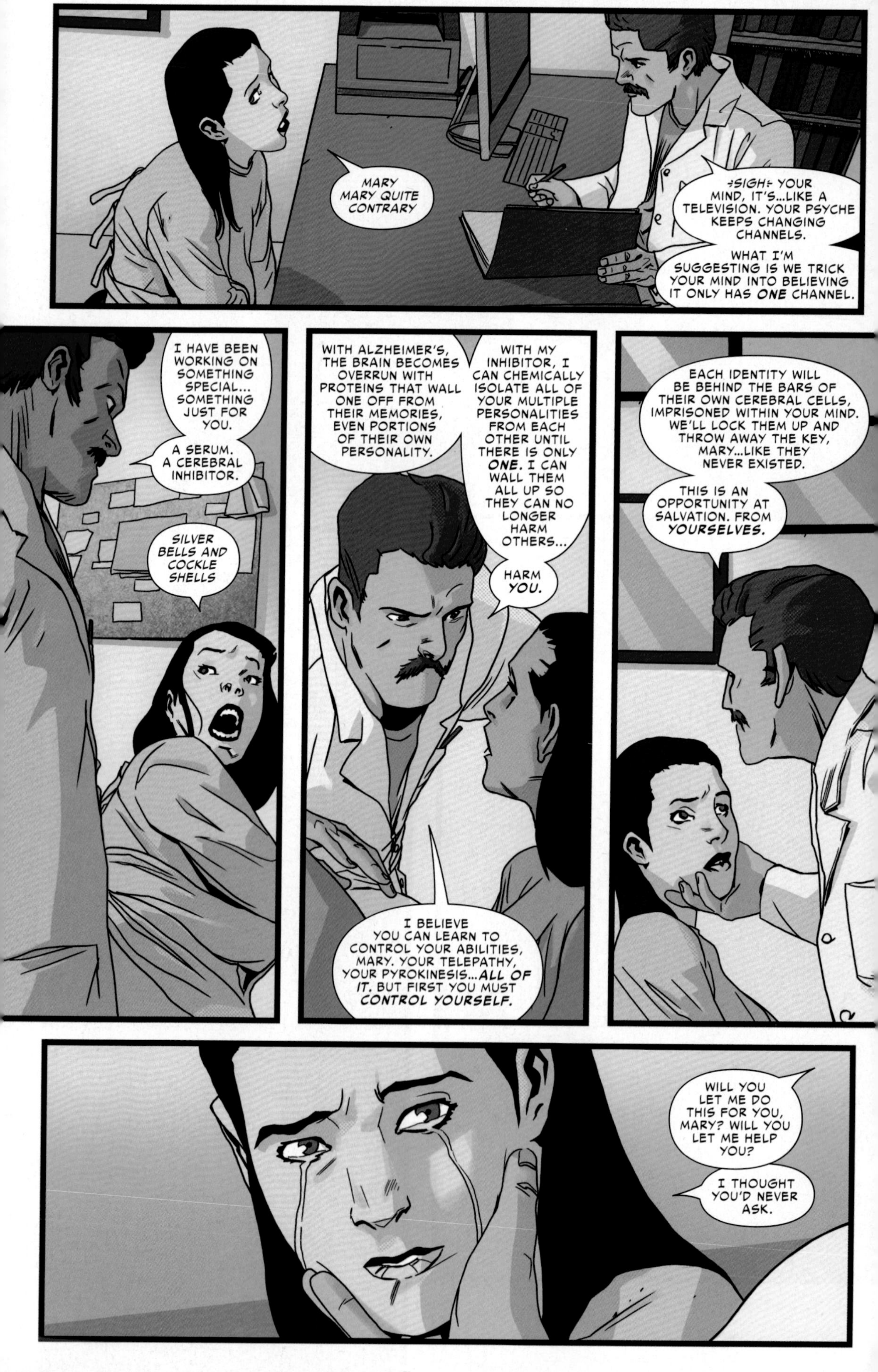
MARY MARY QUITE CONTRARY
SIGH YOUR MIND, IT'S...LIKE A TELEVISION. YOUR PSYCHE KEEPS CHANGING CHANNELS.
WHAT I'M SUGGESTING IS WE TRICK YOUR MIND INTO BELIEVING IT ONLY HAS ONE CHANNEL.
I HAVE BEEN WORKING ON SOMETHING SPECIAL... SOMETHING JUST FOR YOU.
A SERUM. A CEREBRAL INHIBITOR.
SILVER BELLS AND COCKLE SHELLS
WITH ALZHEIMER'S, THE BRAIN BECOMES OVERRUN WITH PROTEINS THAT WALL ONE OFF FROM THEIR MEMORIES, EVEN PORTIONS OF THEIR OWN PERSONALITY.
WITH MY INHIBITOR, I CAN CHEMICALLY ISOLATE ALL OF YOUR MULTIPLE PERSONALITIES FROM EACH OTHER UNTIL THERE IS ONLY ONE. I CAN WALL THEM ALL UP SO THEY CAN NO LONGER HARM OTHERS...
HARM YOU.
I BELIEVE YOU CAN LEARN TO CONTROL YOUR ABILITIES, MARY. YOUR TELEPATHY, YOUR PYROKINESIS...ALL OF IT. BUT FIRST YOU MUST CONTROL YOURSELF.
EACH IDENTITY WILL BE BEHIND THE BARS OF THEIR OWN CEREBRAL CELLS, IMPRISONED WITHIN YOUR MIND. WE'LL LOCK THEM UP AND THROW AWAY THE KEY, MARY...LIKE THEY NEVER EXISTED.
THIS IS AN OPPORTUNITY AT SALVATION. FROM YOURSELVES.
WILL YOU LET ME DO THIS FOR YOU, MARY? WILL YOU LET ME HELP YOU?
I THOUGHT YOU'D NEVER ASK.

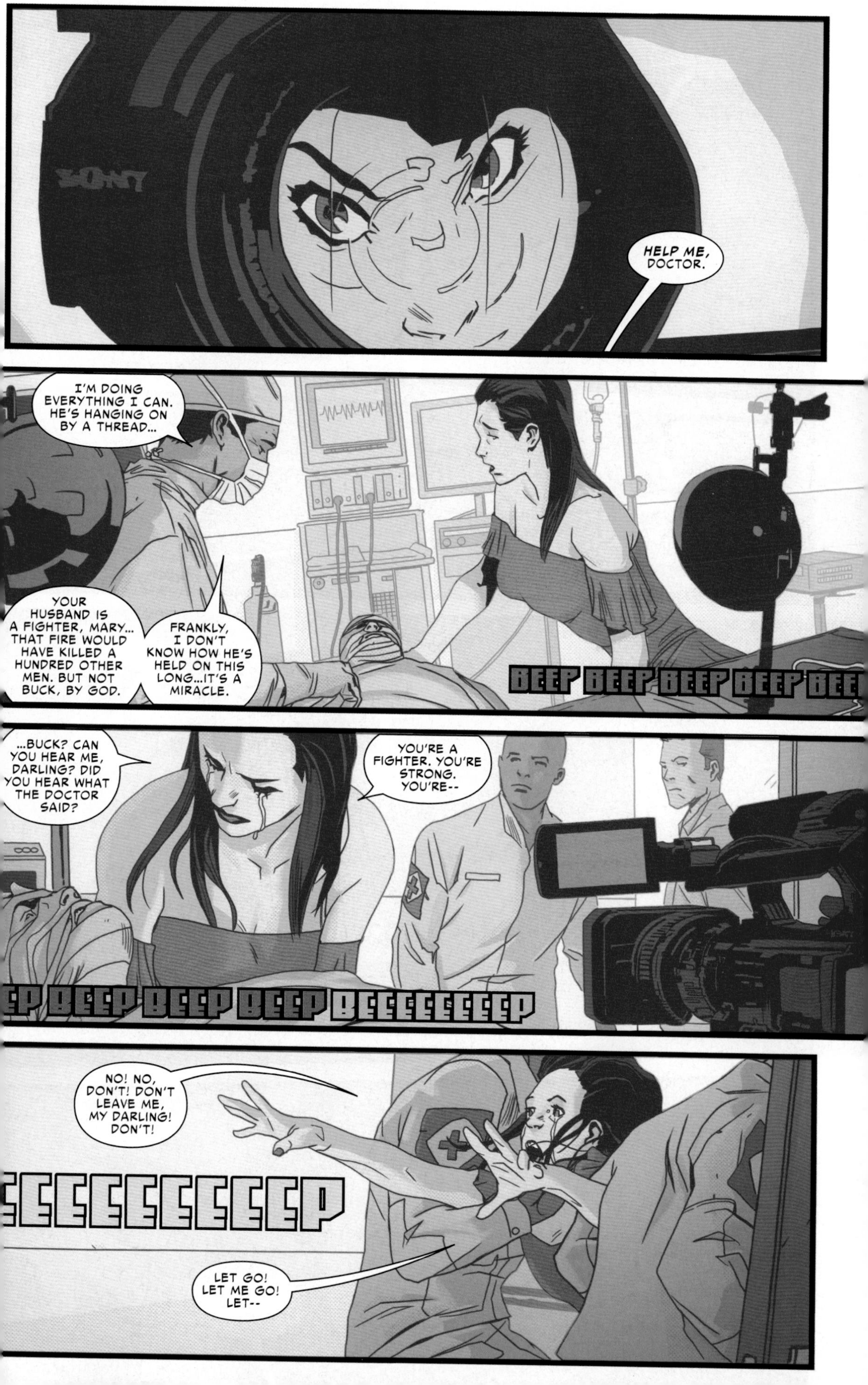
HELP ME, DOCTOR.
I'M DOING EVERYTHING I CAN. HE'S HANGING ON BY A THREAD...
YOUR HUSBAND IS A FIGHTER, MARY... THAT FIRE WOULD HAVE KILLED A HUNDRED OTHER MEN. BUT NOT BUCK, BY GOD.
FRANKLY, I DON'T KNOW HOW HE'S HELD ON THIS LONG...IT'S A MIRACLE.
BEEP BEEP BEEP BEEP BEE
...BUCK? CAN YOU HEAR ME, DARLING? DID YOU HEAR WHAT THE DOCTOR SAID?
YOU'RE A FIGHTER. YOU'RE STRONG. YOU'RE--
EP BEEP BEEP BEEP BEEEEEEEEP
NO! NO, DON'T! DON'T LEAVE ME, MY DARLING! DON'T!
EEEEEEEEEEEP
LET GO! LET ME GO! LET--

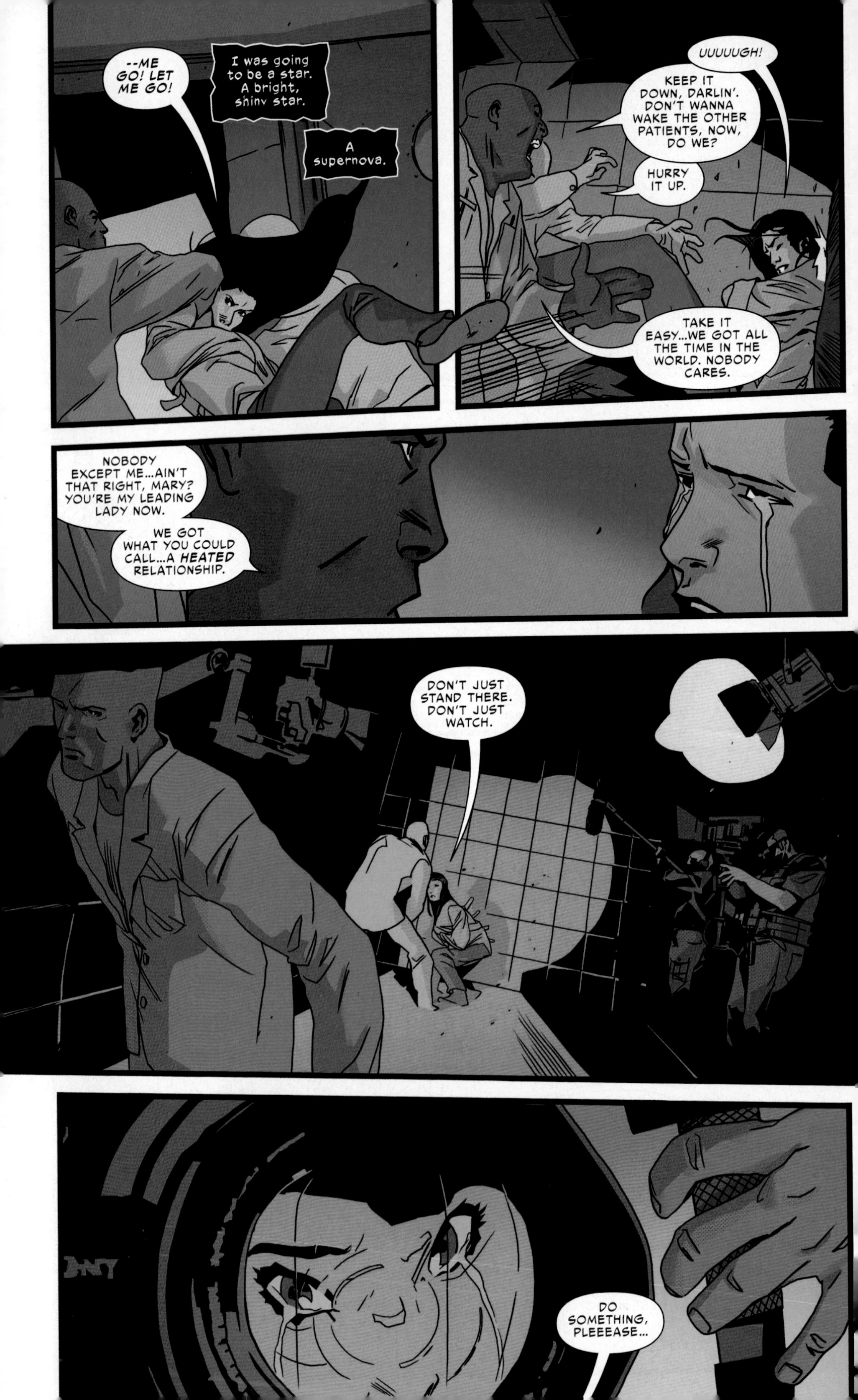
--ME GO! LET ME GO!
I was going to be a star. A bright, shiny star.
A supernova.
UUUUUGH!
KEEP IT DOWN, DARLIN'. DON'T WANNA WAKE THE OTHER PATIENTS, NOW, DO WE?
HURRY IT UP.
TAKE IT EASY...WE GOT ALL THE TIME IN THE WORLD. NOBODY CARES.
NOBODY EXCEPT ME...AIN'T THAT RIGHT, MARY? YOU'RE MY LEADING LADY NOW.
WE GOT WHAT YOU COULD CALL...A *HEATED* RELATIONSHIP.
DON'T JUST STAND THERE. DON'T JUST WATCH.
DO SOMETHING, PLEEEASE...

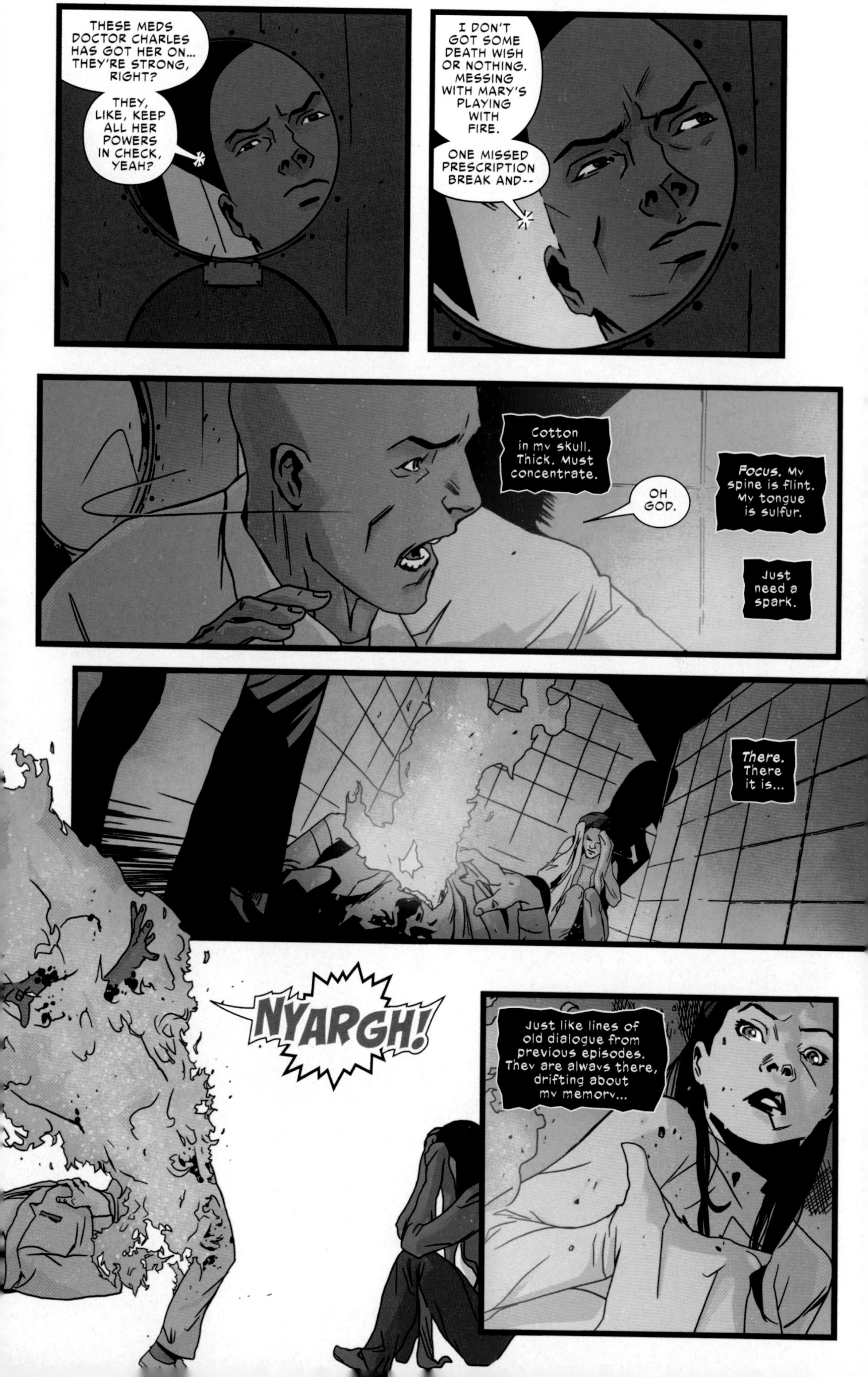
THESE MEDS DOCTOR CHARLES HAS GOT HER ON... THEY'RE STRONG, RIGHT?
THEY, LIKE, KEEP ALL HER POWERS IN CHECK, YEAH?
I DON'T GOT SOME DEATH WISH OR NOTHING. MESSING WITH MARY'S PLAYING WITH FIRE.
ONE MISSED PRESCRIPTION BREAK AND--
Cotton in my skull. Thick. Must concentrate.
OH GOD.
Focus. My spine is flint. My tongue is sulfur.
Just need a spark.
There. There it is...
NYARGH!
Just like lines of old dialogue from previous episodes. They are always there, drifting about my memory...

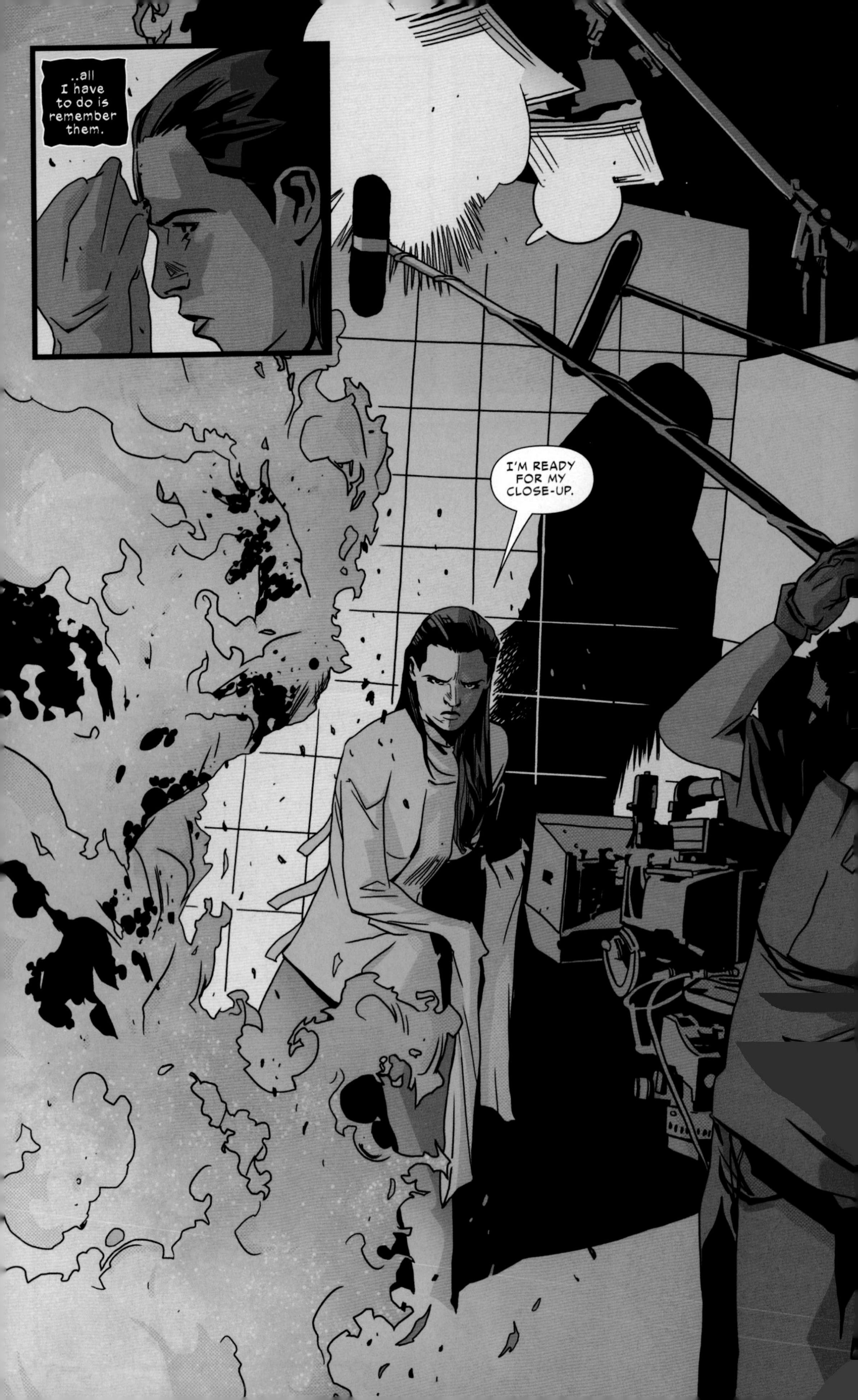
..all I have to do is remember them.
I'M READY FOR MY CLOSE-UP.

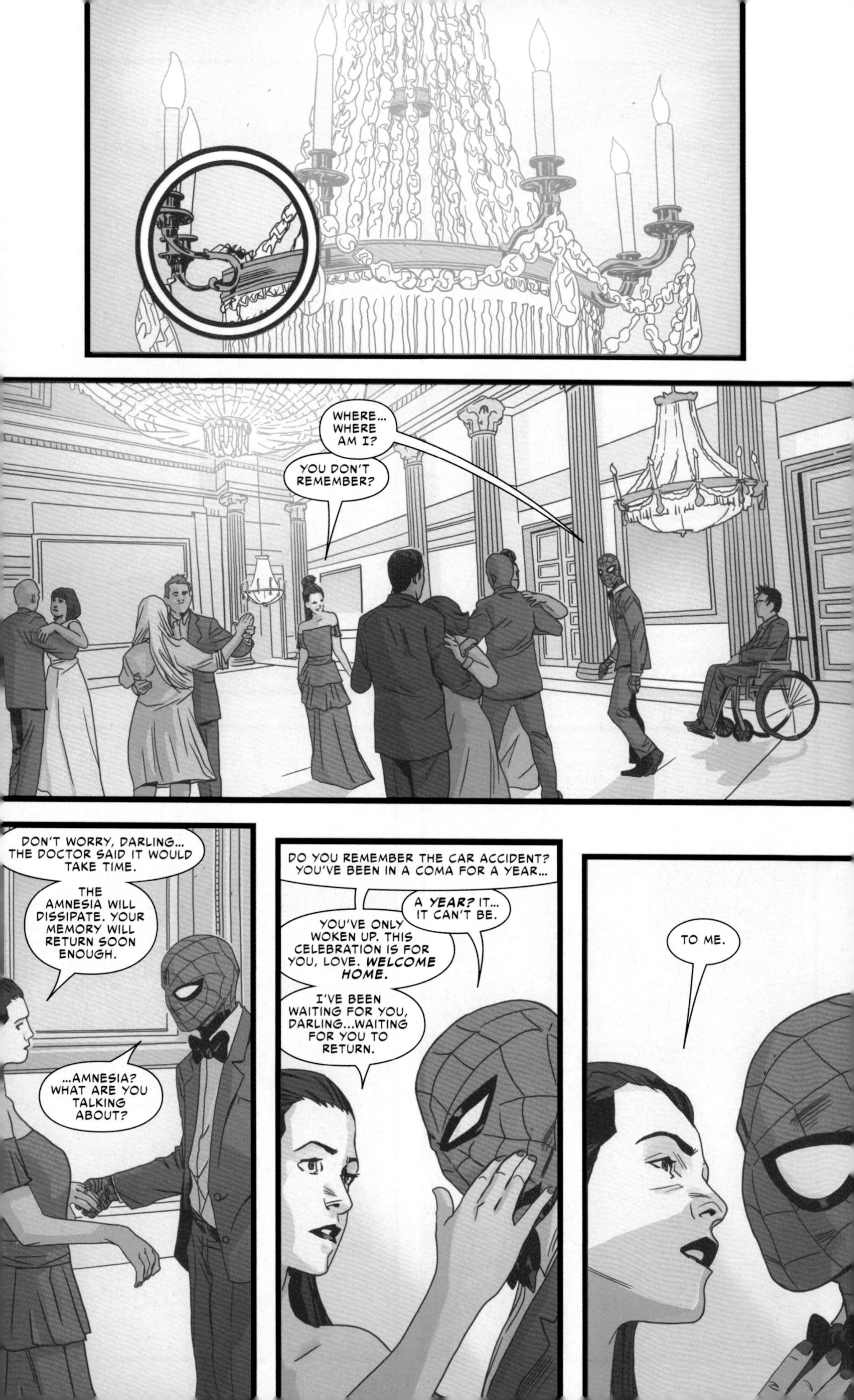
WHERE... WHERE AM I?
YOU DON'T REMEMBER?
DON'T WORRY, DARLING... THE DOCTOR SAID IT WOULD TAKE TIME.
THE AMNESIA WILL DISSIPATE. YOUR MEMORY WILL RETURN SOON ENOUGH.
...AMNESIA? WHAT ARE YOU TALKING ABOUT?
DO YOU REMEMBER THE CAR ACCIDENT? YOU'VE BEEN IN A COMA FOR A YEAR...
A *YEAR?* IT... IT CAN'T BE.
YOU'VE ONLY WOKEN UP. THIS CELEBRATION IS FOR YOU, LOVE. ***WELCOME HOME.***
I'VE BEEN WAITING FOR YOU, DARLING...WAITING FOR YOU TO RETURN.
TO ME.

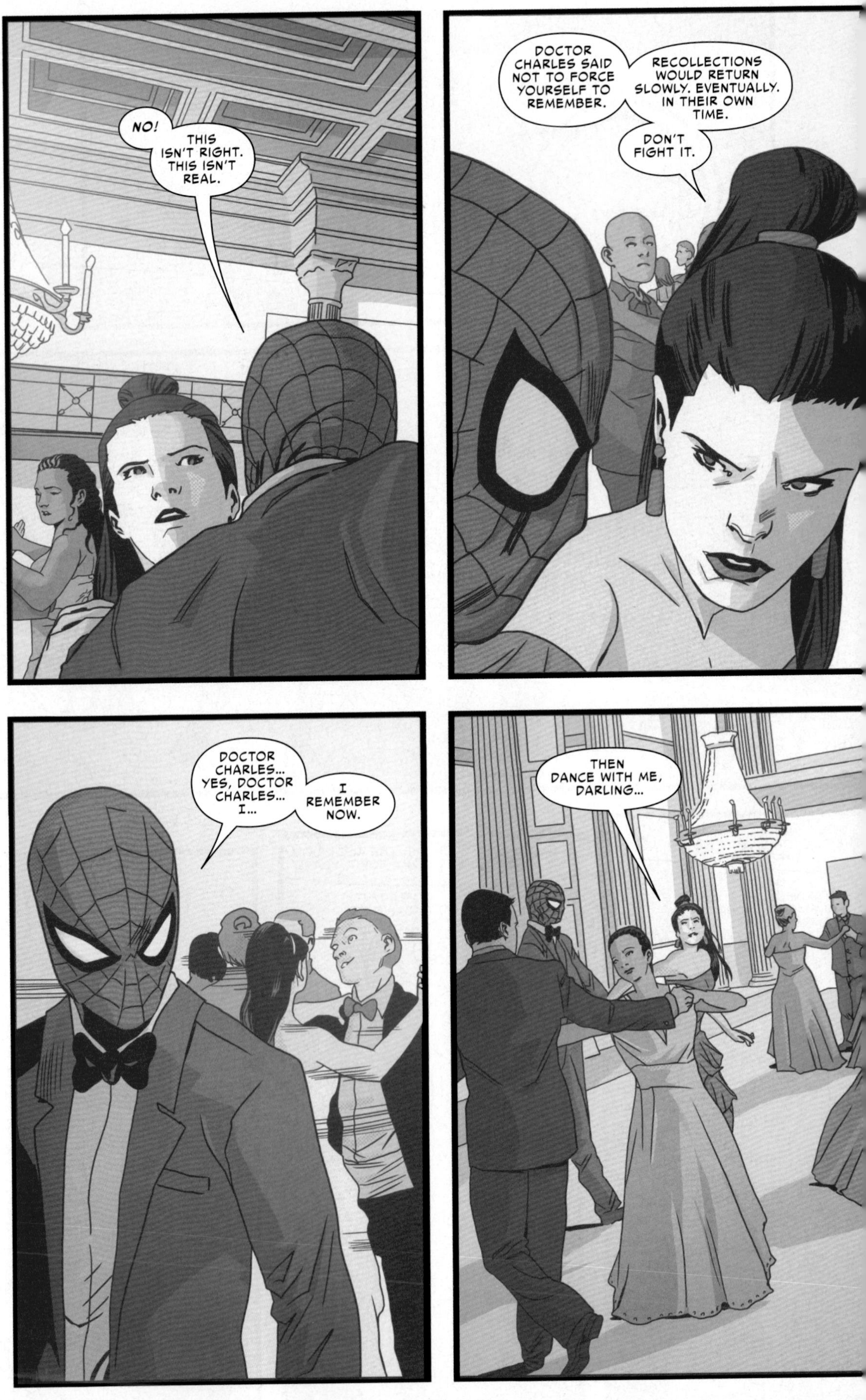
NO!
THIS ISN'T RIGHT. THIS ISN'T REAL.
DOCTOR CHARLES SAID NOT TO FORCE YOURSELF TO REMEMBER.
RECOLLECTIONS WOULD RETURN SLOWLY. EVENTUALLY. IN THEIR OWN TIME.
DON'T FIGHT IT.
DOCTOR CHARLES... YES, DOCTOR CHARLES... I...
I REMEMBER NOW.
THEN DANCE WITH ME, DARLING...

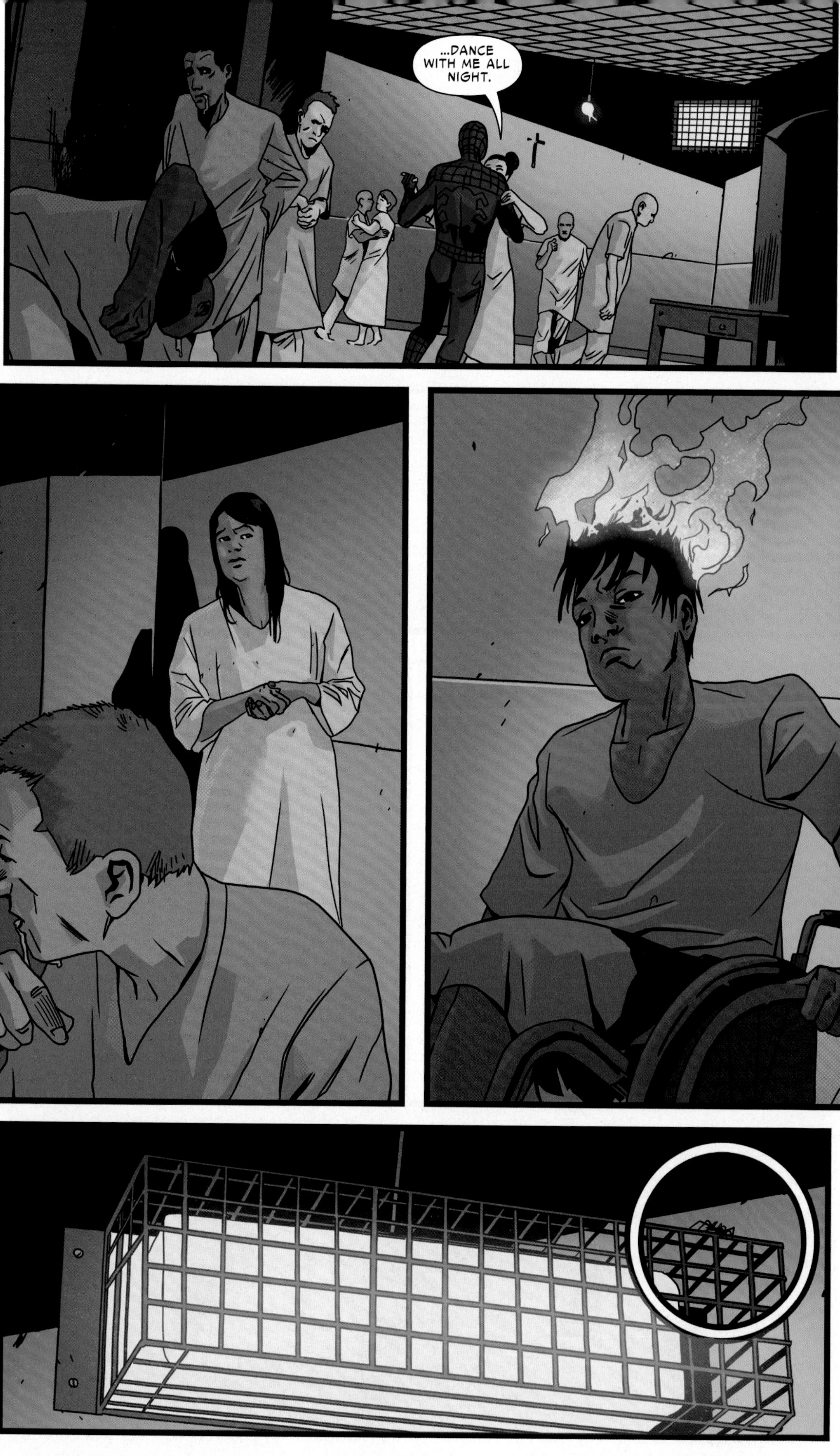
...DANCE WITH ME ALL NIGHT.

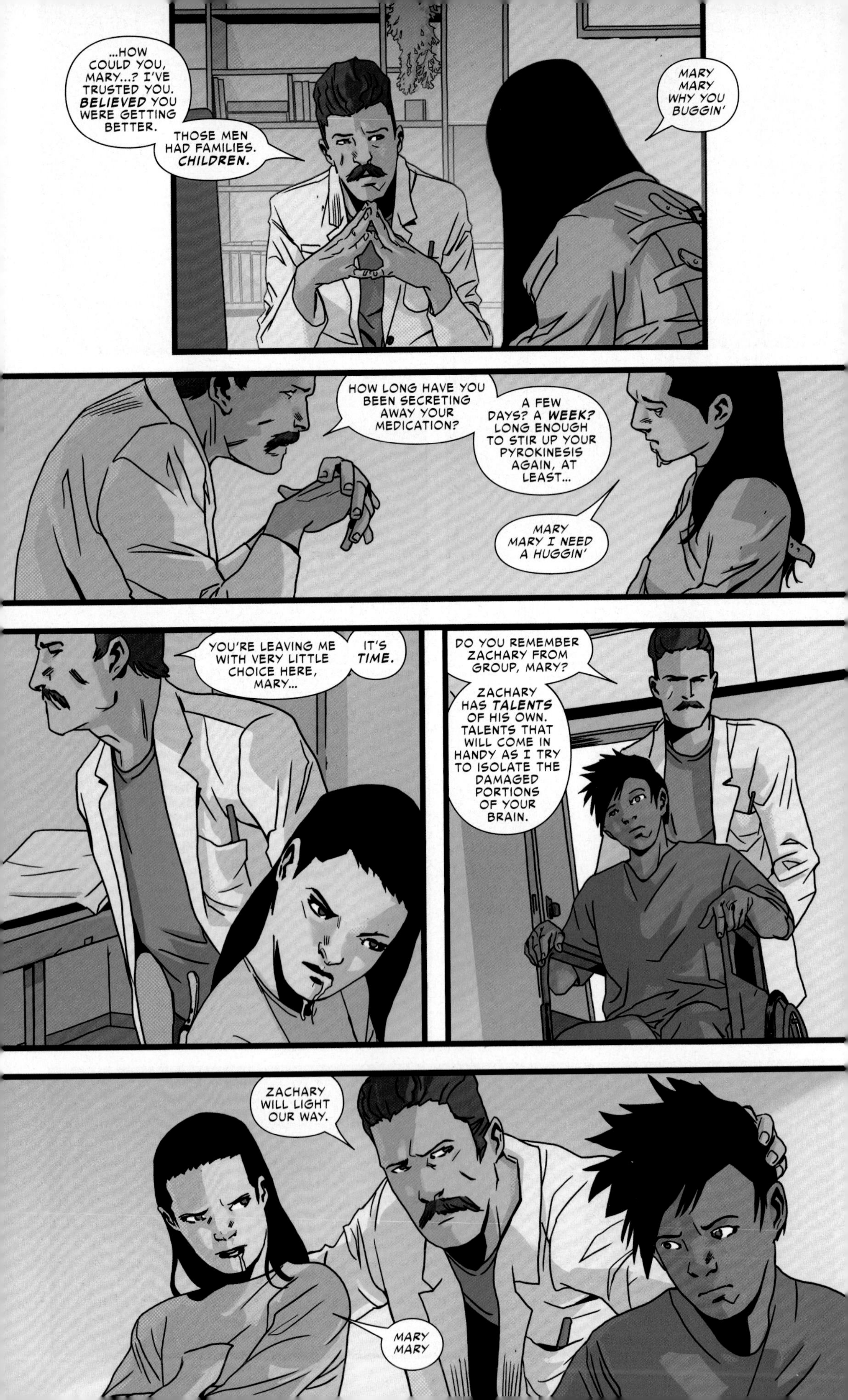
...HOW COULD YOU, MARY...? I'VE TRUSTED YOU. BELIEVED YOU WERE GETTING BETTER.
THOSE MEN HAD FAMILIES. CHILDREN.
MARY MARY WHY YOU BUGGIN'
HOW LONG HAVE YOU BEEN SECRETING AWAY YOUR MEDICATION?
A FEW DAYS? A WEEK? LONG ENOUGH TO STIR UP YOUR PYROKINESIS AGAIN, AT LEAST...
MARY MARY I NEED A HUGGIN'
YOU'RE LEAVING ME WITH VERY LITTLE CHOICE HERE, MARY...
IT'S TIME.
DO YOU REMEMBER ZACHARY FROM GROUP, MARY?
ZACHARY HAS TALENTS OF HIS OWN. TALENTS THAT WILL COME IN HANDY AS I TRY TO ISOLATE THE DAMAGED PORTIONS OF YOUR BRAIN.
ZACHARY WILL LIGHT OUR WAY.
MARY MARY

WHY YOU BUGGIN'

PATIENT IS PREPPED. BEGIN GENERAL ANESTHESIA.

MARY MMARY... I...NNEEED YRR...

I SWEAR I RECOGNIZE HER FROM SOMEWHERE. SHE LOOKS SO FAMILIAR...

EVER WATCH LOVERS AND STRANGERS? SHE USED TO BE ON IT...

OH MY GOD, I LOVED THAT SHOW! WAS SHE THE LADY WITH THE--

ENOUGH CHIT CHAT, LADIES...WE NEED TO WORK FAST. BEFORE SHE WAKES.

ZACHARY? IT'S TIME... I NEED YOU TO USE YOUR AMPLIFICATION POWERS TO LIGHT UP HER MIND. SHOW ME WHERE MARY'S OTHER PERSONALITIES ARE HIDING.

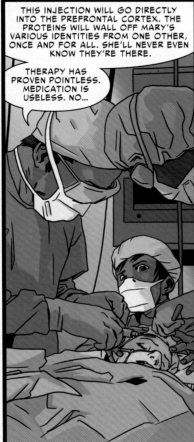

THIS INJECTION WILL GO DIRECTLY INTO THE PREFRONTAL CORTEX. THE PROTEINS WILL WALL OFF MARY'S VARIOUS IDENTITIES FROM ONE OTHER, ONCE AND FOR ALL. SHE'LL NEVER EVEN KNOW THEY'RE THERE.

THERAPY HAS PROVEN POINTLESS. MEDICATION IS USELESS. NO...

...WE WILL BUILD WALLS IN HER BRAIN NOW. DUNGEONS FOR HER MULTIPLE PERSONALITIES.

GOODBYE, TYPHOID...FAREWELL, BLOODY...

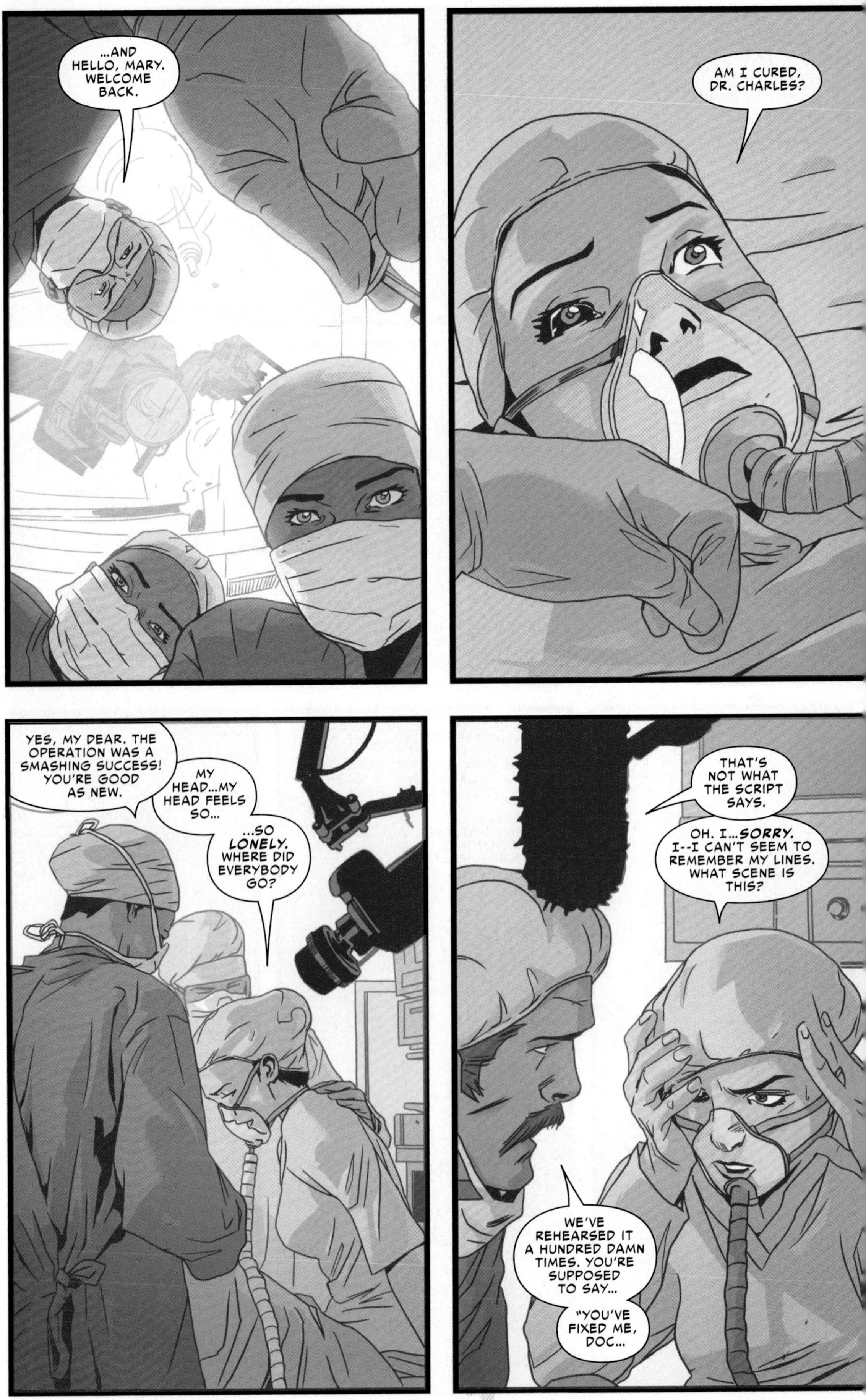
...AND HELLO, MARY. WELCOME BACK.
AM I CURED, DR. CHARLES?
YES, MY DEAR. THE OPERATION WAS A SMASHING SUCCESS! YOU'RE GOOD AS NEW.
MY HEAD...MY HEAD FEELS SO...
...SO *LONELY.* WHERE DID EVERYBODY GO?
THAT'S NOT WHAT THE SCRIPT SAYS.
OH. I...*SORRY.* I--I CAN'T SEEM TO REMEMBER MY LINES. WHAT SCENE IS THIS?
WE'VE REHEARSED IT A HUNDRED DAMN TIMES. YOU'RE SUPPOSED TO SAY...
"YOU'VE FIXED ME, DOC...

"...HOW SHALL I EVER REPAY YOU?"

HOW SHALL I... EVER REPAY YOU?

SIMPLE. JUST LEAN BACK, CLOSE YOUR EYES AND...

...LEAVE THE REST TO ME.

WAIT. HOLD UP. I'M...I'M CONFUSED. HOW DID I GET HERE AGAIN?

DON'T STRAIN YOURSELF, DEAR. THE DOCTOR SAID YOU NEED TO REST.

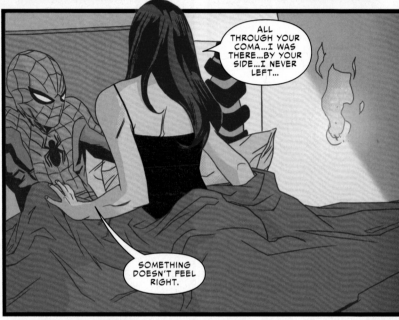

ALL THROUGH YOUR COMA...I WAS THERE...BY YOUR SIDE...I NEVER LEFT...

SOMETHING DOESN'T FEEL RIGHT.

LIKE SOMETHING'S TELLING ME...I'M IN DANGER.

SHHH, DARLING. EVERYTHING IS ALL RIGHT.

THERE WAS A YOUNG WOMAN WHO SWALLOWED A FLY...

I DON'T KNOW WHY SHE SWALLOWED A FLY...

PERHAPS SHE'LL--

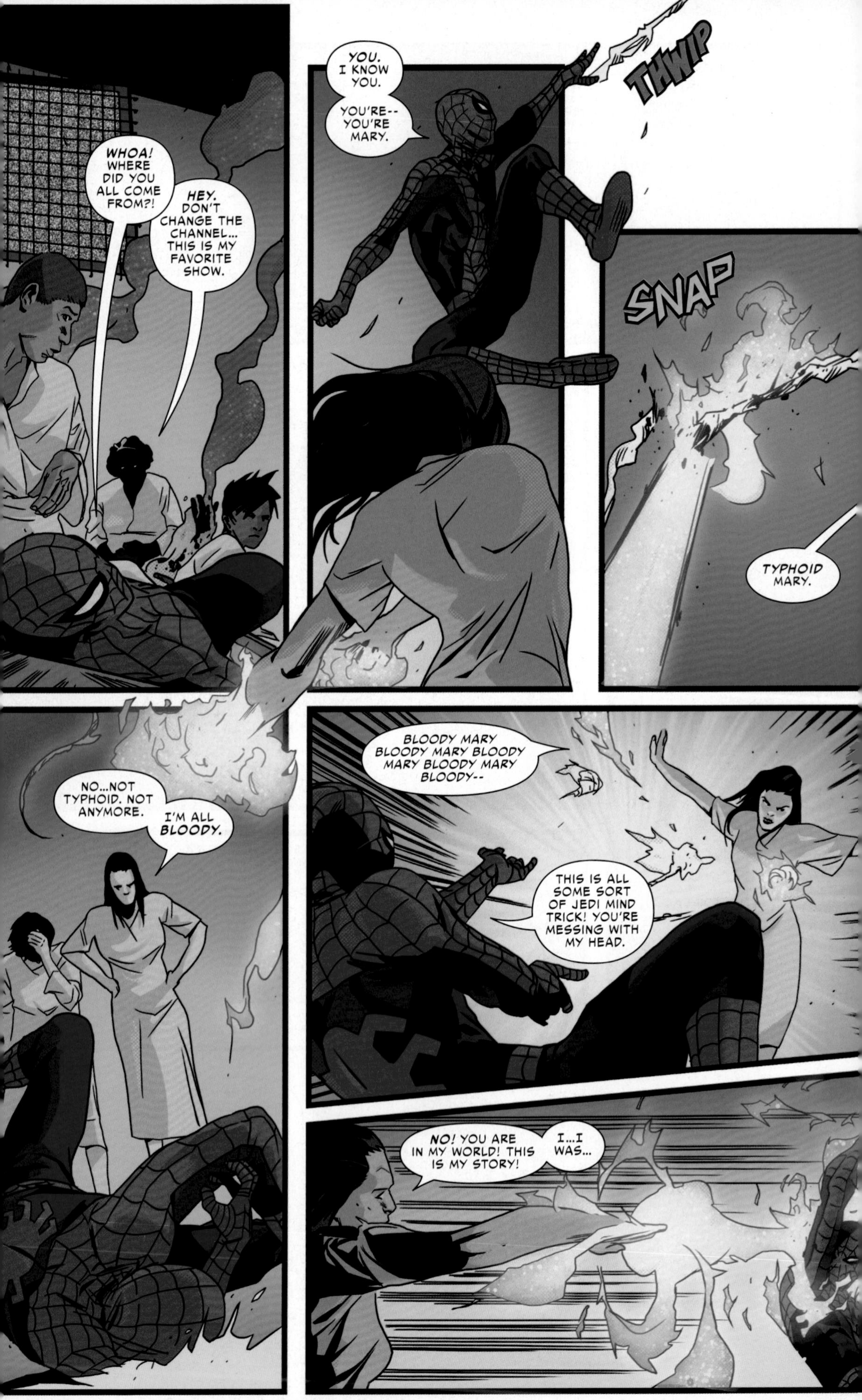
WHOA! WHERE DID YOU ALL COME FROM?!
HEY. DON'T CHANGE THE CHANNEL... THIS IS MY FAVORITE SHOW.
YOU. I KNOW YOU.
YOU'RE-- YOU'RE MARY.
THWIP
SNAP
TYPHOID MARY.
NO...NOT TYPHOID. NOT ANYMORE.
I'M ALL BLOODY.
BLOODY MARY BLOODY MARY BLOODY MARY BLOODY MARY BLOODY--
THIS IS ALL SOME SORT OF JEDI MIND TRICK! YOU'RE MESSING WITH MY HEAD.
NO! YOU ARE IN MY WORLD! THIS IS MY STORY!
I...I WAS...

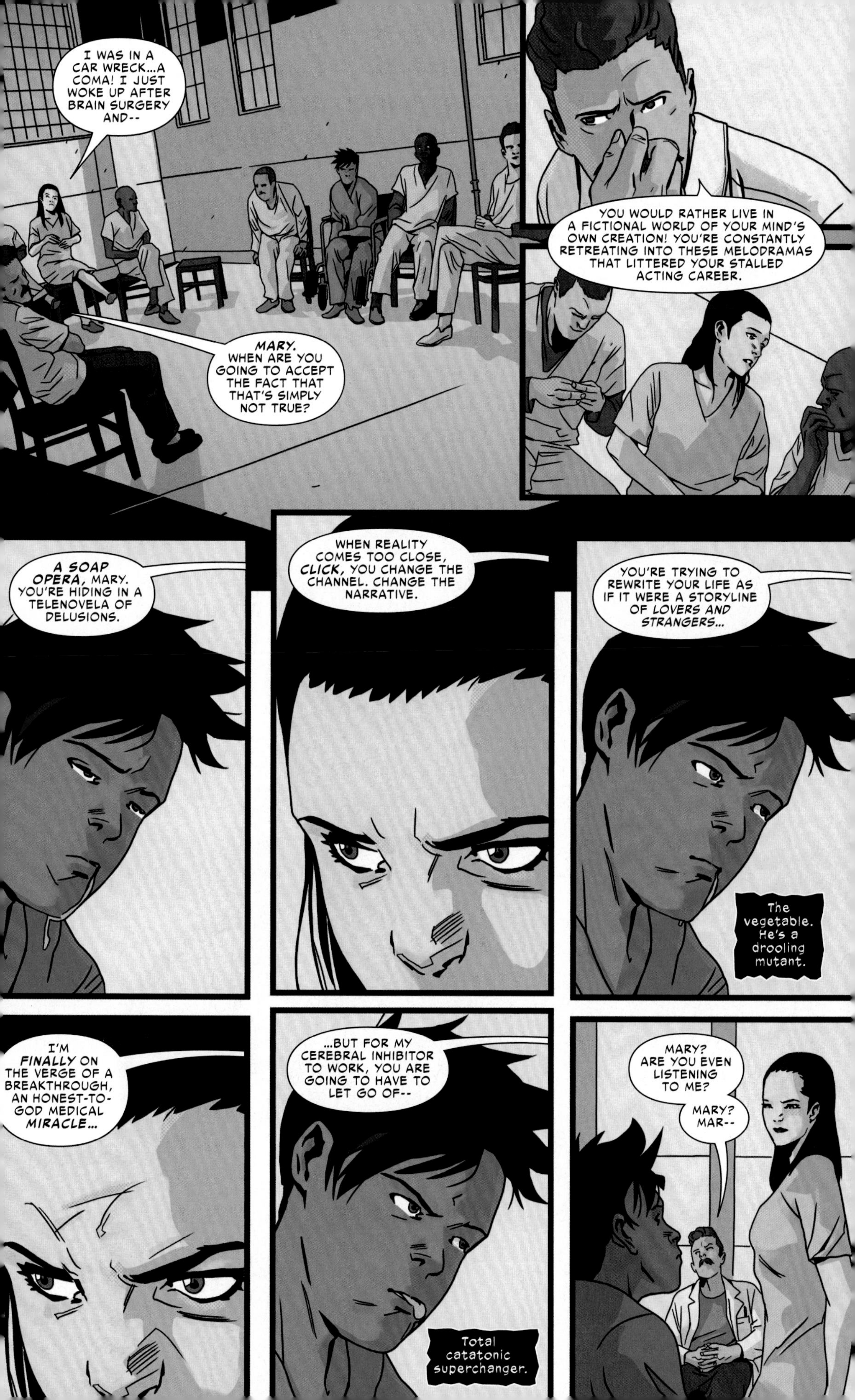
I WAS IN A CAR WRECK...A COMA! I JUST WOKE UP AFTER BRAIN SURGERY AND--
MARY. WHEN ARE YOU GOING TO ACCEPT THE FACT THAT THAT'S SIMPLY NOT TRUE?
YOU WOULD RATHER LIVE IN A FICTIONAL WORLD OF YOUR MIND'S OWN CREATION! YOU'RE CONSTANTLY RETREATING INTO THESE MELODRAMAS THAT LITTERED YOUR STALLED ACTING CAREER.
A SOAP OPERA, MARY. YOU'RE HIDING IN A TELENOVELA OF DELUSIONS.
WHEN REALITY COMES TOO CLOSE, CLICK, YOU CHANGE THE CHANNEL. CHANGE THE NARRATIVE.
YOU'RE TRYING TO REWRITE YOUR LIFE AS IF IT WERE A STORYLINE OF LOVERS AND STRANGERS...
The vegetable. He's a drooling mutant.
I'M FINALLY ON THE VERGE OF A BREAKTHROUGH, AN HONEST-TO-GOD MEDICAL MIRACLE...
...BUT FOR MY CEREBRAL INHIBITOR TO WORK, YOU ARE GOING TO HAVE TO LET GO OF--
Total catatonic superchanger.
MARY? ARE YOU EVEN LISTENING TO ME?
MARY? MAR--

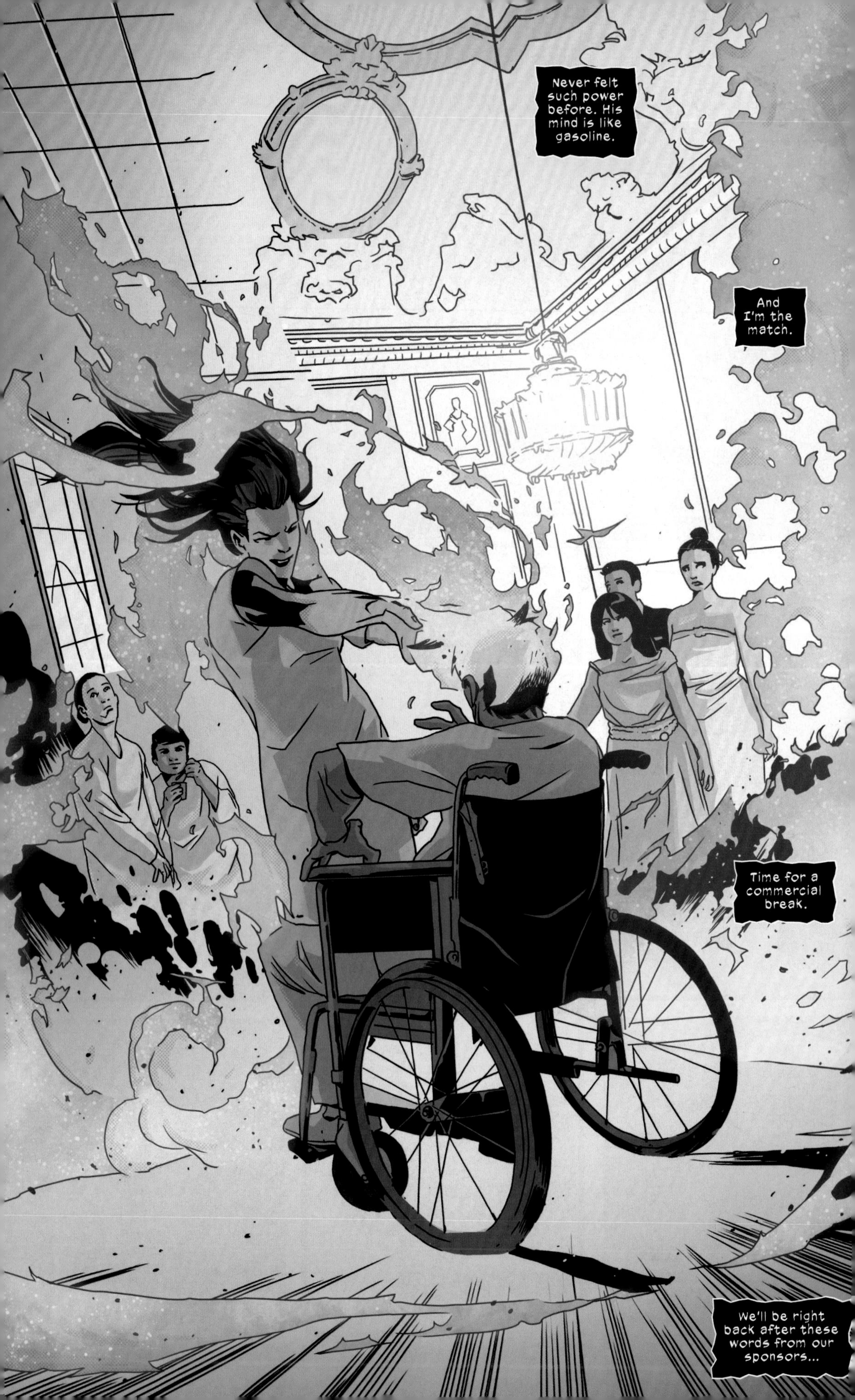
Never felt such power before. His mind is like gasoline.
And I'm the match.
Time for a commercial break.
We'll be right back after these words from our sponsors...

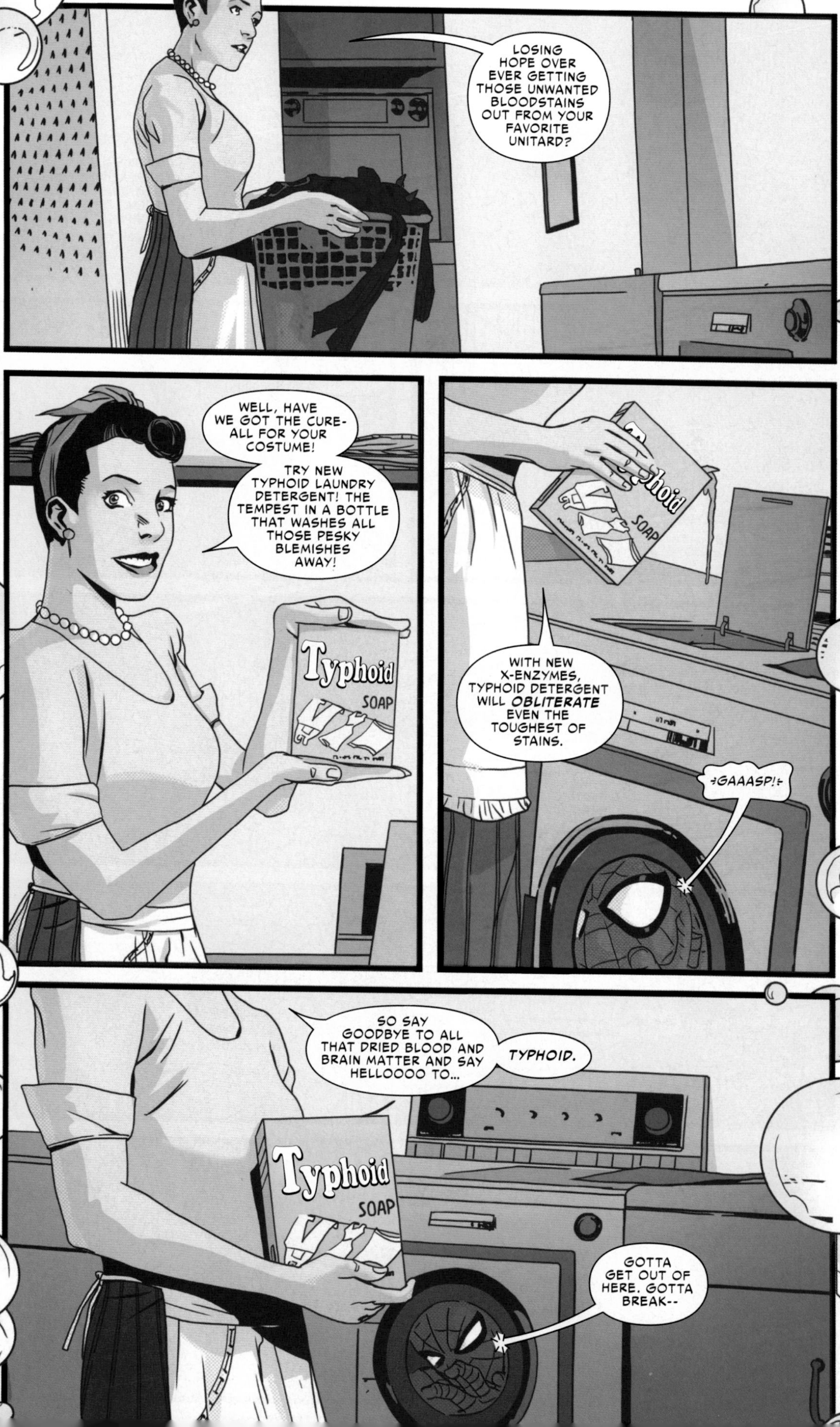
LOSING HOPE OVER EVER GETTING THOSE UNWANTED BLOODSTAINS OUT FROM YOUR FAVORITE UNITARD?
WELL, HAVE WE GOT THE CURE-ALL FOR YOUR COSTUME!
TRY NEW TYPHOID LAUNDRY DETERGENT! THE TEMPEST IN A BOTTLE THAT WASHES ALL THOSE PESKY BLEMISHES AWAY!
Typhoid
SOAP
Typhoid
SOAP
WITH NEW X-ENZYMES, TYPHOID DETERGENT WILL OBLITERATE EVEN THE TOUGHEST OF STAINS.
GAAASP!
SO SAY GOODBYE TO ALL THAT DRIED BLOOD AND BRAIN MATTER AND SAY HELLOOOO TO...
TYPHOID.
Typhoid
SOAP
GOTTA GET OUT OF HERE. GOTTA BREAK--

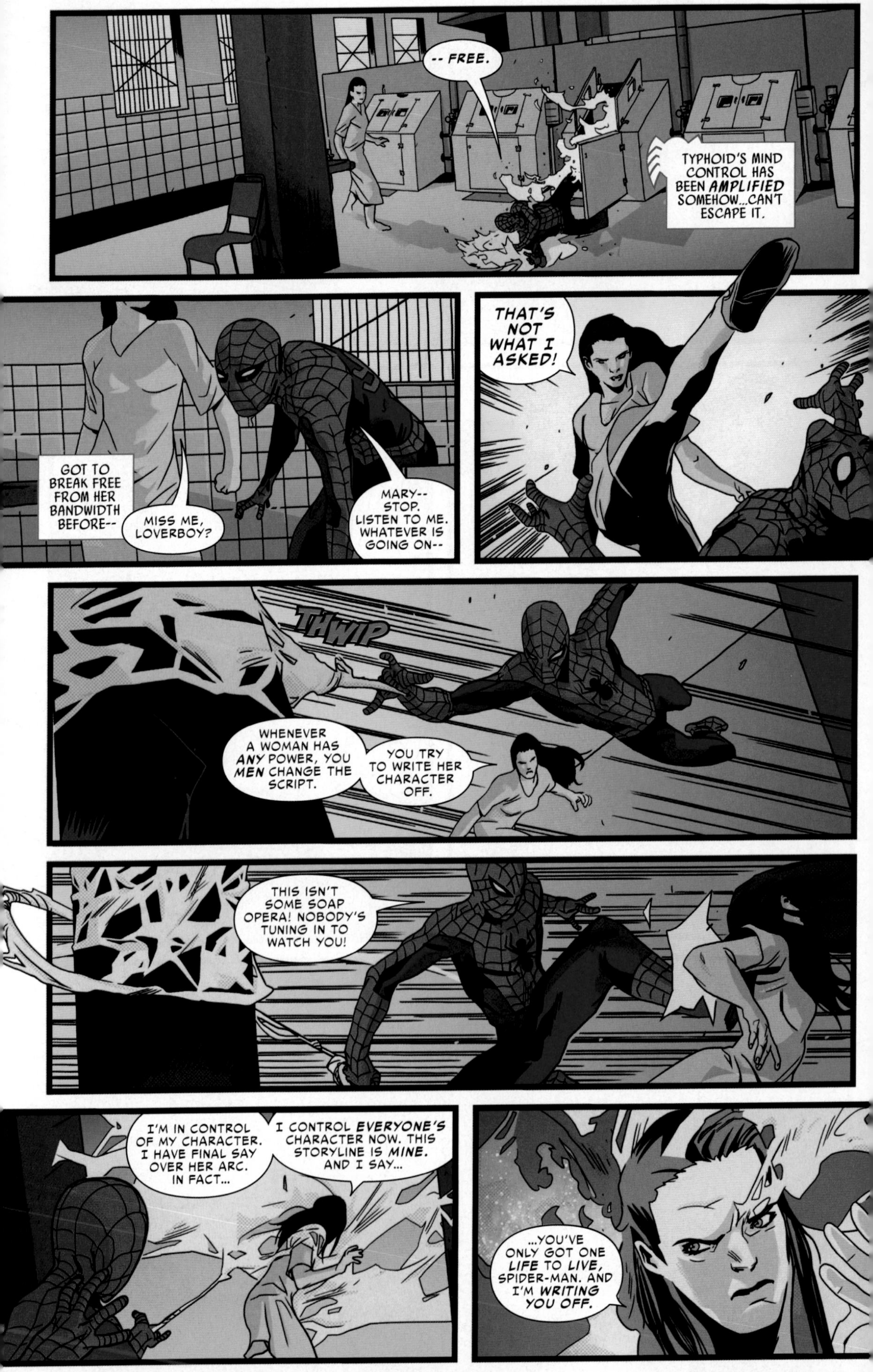
-- FREE.
TYPHOID'S MIND CONTROL HAS BEEN AMPLIFIED SOMEHOW...CAN'T ESCAPE IT.
GOT TO BREAK FREE FROM HER BANDWIDTH BEFORE--
MISS ME, LOVERBOY?
MARY-- STOP. LISTEN TO ME. WHATEVER IS GOING ON--
THAT'S NOT WHAT I ASKED!
THWIP
WHENEVER A WOMAN HAS ANY POWER, YOU MEN CHANGE THE SCRIPT.
YOU TRY TO WRITE HER CHARACTER OFF.
THIS ISN'T SOME SOAP OPERA! NOBODY'S TUNING IN TO WATCH YOU!
I'M IN CONTROL OF MY CHARACTER. I HAVE FINAL SAY OVER HER ARC. IN FACT...
I CONTROL EVERYONE'S CHARACTER NOW. THIS STORYLINE IS MINE. AND I SAY...
...YOU'VE ONLY GOT ONE LIFE TO LIVE, SPIDER-MAN. AND I'M WRITING YOU OFF.

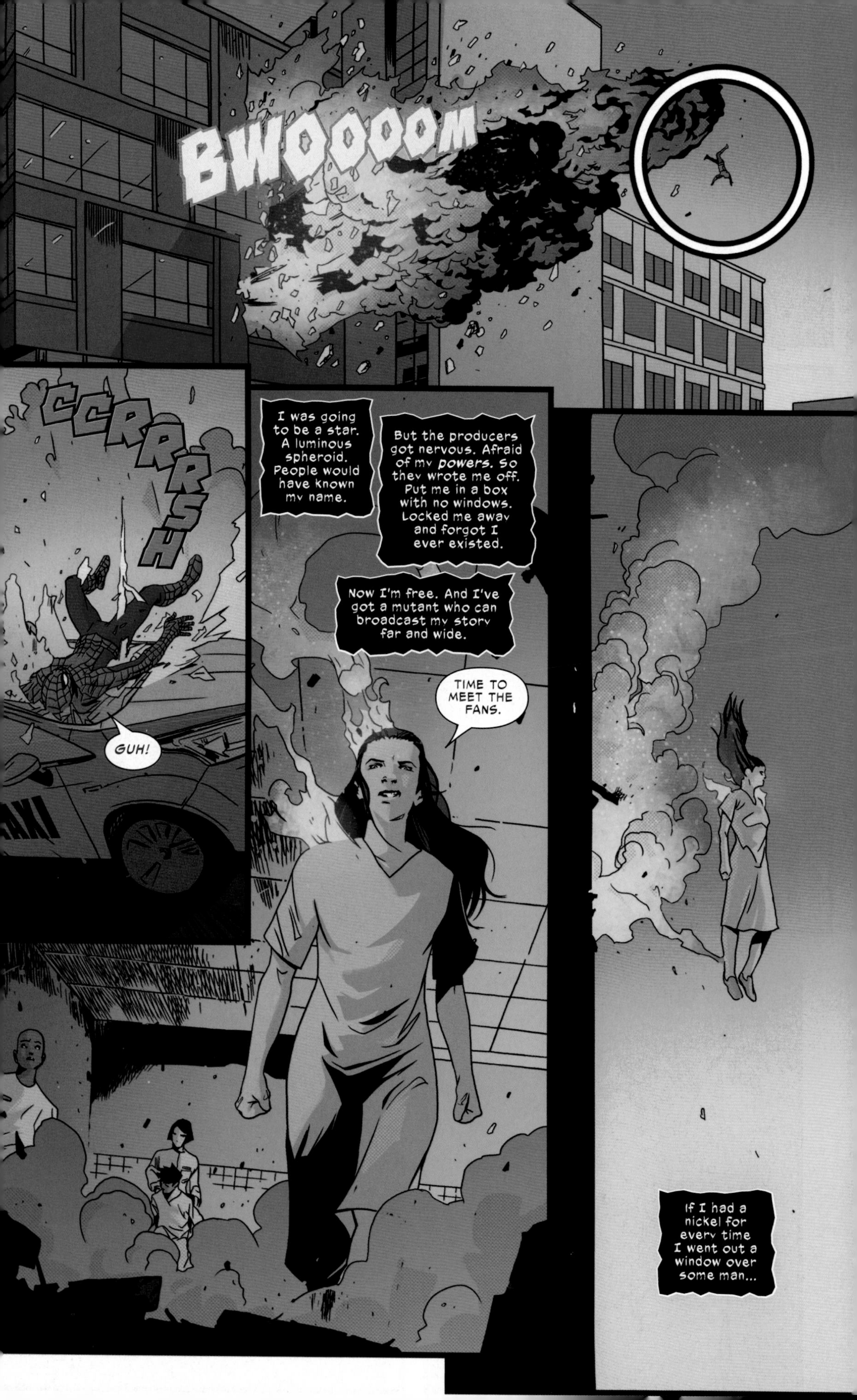
BWOOOOM
CCRRRRSH
GUH!
I was going to be a star. A luminous spheroid. People would have known my name.
But the producers got nervous. Afraid of my *powers.* So they wrote me off. Put me in a box with no windows. Locked me away and forgot I ever existed.
Now I'm free. And I've got a mutant who can broadcast my story far and wide.
TIME TO MEET THE FANS.
If I had a nickel for every time I went out a window over some man...

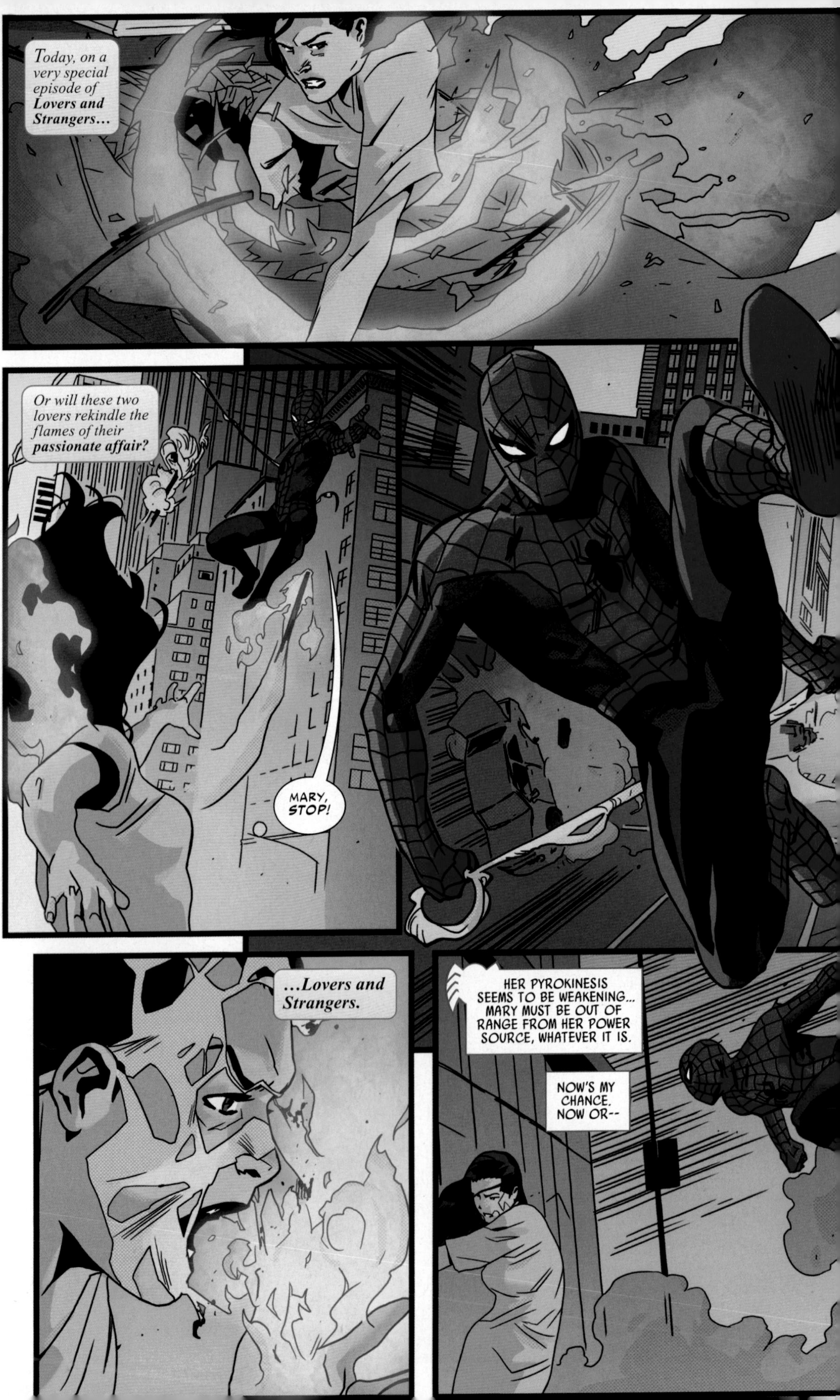

Today, on a very special episode of Lovers and Strangers...
Or will these two lovers rekindle the flames of their passionate affair?
MARY, STOP!
...Lovers and Strangers.
HER PYROKINESIS SEEMS TO BE WEAKENING... MARY MUST BE OUT OF RANGE FROM HER POWER SOURCE, WHATEVER IT IS.
NOW'S MY CHANCE. NOW OR--

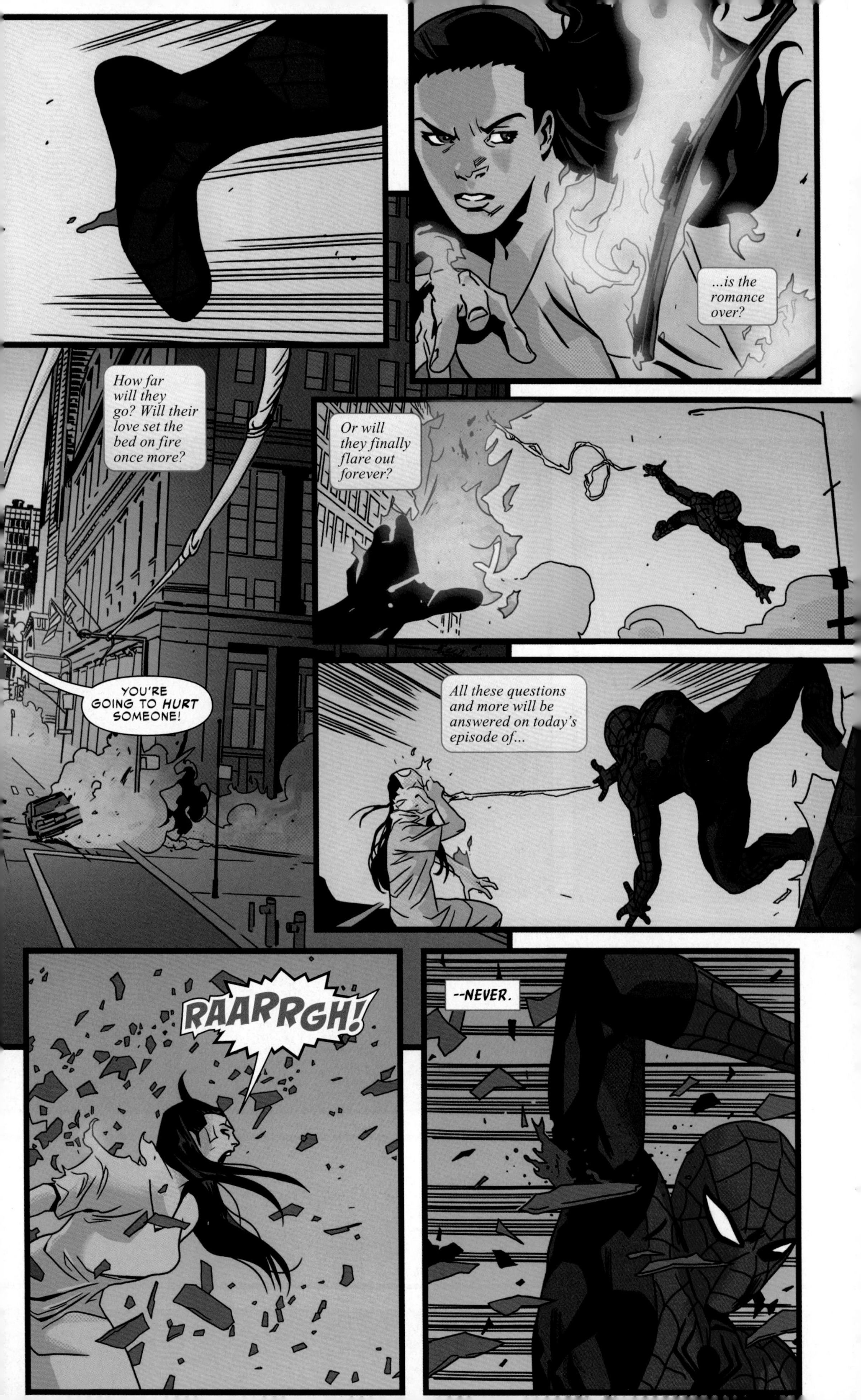
...is the
romance
over?
How far
will they
go? Will their
love set the
bed on fire
once more?
YOU'RE
GOING TO HURT
SOMEONE!
Or will
they finally
flare out
forever?
All these questions
and more will be
answered on today's
episode of...
RAARRGH!
--NEVER.

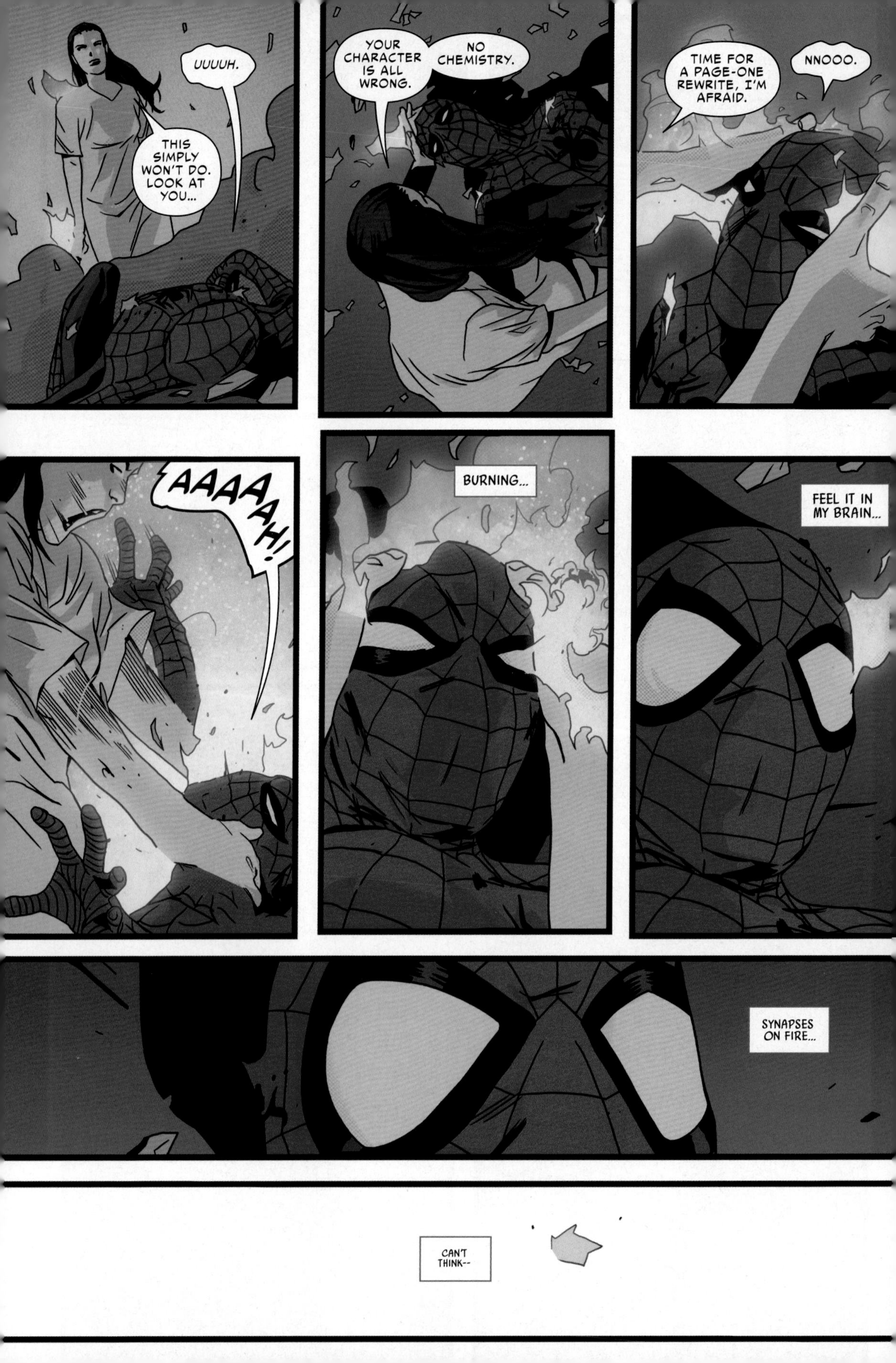
UUUUH.
THIS SIMPLY WON'T DO. LOOK AT YOU...
YOUR CHARACTER IS ALL WRONG.
NO CHEMISTRY.
TIME FOR A PAGE-ONE REWRITE, I'M AFRAID.
NNOOO.
AAAAAH!
BURNING...
FEEL IT IN MY BRAIN...
SYNAPSES ON FIRE...
CAN'T THINK--

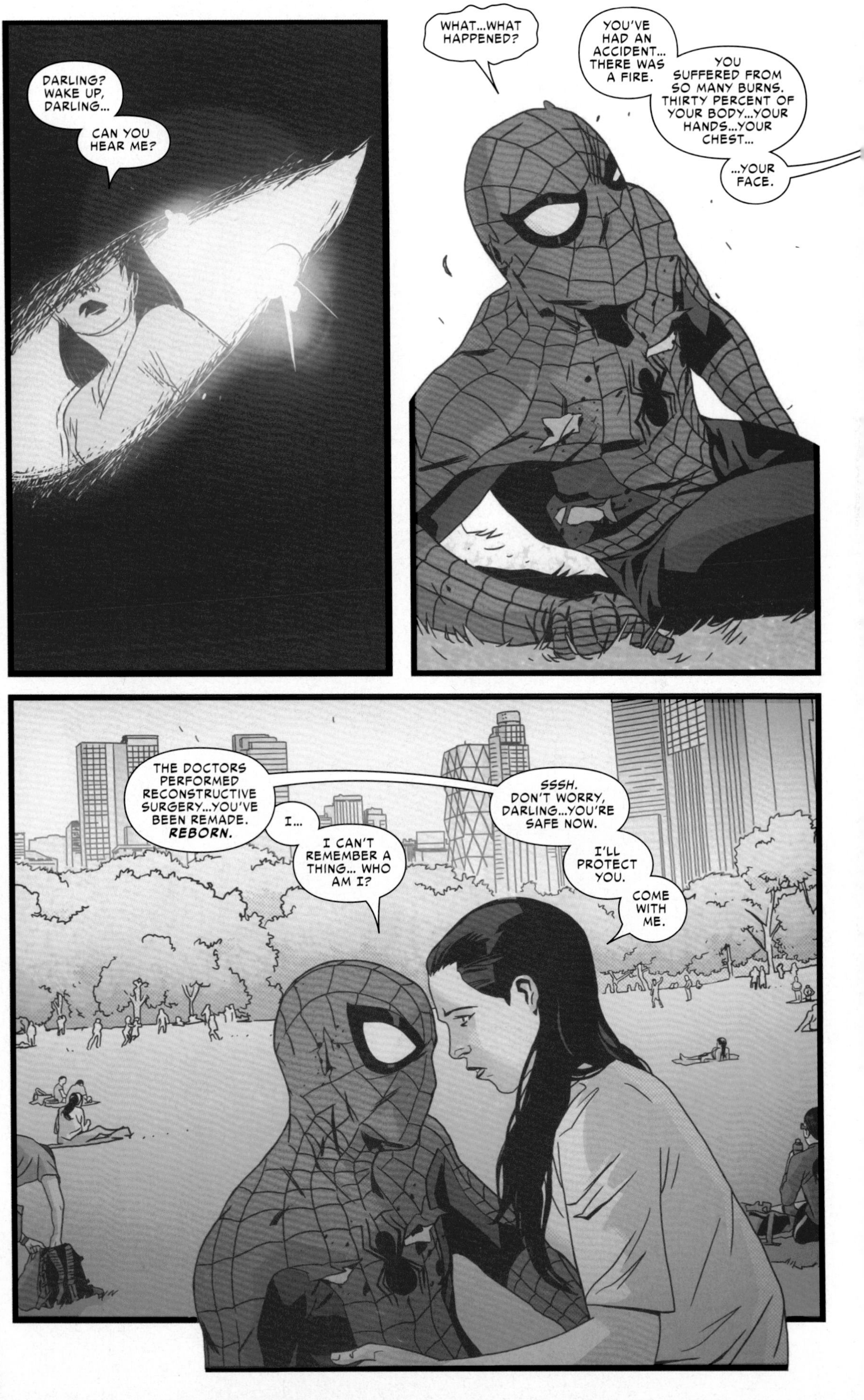
DARLING? WAKE UP, DARLING...
CAN YOU HEAR ME?
WHAT...WHAT HAPPENED?
YOU'VE HAD AN ACCIDENT... THERE WAS A FIRE.
YOU SUFFERED FROM SO MANY BURNS. THIRTY PERCENT OF YOUR BODY...YOUR HANDS...YOUR CHEST...
...YOUR FACE.
THE DOCTORS PERFORMED RECONSTRUCTIVE SURGERY...YOU'VE BEEN REMADE. REBORN.
I...
I CAN'T REMEMBER A THING... WHO AM I?
SSSH. DON'T WORRY, DARLING...YOU'RE SAFE NOW.
I'LL PROTECT YOU.
COME WITH ME.

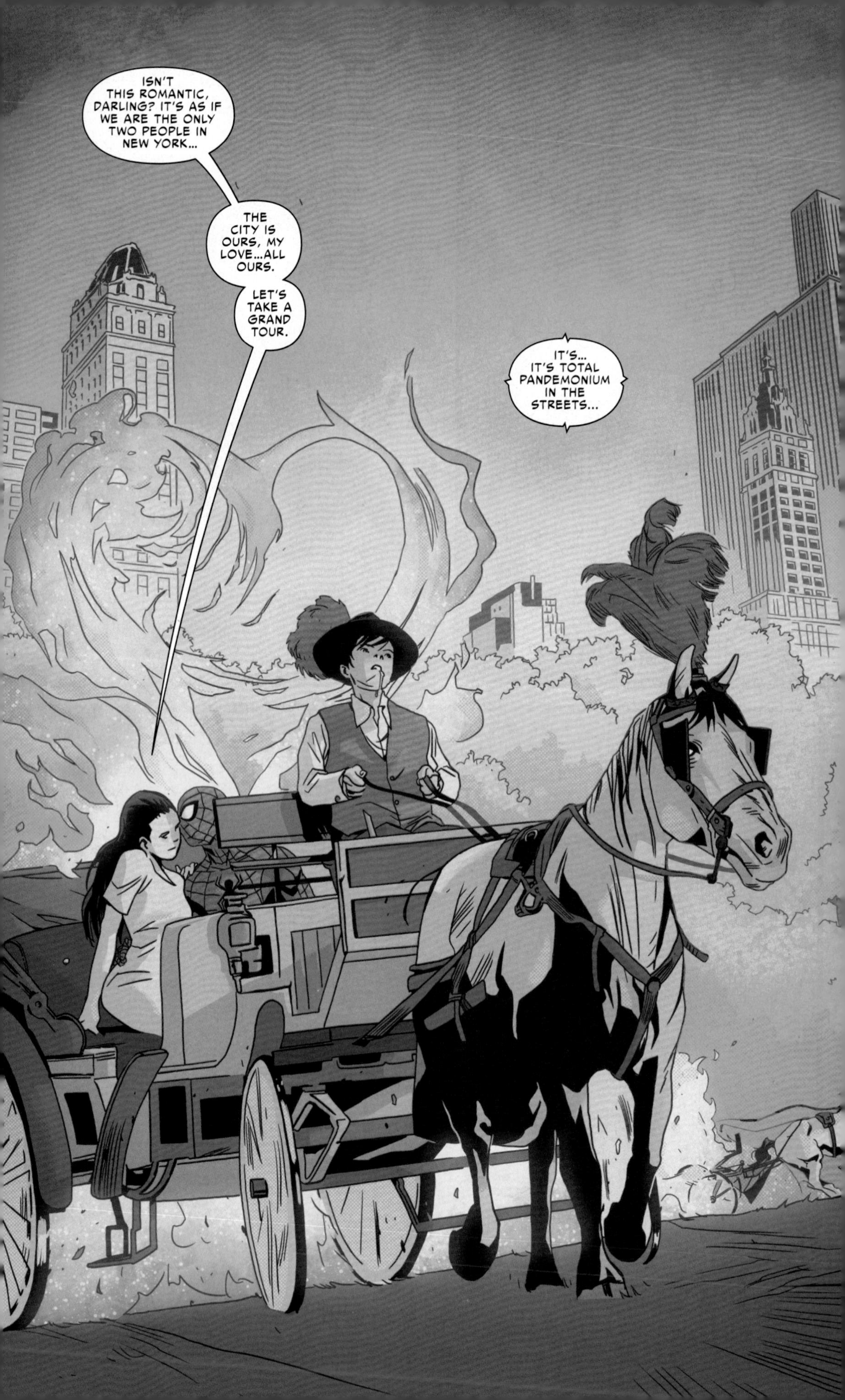
ISN'T THIS ROMANTIC, DARLING? IT'S AS IF WE ARE THE ONLY TWO PEOPLE IN NEW YORK...
THE CITY IS OURS, MY LOVE...ALL OURS.
LET'S TAKE A GRAND TOUR.
IT'S... IT'S TOTAL PANDEMONIUM IN THE STREETS...

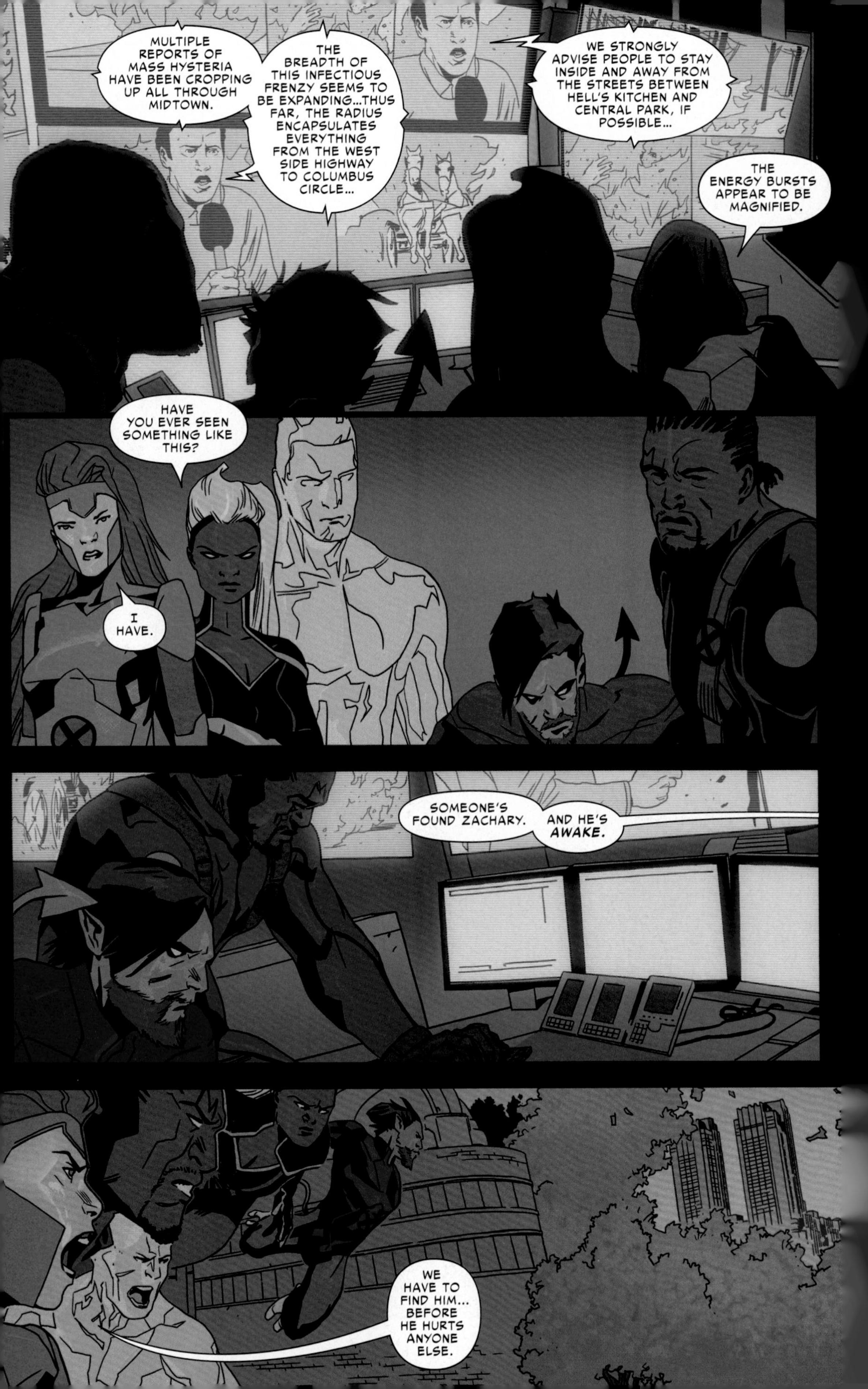
MULTIPLE REPORTS OF MASS HYSTERIA HAVE BEEN CROPPING UP ALL THROUGH MIDTOWN.
THE BREADTH OF THIS INFECTIOUS FRENZY SEEMS TO BE EXPANDING...THUS FAR, THE RADIUS ENCAPSULATES EVERYTHING FROM THE WEST SIDE HIGHWAY TO COLUMBUS CIRCLE...
WE STRONGLY ADVISE PEOPLE TO STAY INSIDE AND AWAY FROM THE STREETS BETWEEN HELL'S KITCHEN AND CENTRAL PARK, IF POSSIBLE...
THE ENERGY BURSTS APPEAR TO BE MAGNIFIED.
HAVE YOU EVER SEEN SOMETHING LIKE THIS?
I HAVE.
SOMEONE'S FOUND ZACHARY.
AND HE'S *AWAKE.*
WE HAVE TO FIND HIM... BEFORE HE HURTS ANYONE ELSE.

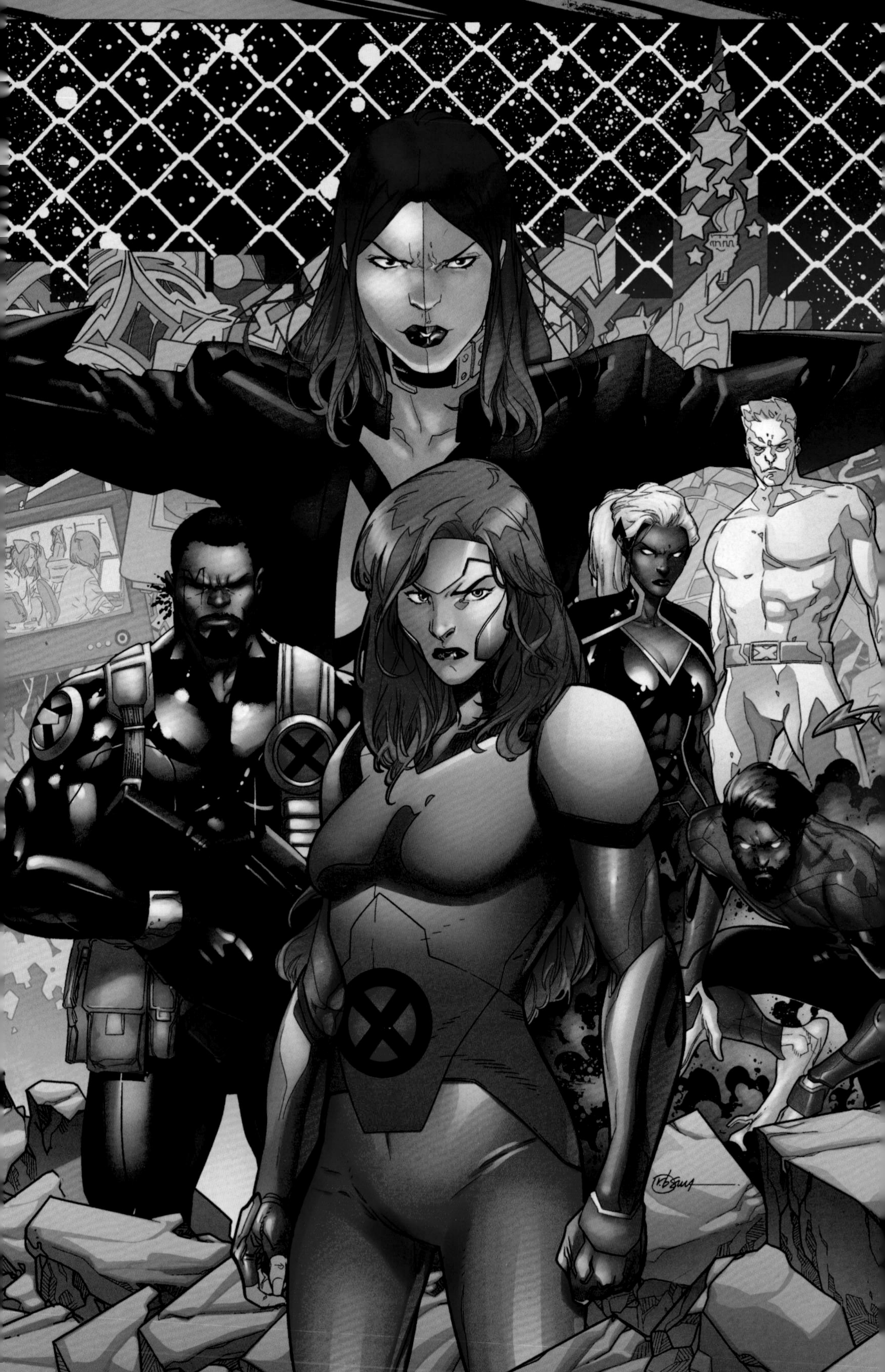

TYPHOID FEVER: X-MEN

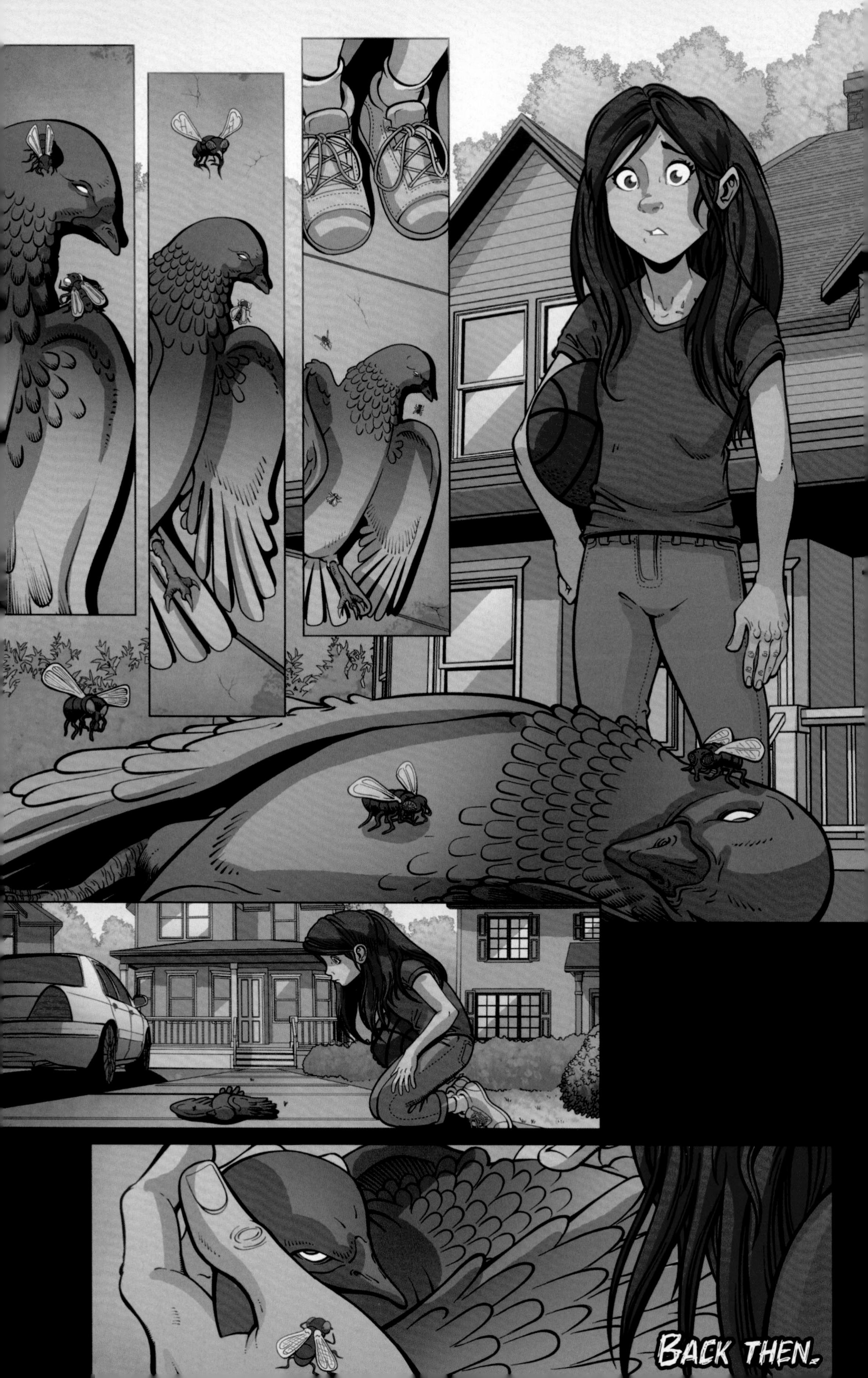
BACK THEN.

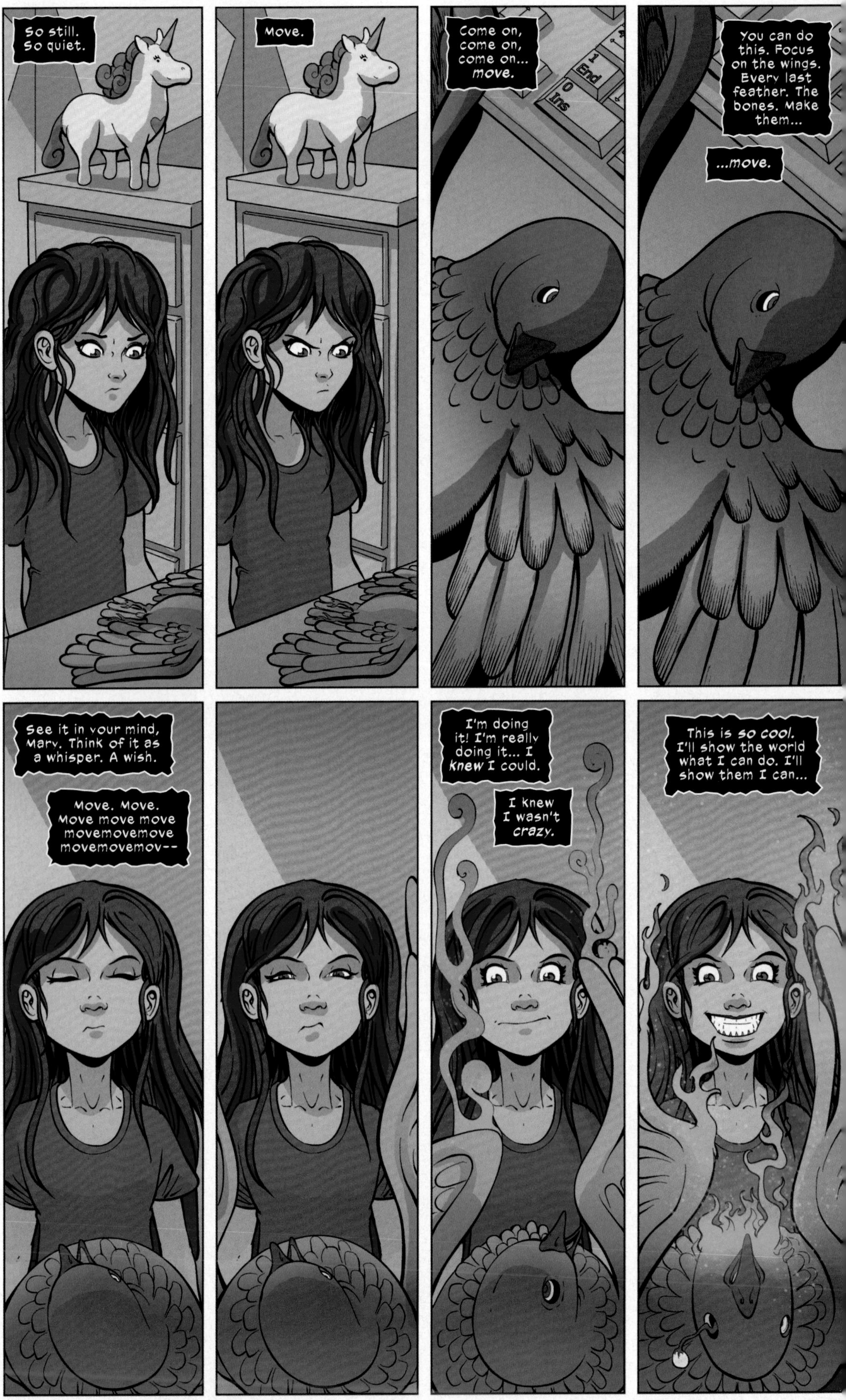
So still. So quiet.
Move.
Come on, come on, come on... *move.*
1 End
0 Ins
You can do this. Focus on the wings. Every last feather. The bones. Make them...
...move.
See it in your mind, Mary. Think of it as a whisper. A wish.
Move. Move. Move move move movemovemove movemovemov--
I'm doing it! I'm really doing it... I *knew* I could.
I knew I wasn't *crazy.*
This is *so cool.* I'll show the world what I can do. I'll show them I can...

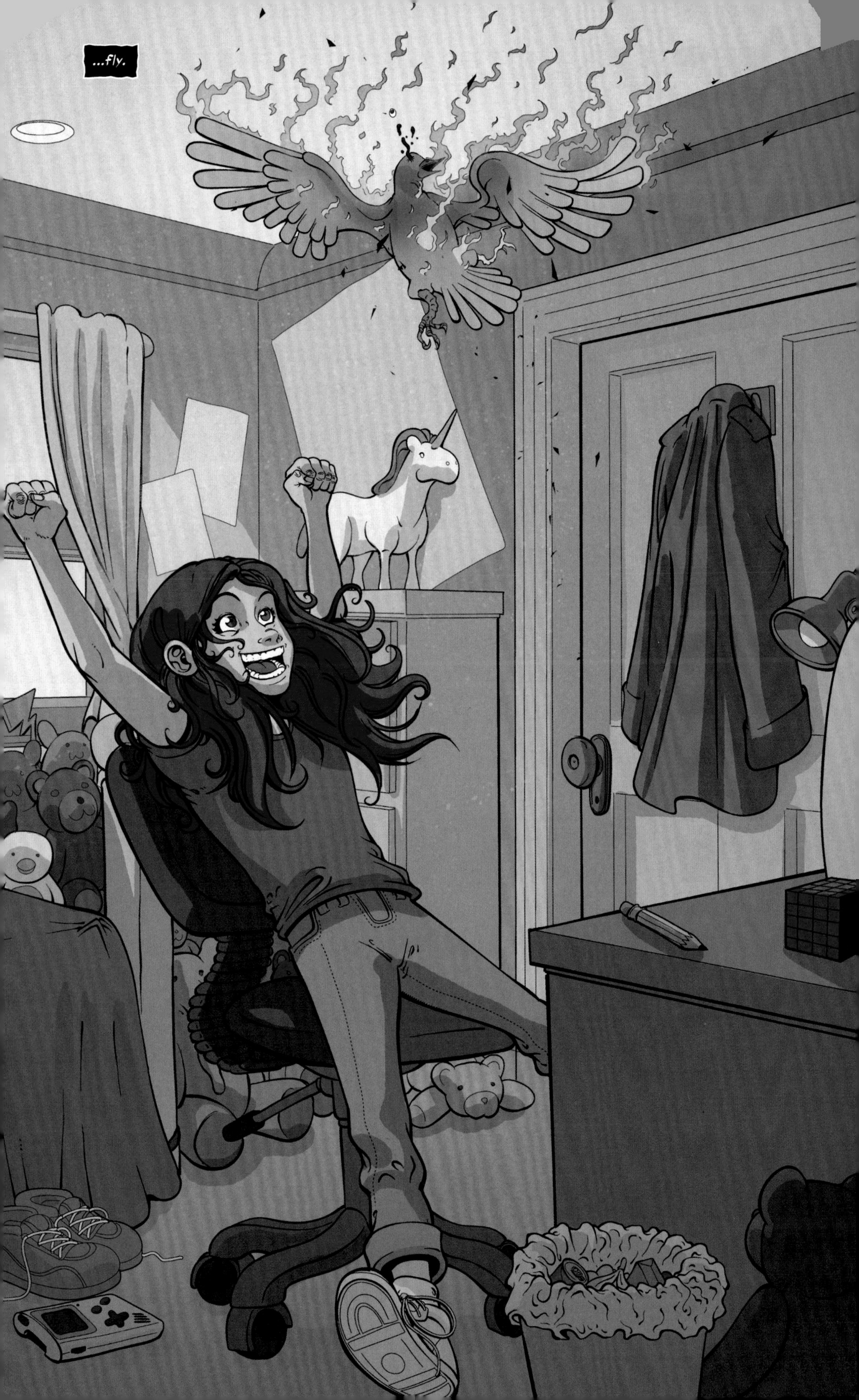
...fly.

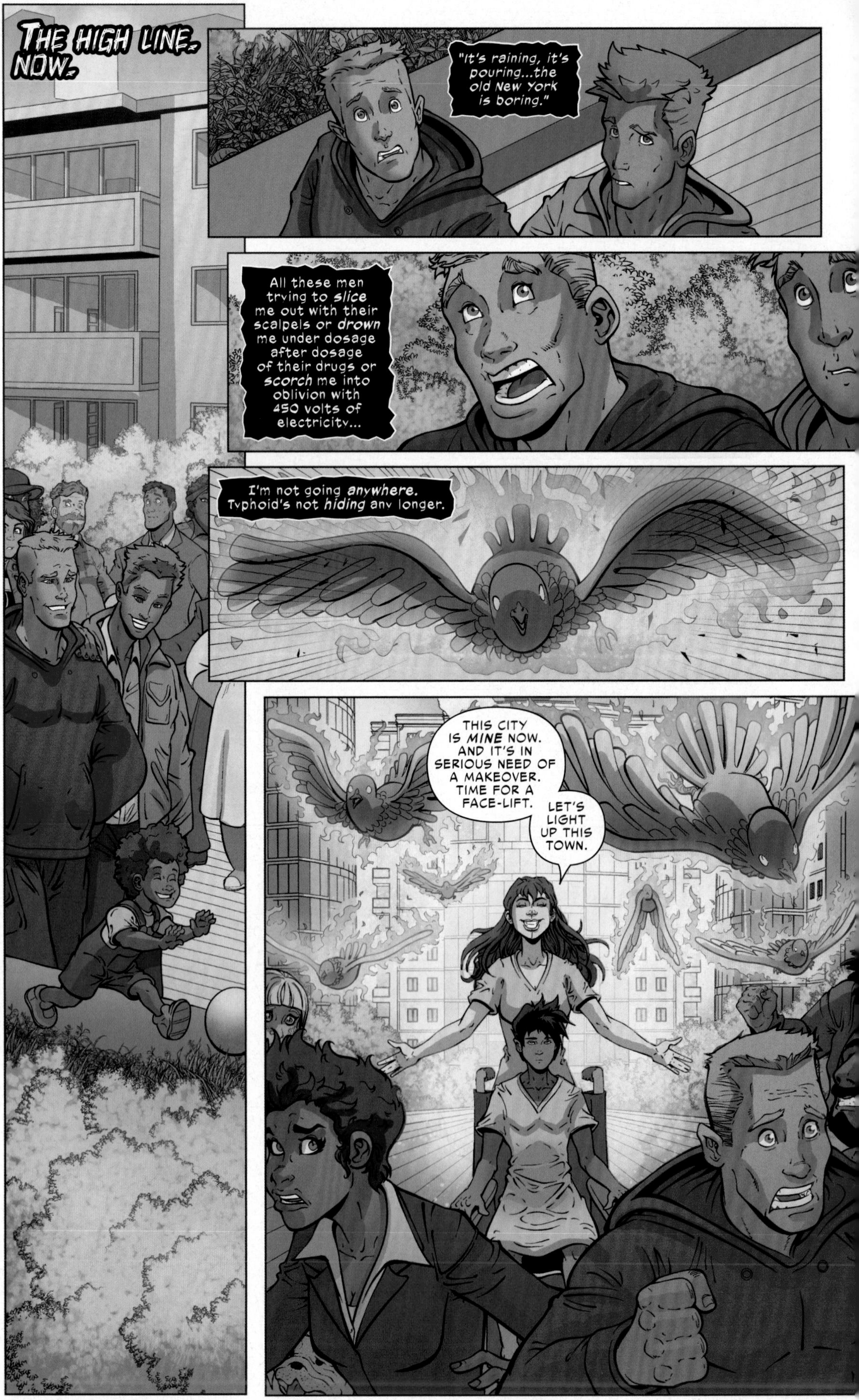
THE HIGH LINE. NOW.
"It's raining, it's pouring...the old New York is boring."
All these men trying to slice me out with their scalpels or drown me under dosage after dosage of their drugs or scorch me into oblivion with 450 volts of electricity...
I'm not going anywhere. Typhoid's not hiding any longer.
THIS CITY IS MINE NOW. AND IT'S IN SERIOUS NEED OF A MAKEOVER. TIME FOR A FACE-LIFT.
LET'S LIGHT UP THIS TOWN.

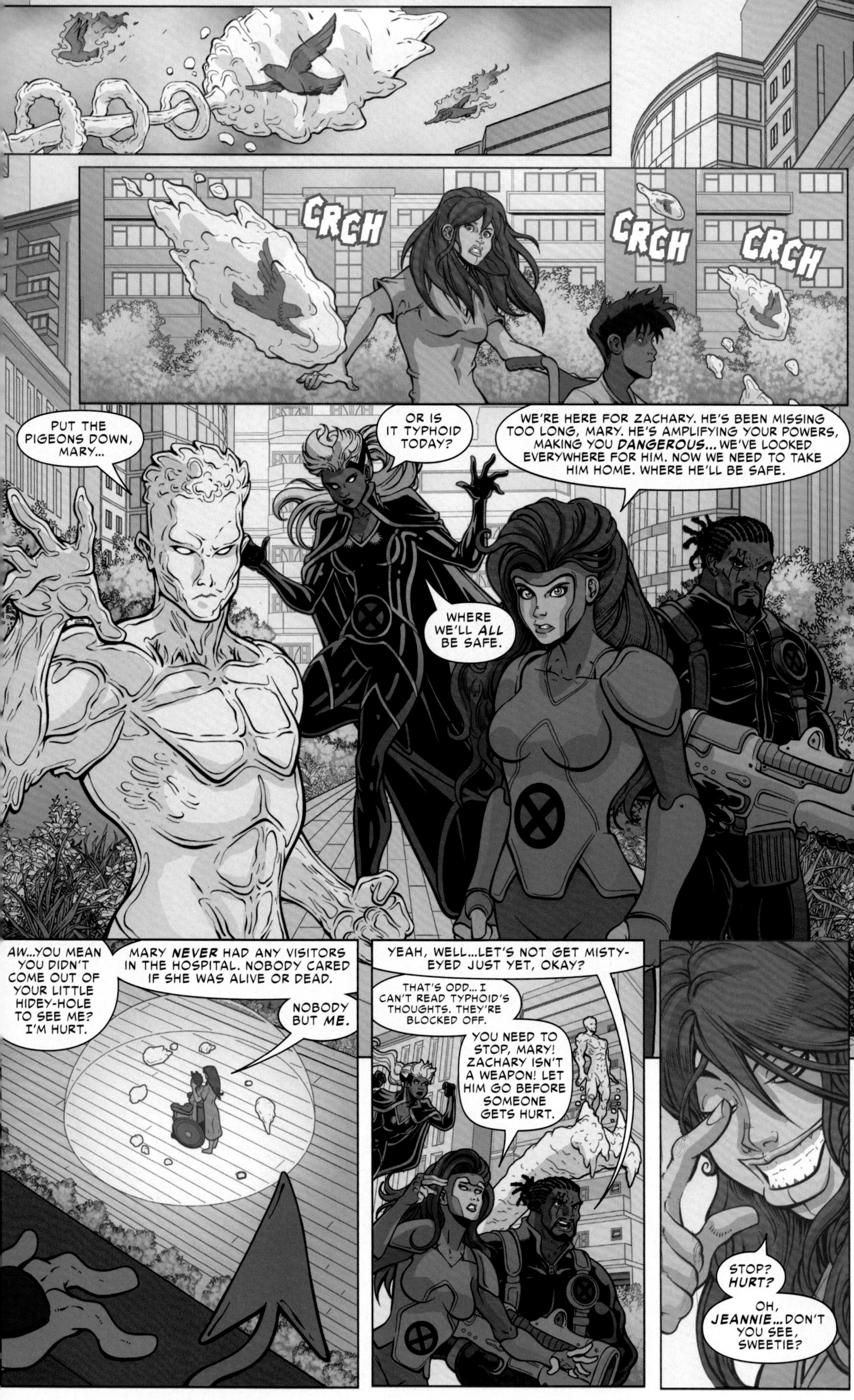
CRCH
CRCH
CRCH
PUT THE PIGEONS DOWN, MARY...
OR IS IT TYPHOID TODAY?
WE'RE HERE FOR ZACHARY. HE'S BEEN MISSING TOO LONG, MARY. HE'S AMPLIFYING YOUR POWERS, MAKING YOU DANGEROUS... WE'VE LOOKED EVERYWHERE FOR HIM. NOW WE NEED TO TAKE HIM HOME. WHERE HE'LL BE SAFE.
WHERE WE'LL ALL BE SAFE.
AW...YOU MEAN YOU DIDN'T COME OUT OF YOUR LITTLE HIDEY-HOLE TO SEE ME? I'M HURT.
MARY NEVER HAD ANY VISITORS IN THE HOSPITAL. NOBODY CARED IF SHE WAS ALIVE OR DEAD.
NOBODY BUT ME.
YEAH, WELL...LET'S NOT GET MISTY-EYED JUST YET, OKAY?
THAT'S ODD... I CAN'T READ TYPHOID'S THOUGHTS. THEY'RE BLOCKED OFF.
YOU NEED TO STOP, MARY! ZACHARY ISN'T A WEAPON! LET HIM GO BEFORE SOMEONE GETS HURT.
STOP? HURT?
OH, JEANNIE... DON'T YOU SEE, SWEETIE?

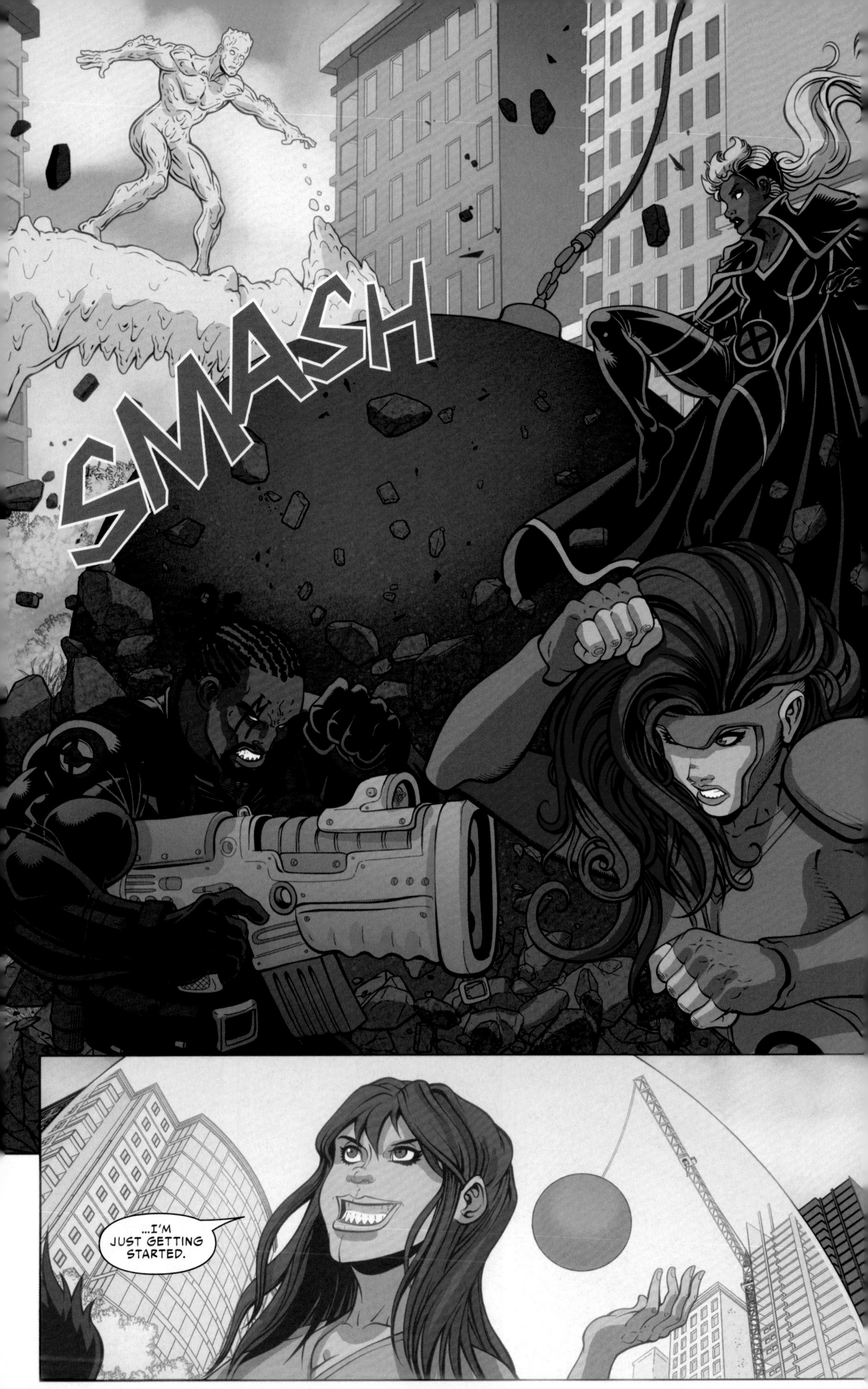
SMASH
...I'M JUST GETTING STARTED.

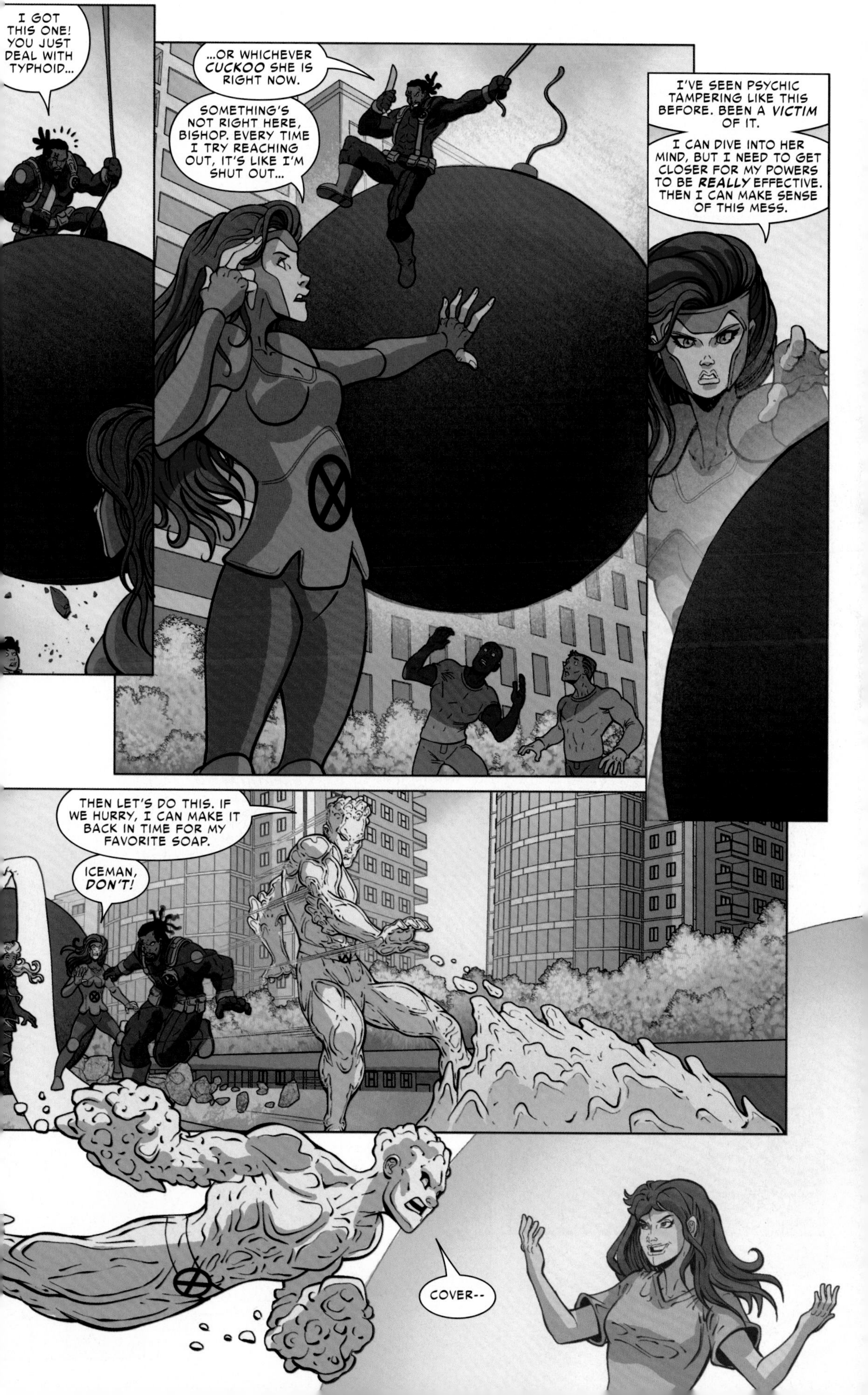
I GOT THIS ONE! YOU JUST DEAL WITH TYPHOID...
...OR WHICHEVER CUCKOO SHE IS RIGHT NOW.
SOMETHING'S NOT RIGHT HERE, BISHOP. EVERY TIME I TRY REACHING OUT, IT'S LIKE I'M SHUT OUT...
I'VE SEEN PSYCHIC TAMPERING LIKE THIS BEFORE. BEEN A VICTIM OF IT.
I CAN DIVE INTO HER MIND, BUT I NEED TO GET CLOSER FOR MY POWERS TO BE REALLY EFFECTIVE. THEN I CAN MAKE SENSE OF THIS MESS.
THEN LET'S DO THIS. IF WE HURRY, I CAN MAKE IT BACK IN TIME FOR MY FAVORITE SOAP.
ICEMAN, DON'T!
COVER--

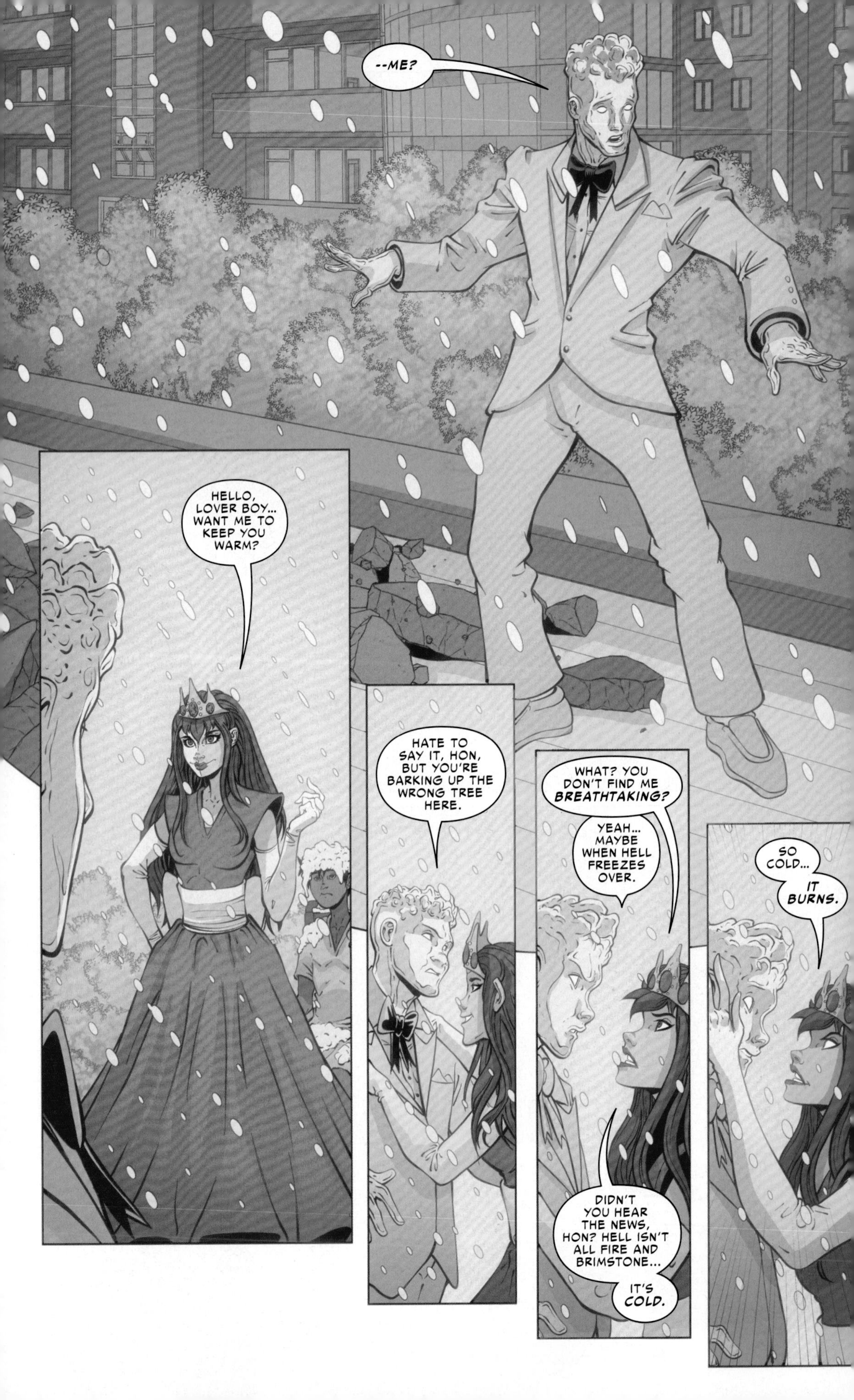
--ME?
HELLO, LOVER BOY... WANT ME TO KEEP YOU WARM?
HATE TO SAY IT, HON, BUT YOU'RE BARKING UP THE WRONG TREE HERE.
WHAT? YOU DON'T FIND ME *BREATHTAKING?*
YEAH... MAYBE WHEN HELL FREEZES OVER.
DIDN'T YOU HEAR THE NEWS, HON? HELL ISN'T ALL FIRE AND BRIMSTONE...
IT'S *COLD.*
SO COLD... IT *BURNS.*

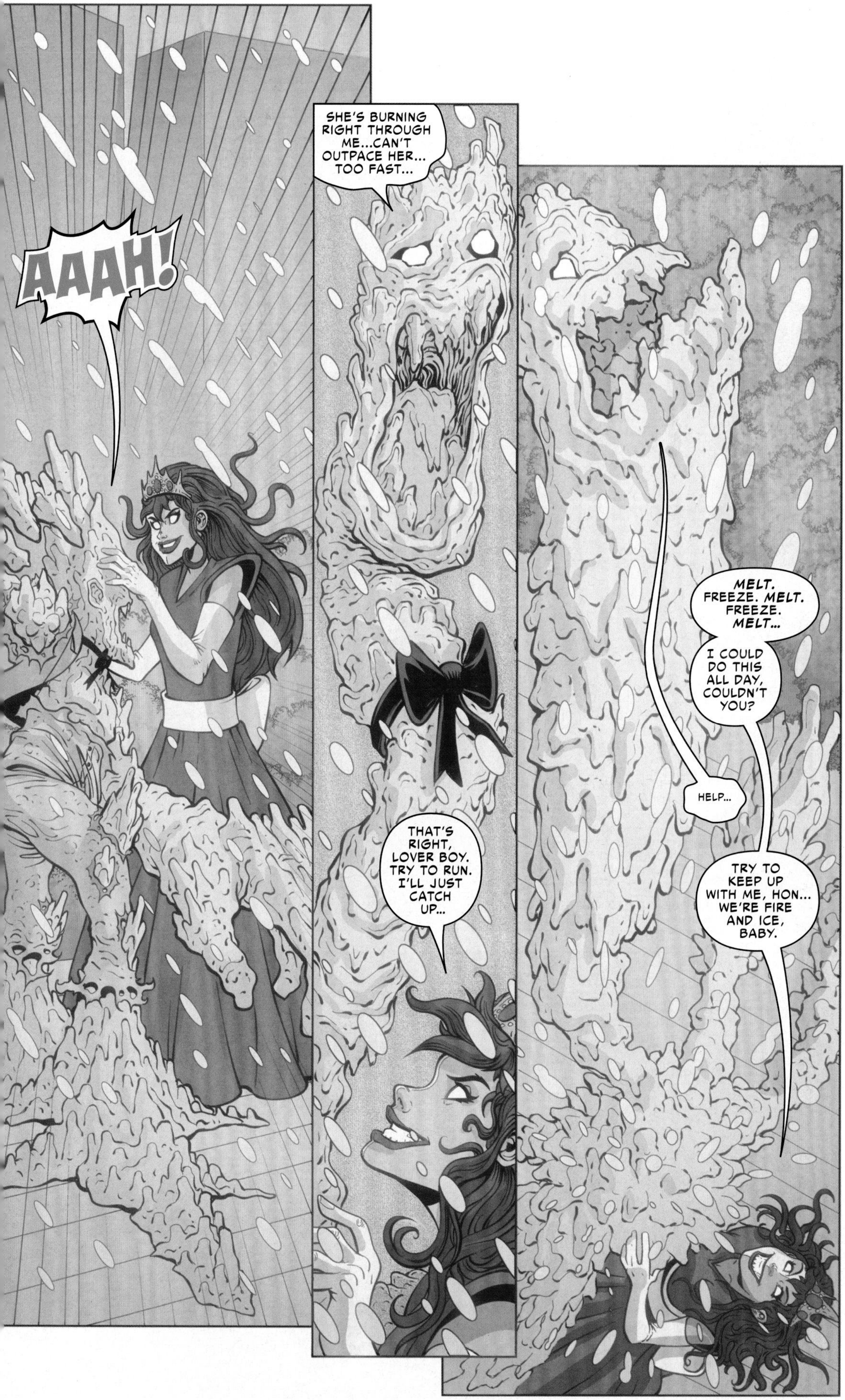
AAAH!
SHE'S BURNING RIGHT THROUGH ME...CAN'T OUTPACE HER... TOO FAST...
THAT'S RIGHT, LOVER BOY. TRY TO RUN. I'LL JUST CATCH UP...
HELP...
MELT. FREEZE. MELT. FREEZE. MELT...
I COULD DO THIS ALL DAY, COULDN'T YOU?
TRY TO KEEP UP WITH ME, HON... WE'RE FIRE AND ICE, BABY.

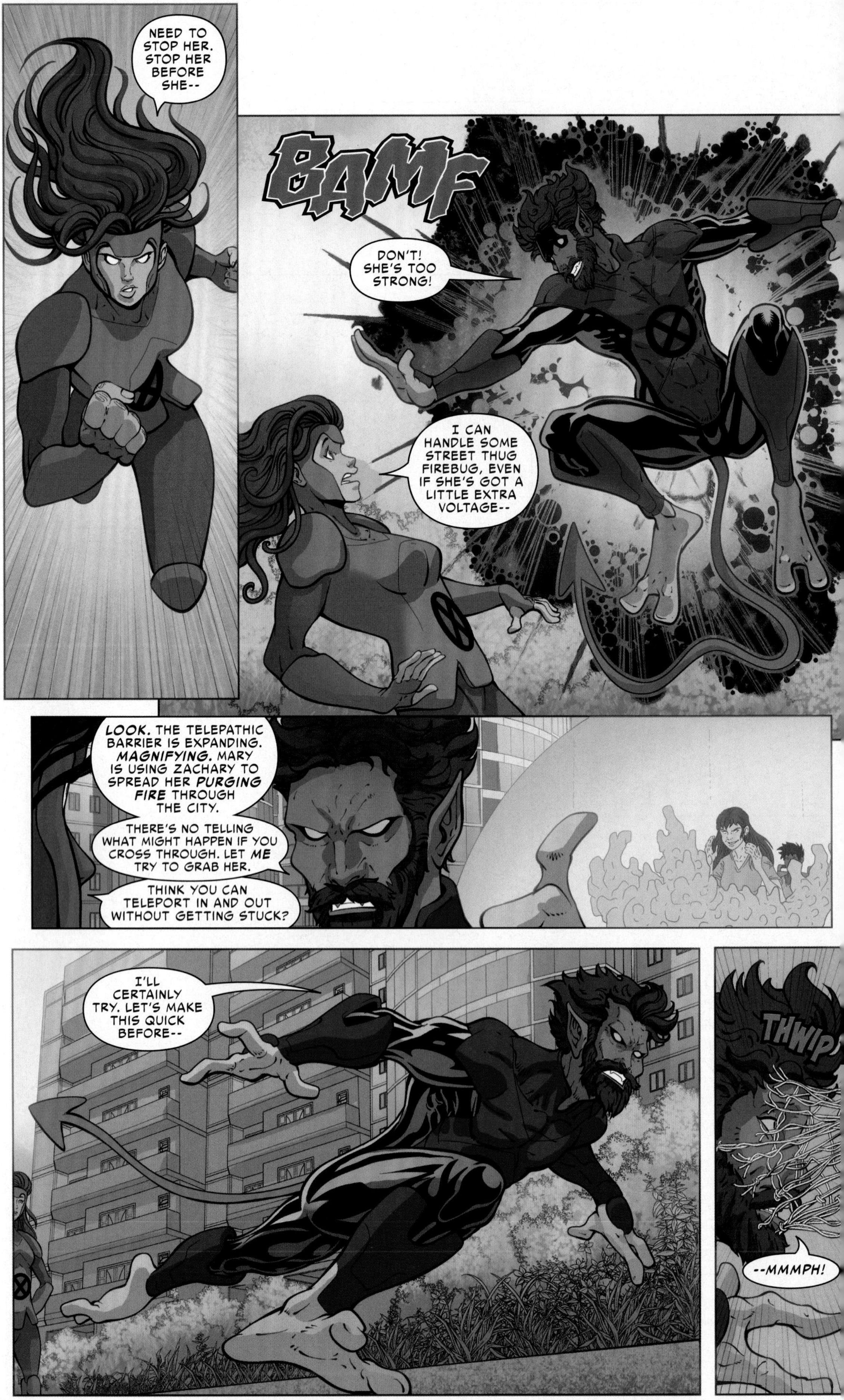
NEED TO STOP HER. STOP HER BEFORE SHE--
BAMF
DON'T! SHE'S TOO STRONG!
I CAN HANDLE SOME STREET THUG FIREBUG, EVEN IF SHE'S GOT A LITTLE EXTRA VOLTAGE--
LOOK. THE TELEPATHIC BARRIER IS EXPANDING. MAGNIFYING. MARY IS USING ZACHARY TO SPREAD HER PURGING FIRE THROUGH THE CITY.
THERE'S NO TELLING WHAT MIGHT HAPPEN IF YOU CROSS THROUGH. LET ME TRY TO GRAB HER.
THINK YOU CAN TELEPORT IN AND OUT WITHOUT GETTING STUCK?
I'LL CERTAINLY TRY. LET'S MAKE THIS QUICK BEFORE--
THWIP
--MMMPH!

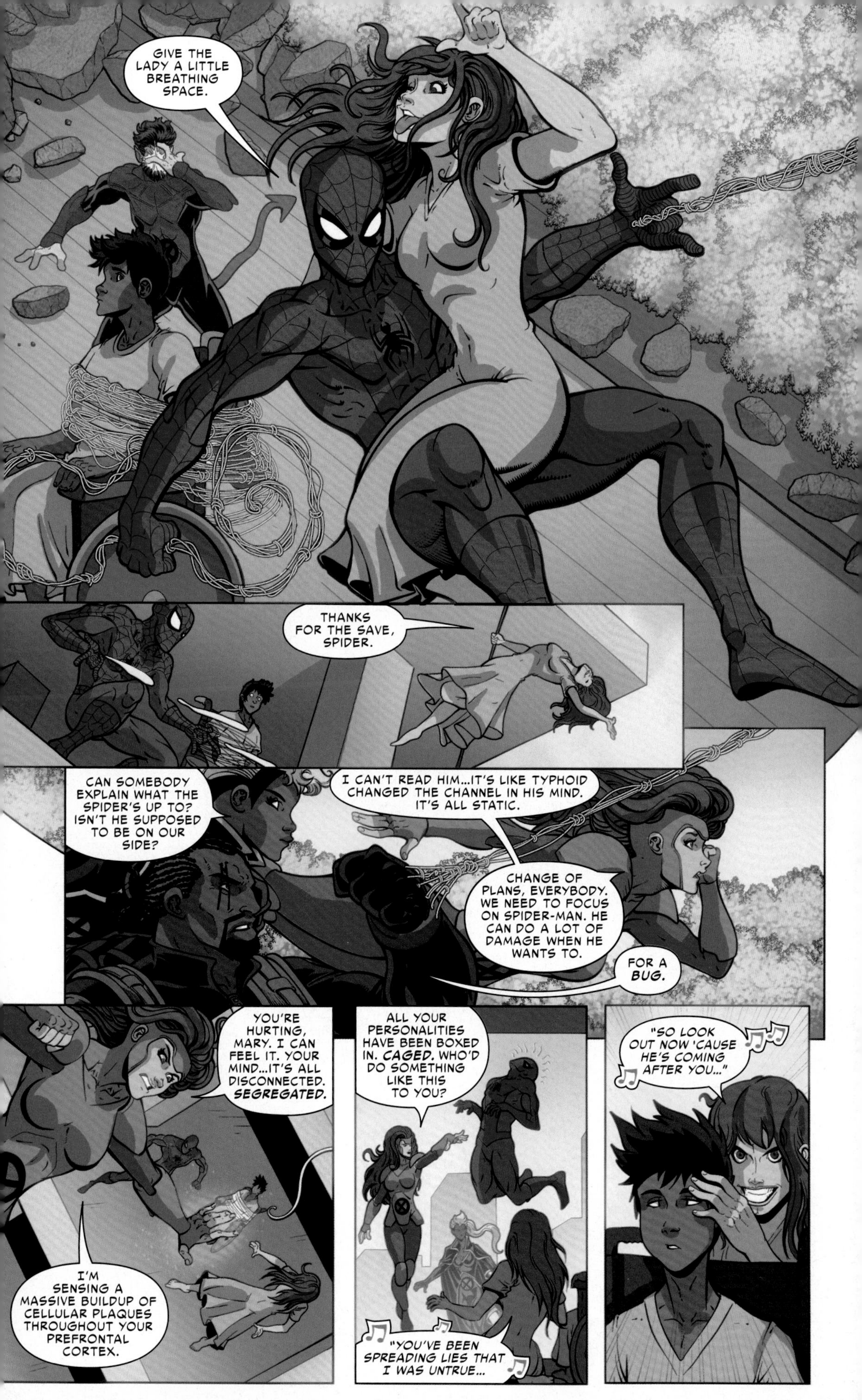
GIVE THE LADY A LITTLE BREATHING SPACE.
THANKS FOR THE SAVE, SPIDER.
CAN SOMEBODY EXPLAIN WHAT THE SPIDER'S UP TO? ISN'T HE SUPPOSED TO BE ON OUR SIDE?
I CAN'T READ HIM...IT'S LIKE TYPHOID CHANGED THE CHANNEL IN HIS MIND. IT'S ALL STATIC.
CHANGE OF PLANS, EVERYBODY. WE NEED TO FOCUS ON SPIDER-MAN. HE CAN DO A LOT OF DAMAGE WHEN HE WANTS TO.
FOR A BUG.
YOU'RE HURTING, MARY. I CAN FEEL IT. YOUR MIND...IT'S ALL DISCONNECTED. SEGREGATED.
I'M SENSING A MASSIVE BUILDUP OF CELLULAR PLAQUES THROUGHOUT YOUR PREFRONTAL CORTEX.
ALL YOUR PERSONALITIES HAVE BEEN BOXED IN. CAGED. WHO'D DO SOMETHING LIKE THIS TO YOU?
"YOU'VE BEEN SPREADING LIES THAT I WAS UNTRUE...
"SO LOOK OUT NOW 'CAUSE HE'S COMING AFTER YOU..."

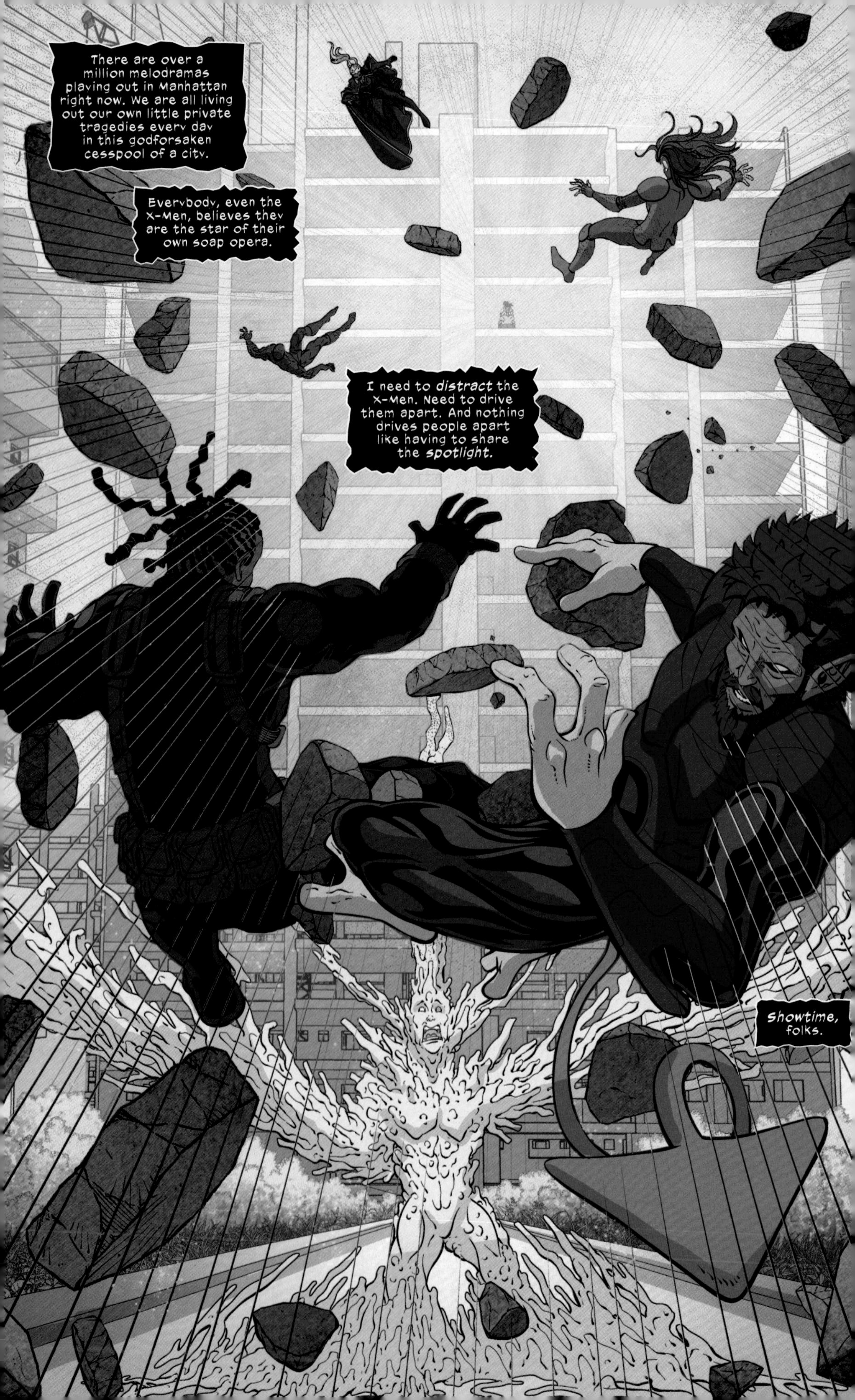
There are over a million melodramas playing out in Manhattan right now. We are all living out our own little private tragedies every day in this godforsaken cesspool of a city.
Everybody, even the X-Men, believes they are the star of their own soap opera.
I need to distract the X-Men. Need to drive them apart. And nothing drives people apart like having to share the spotlight.
Showtime, folks.

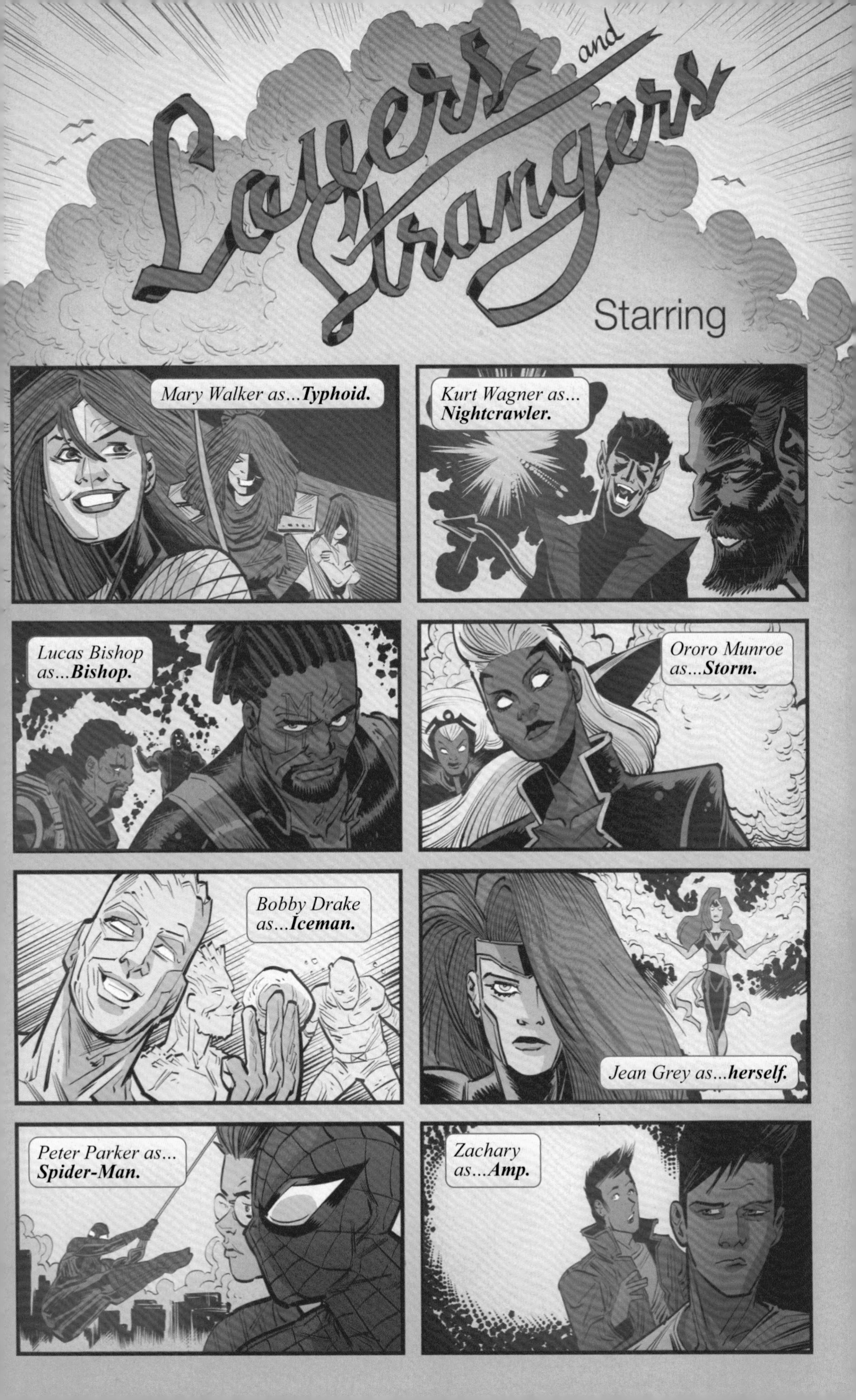
Lovers and Strangers
Starring
Mary Walker as...Typhoid.
Kurt Wagner as... Nightcrawler.
Lucas Bishop as...Bishop.
Ororo Munroe as...Storm.
Bobby Drake as...Iceman.
Jean Grey as...herself.
Peter Parker as... Spider-Man.
Zachary as...Amp.

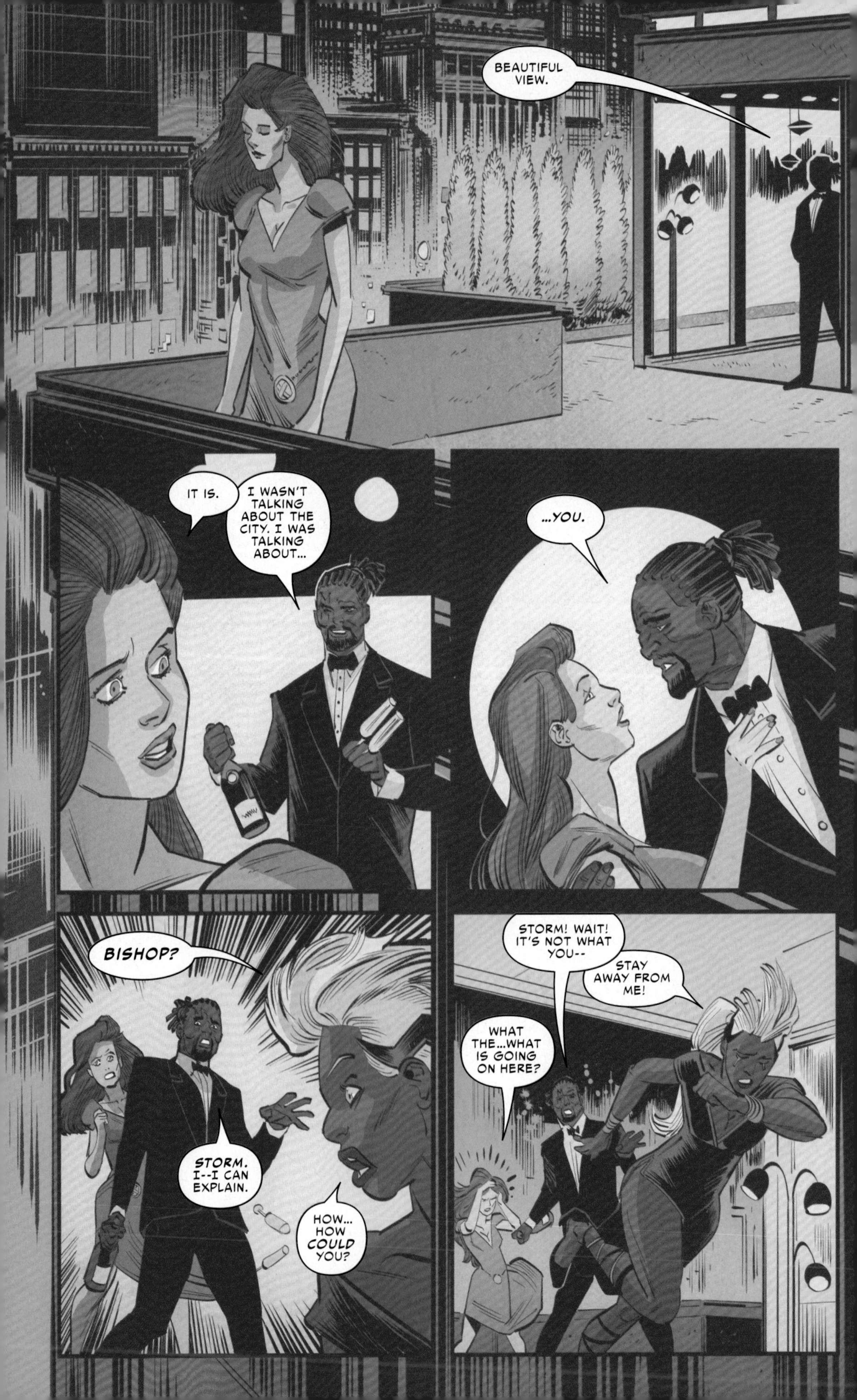
BEAUTIFUL VIEW.
IT IS.
I WASN'T TALKING ABOUT THE CITY. I WAS TALKING ABOUT...
...YOU.
BISHOP?
STORM. I--I CAN EXPLAIN.
HOW... HOW COULD YOU?
STORM! WAIT! IT'S NOT WHAT YOU--
STAY AWAY FROM ME!
WHAT THE...WHAT IS GOING ON HERE?

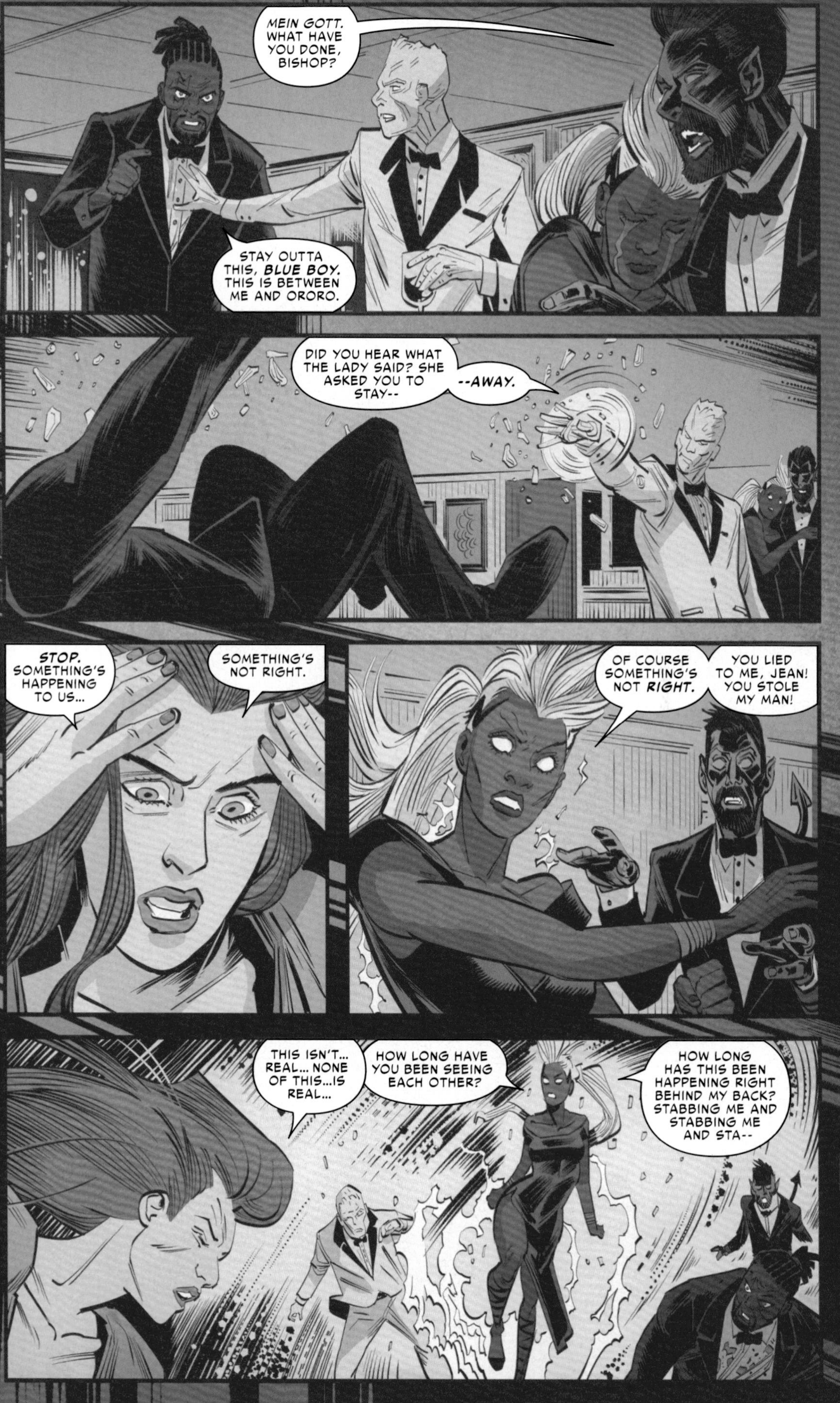
MEIN GOTT. WHAT HAVE YOU DONE, BISHOP?
STAY OUTTA THIS, BLUE BOY. THIS IS BETWEEN ME AND ORORO.
DID YOU HEAR WHAT THE LADY SAID? SHE ASKED YOU TO STAY--
--AWAY.
STOP. SOMETHING'S HAPPENING TO US...
SOMETHING'S NOT RIGHT.
OF COURSE SOMETHING'S NOT RIGHT.
YOU LIED TO ME, JEAN! YOU STOLE MY MAN!
THIS ISN'T... REAL... NONE OF THIS...IS REAL...
HOW LONG HAVE YOU BEEN SEEING EACH OTHER?
HOW LONG HAS THIS BEEN HAPPENING RIGHT BEHIND MY BACK? STABBING ME AND STABBING ME AND STA--

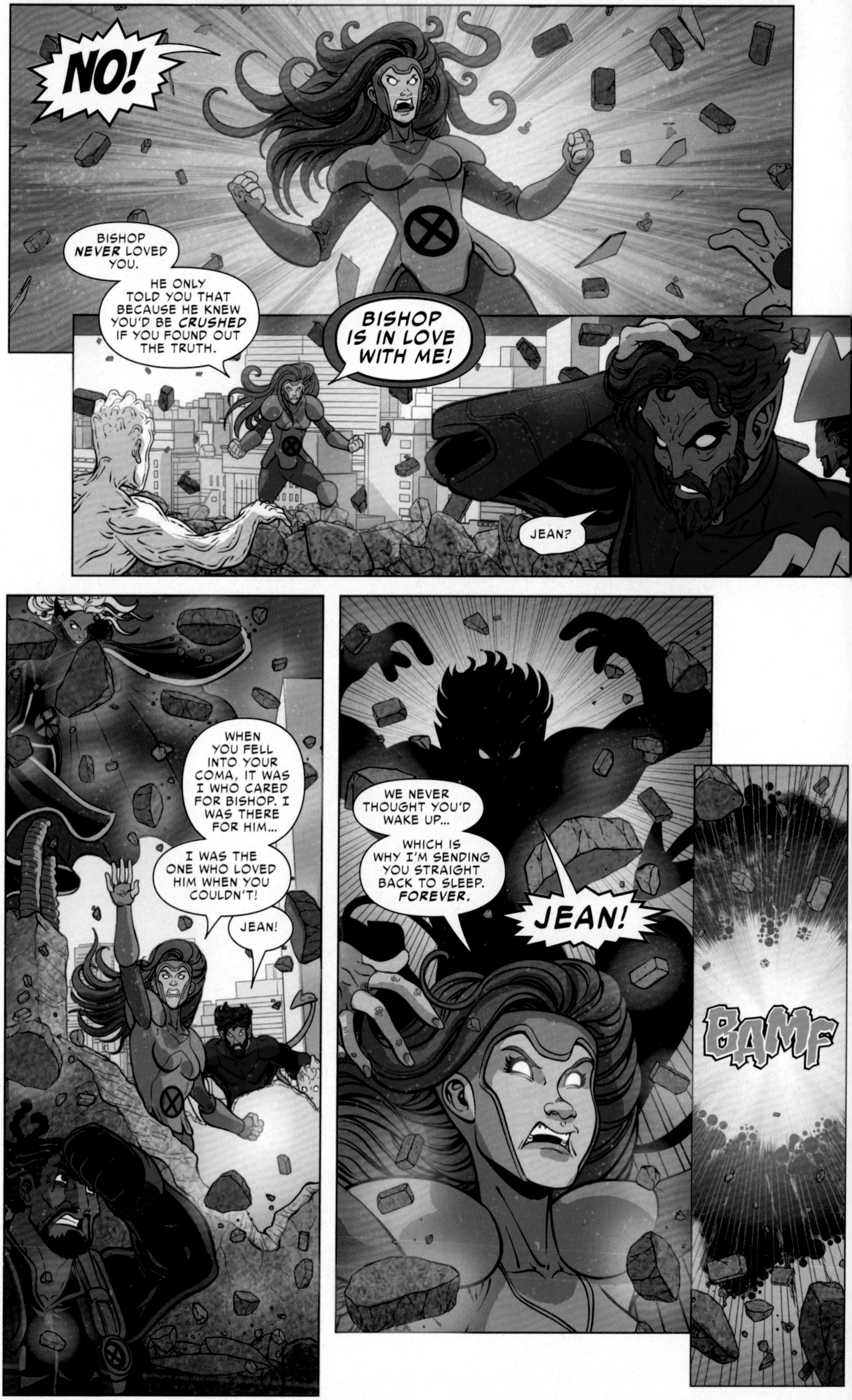
NO!
BISHOP NEVER LOVED YOU.
HE ONLY TOLD YOU THAT BECAUSE HE KNEW YOU'D BE CRUSHED IF YOU FOUND OUT THE TRUTH.
BISHOP IS IN LOVE WITH ME!
JEAN?
WHEN YOU FELL INTO YOUR COMA, IT WAS I WHO CARED FOR BISHOP. I WAS THERE FOR HIM...
I WAS THE ONE WHO LOVED HIM WHEN YOU COULDN'T!
JEAN!
WE NEVER THOUGHT YOU'D WAKE UP...
WHICH IS WHY I'M SENDING YOU STRAIGHT BACK TO SLEEP. FOREVER.
JEAN!
BAMF

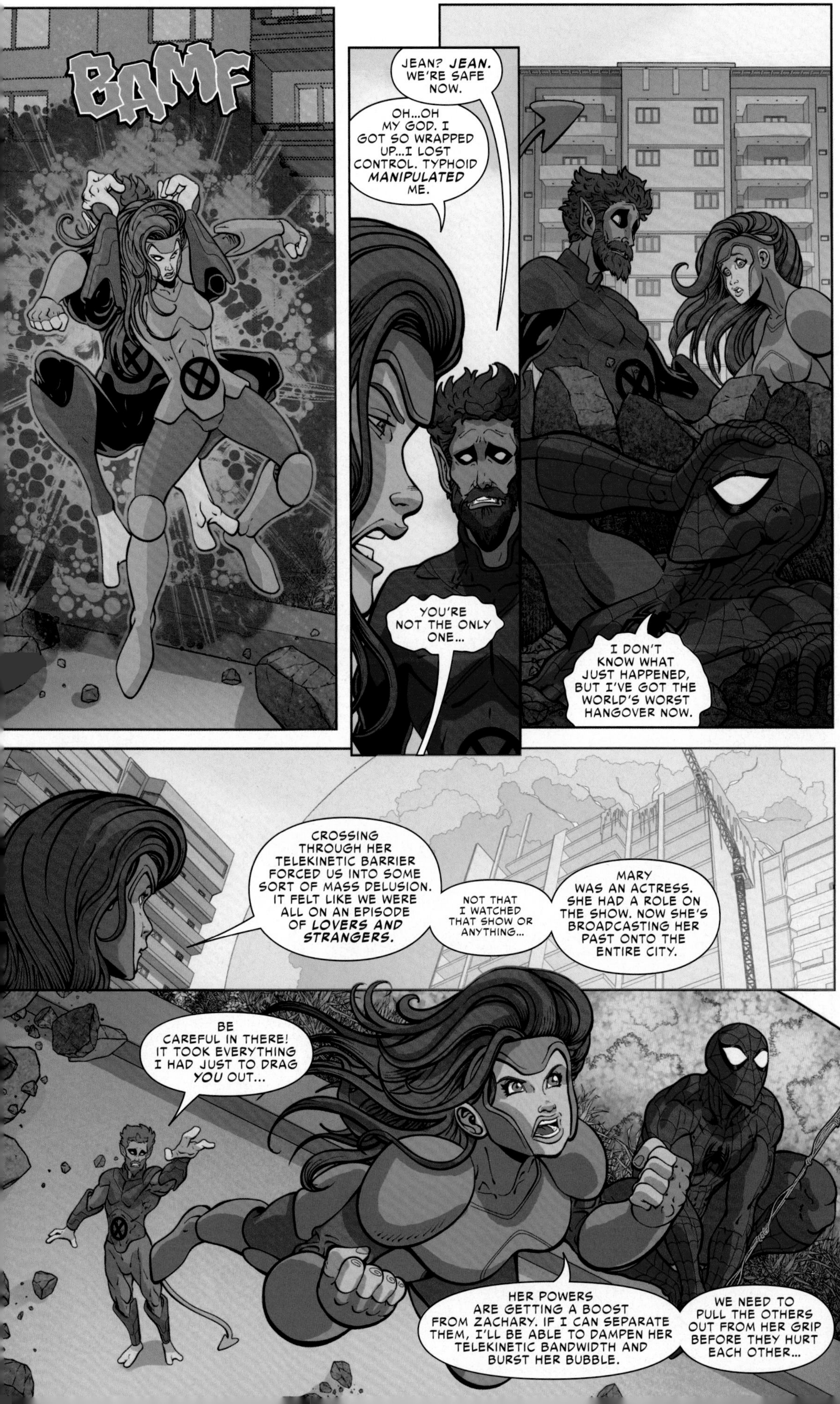
BAMF
JEAN? JEAN. WE'RE SAFE NOW.
OH...OH MY GOD. I GOT SO WRAPPED UP...I LOST CONTROL. TYPHOID MANIPULATED ME.
YOU'RE NOT THE ONLY ONE...
I DON'T KNOW WHAT JUST HAPPENED, BUT I'VE GOT THE WORLD'S WORST HANGOVER NOW.
CROSSING THROUGH HER TELEKINETIC BARRIER FORCED US INTO SOME SORT OF MASS DELUSION. IT FELT LIKE WE WERE ALL ON AN EPISODE OF LOVERS AND STRANGERS.
NOT THAT I WATCHED THAT SHOW OR ANYTHING...
MARY WAS AN ACTRESS. SHE HAD A ROLE ON THE SHOW. NOW SHE'S BROADCASTING HER PAST ONTO THE ENTIRE CITY.
BE CAREFUL IN THERE! IT TOOK EVERYTHING I HAD JUST TO DRAG YOU OUT...
HER POWERS ARE GETTING A BOOST FROM ZACHARY. IF I CAN SEPARATE THEM, I'LL BE ABLE TO DAMPEN HER TELEKINETIC BANDWIDTH AND BURST HER BUBBLE.
WE NEED TO PULL THE OTHERS OUT FROM HER GRIP BEFORE THEY HURT EACH OTHER...

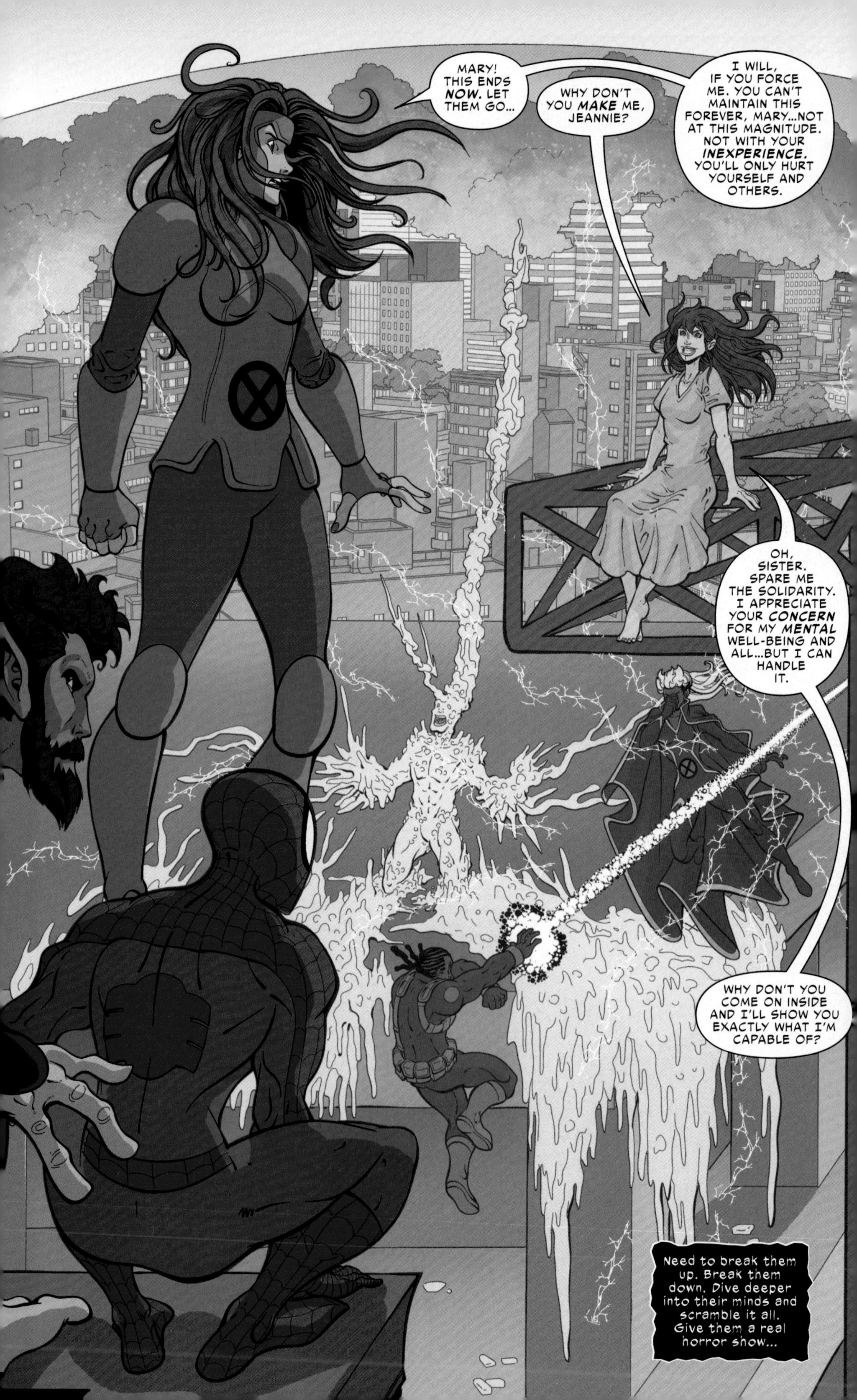

MARY! THIS ENDS **NOW.** LET THEM GO...
WHY DON'T YOU ***MAKE*** ME, JEANNIE?
I WILL, IF YOU FORCE ME. YOU CAN'T MAINTAIN THIS FOREVER, MARY...NOT AT THIS MAGNITUDE. NOT WITH YOUR ***INEXPERIENCE.*** YOU'LL ONLY HURT YOURSELF AND OTHERS.
OH, SISTER. SPARE ME THE SOLIDARITY. I APPRECIATE YOUR ***CONCERN*** FOR MY ***MENTAL*** WELL-BEING AND ALL...BUT I CAN HANDLE IT.
WHY DON'T YOU COME ON INSIDE AND I'LL SHOW YOU EXACTLY WHAT I'M CAPABLE OF?
Need to break them up. Break them down. Dive deeper into their minds and scramble it all. Give them a real horror show...

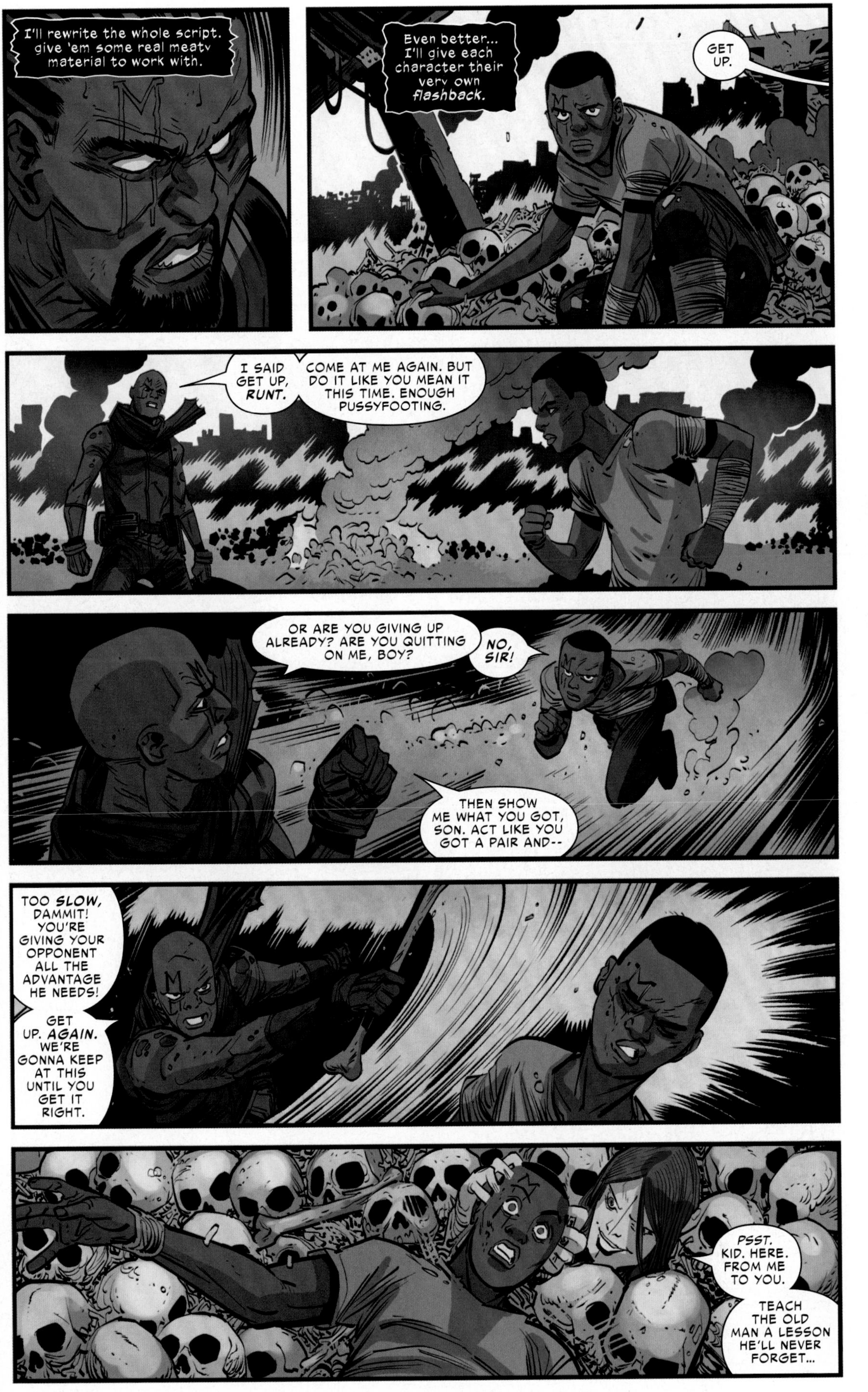
I'll rewrite the whole script. give 'em some real meaty material to work with.
Even better... I'll give each character their very own flashback.
GET UP.
I SAID GET UP, RUNT.
COME AT ME AGAIN. BUT DO IT LIKE YOU MEAN IT THIS TIME. ENOUGH PUSSYFOOTING.
OR ARE YOU GIVING UP ALREADY? ARE YOU QUITTING ON ME, BOY?
NO, SIR!
THEN SHOW ME WHAT YOU GOT, SON. ACT LIKE YOU GOT A PAIR AND--
TOO SLOW, DAMMIT! YOU'RE GIVING YOUR OPPONENT ALL THE ADVANTAGE HE NEEDS!
GET UP. AGAIN. WE'RE GONNA KEEP AT THIS UNTIL YOU GET IT RIGHT.
PSST. KID. HERE. FROM ME TO YOU.
TEACH THE OLD MAN A LESSON HE'LL NEVER FORGET...

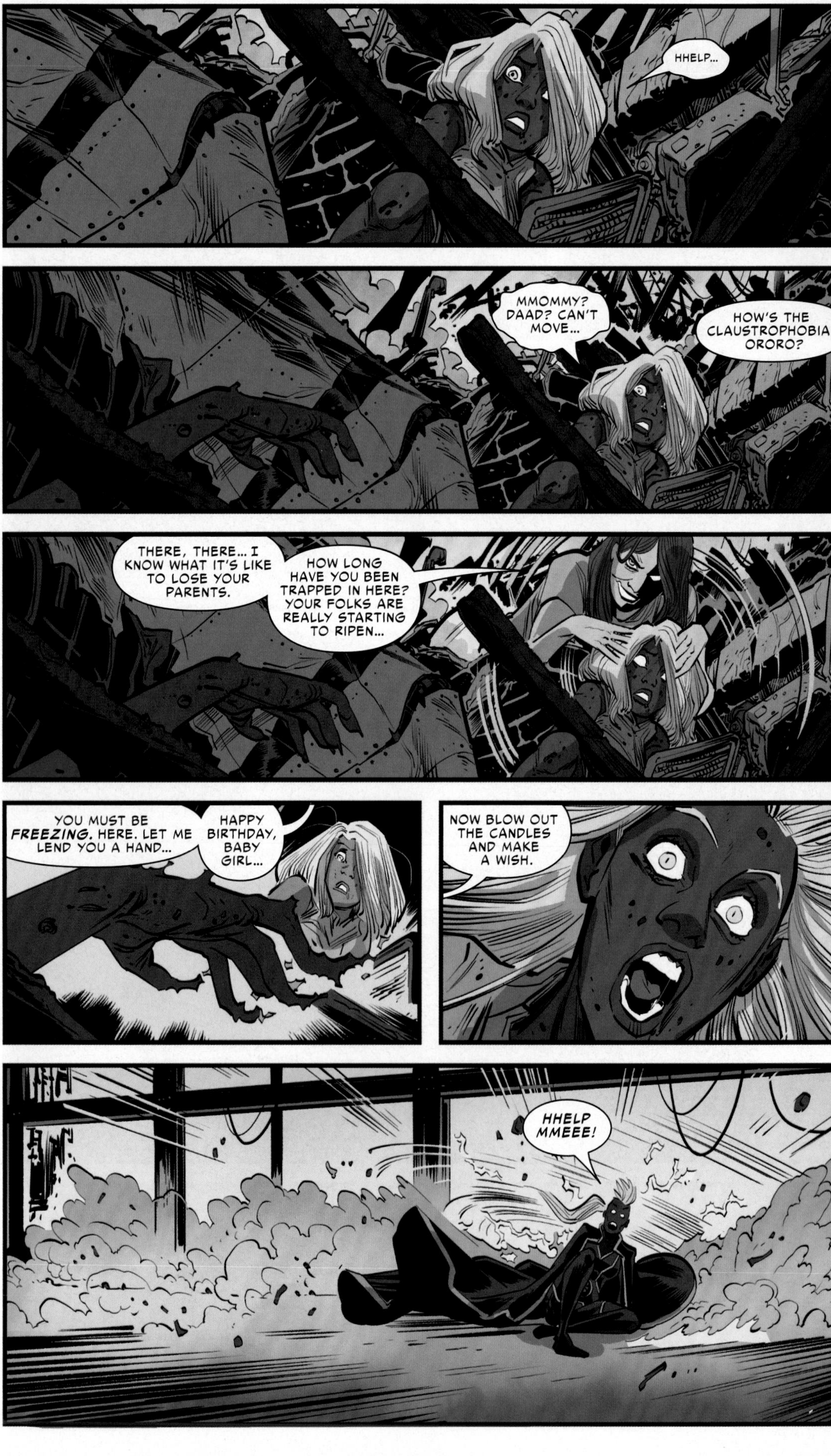
HHELP...
MMOMMY? DAAD? CAN'T MOVE...
HOW'S THE CLAUSTROPHOBIA, ORORO?
THERE, THERE... I KNOW WHAT IT'S LIKE TO LOSE YOUR PARENTS.
HOW LONG HAVE YOU BEEN TRAPPED IN HERE? YOUR FOLKS ARE REALLY STARTING TO RIPEN...
YOU MUST BE FREEZING. HERE. LET ME LEND YOU A HAND...
HAPPY BIRTHDAY, BABY GIRL...
NOW BLOW OUT THE CANDLES AND MAKE A WISH.
HHELP MMEEE!

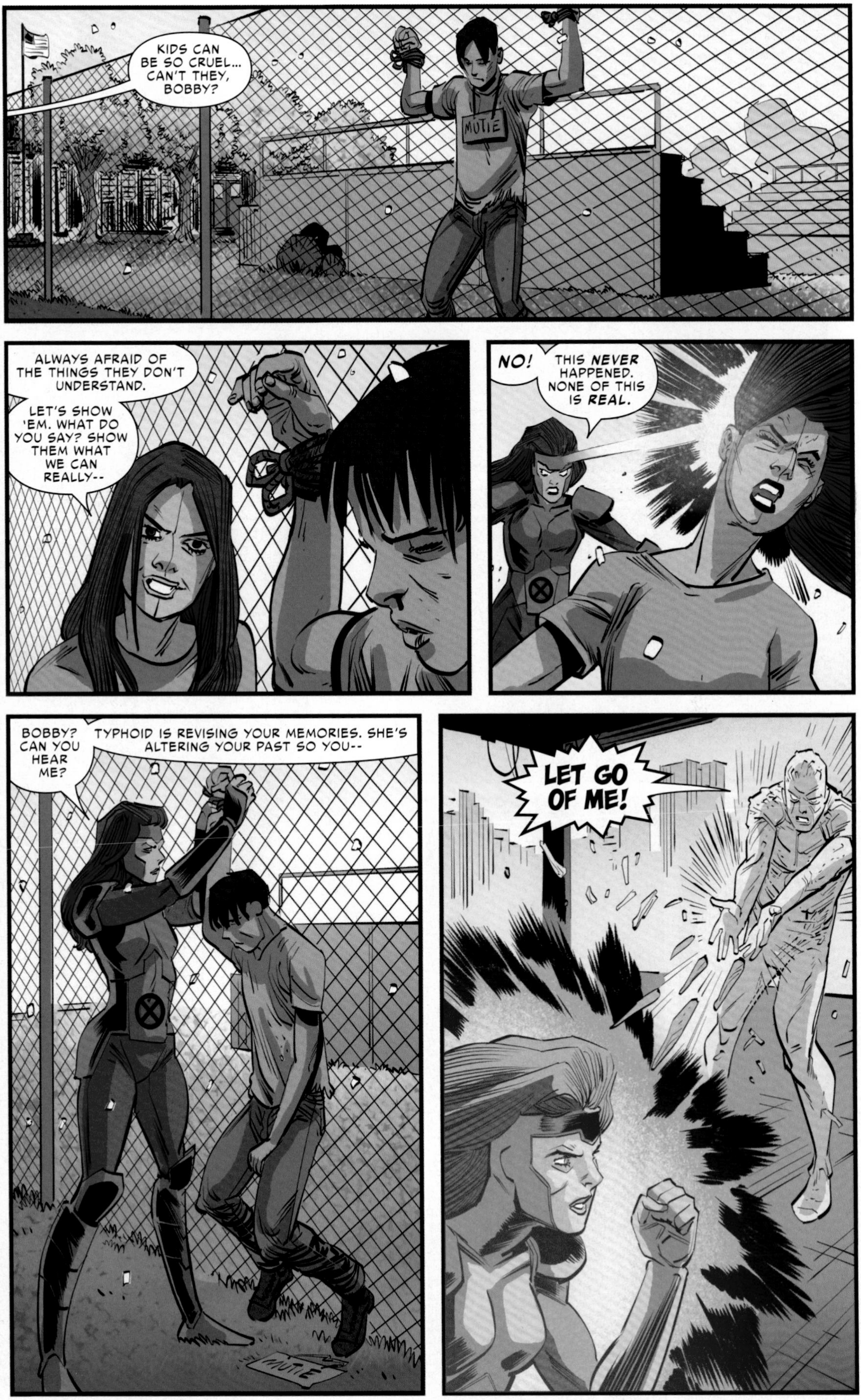
KIDS CAN BE SO CRUEL... CAN'T THEY, BOBBY?
MUTIE
ALWAYS AFRAID OF THE THINGS THEY DON'T UNDERSTAND.
LET'S SHOW 'EM. WHAT DO YOU SAY? SHOW THEM WHAT WE CAN REALLY--
NO!
THIS NEVER HAPPENED. NONE OF THIS IS REAL.
BOBBY? CAN YOU HEAR ME?
TYPHOID IS REVISING YOUR MEMORIES. SHE'S ALTERING YOUR PAST SO YOU--
MUTIE
LET GO OF ME!

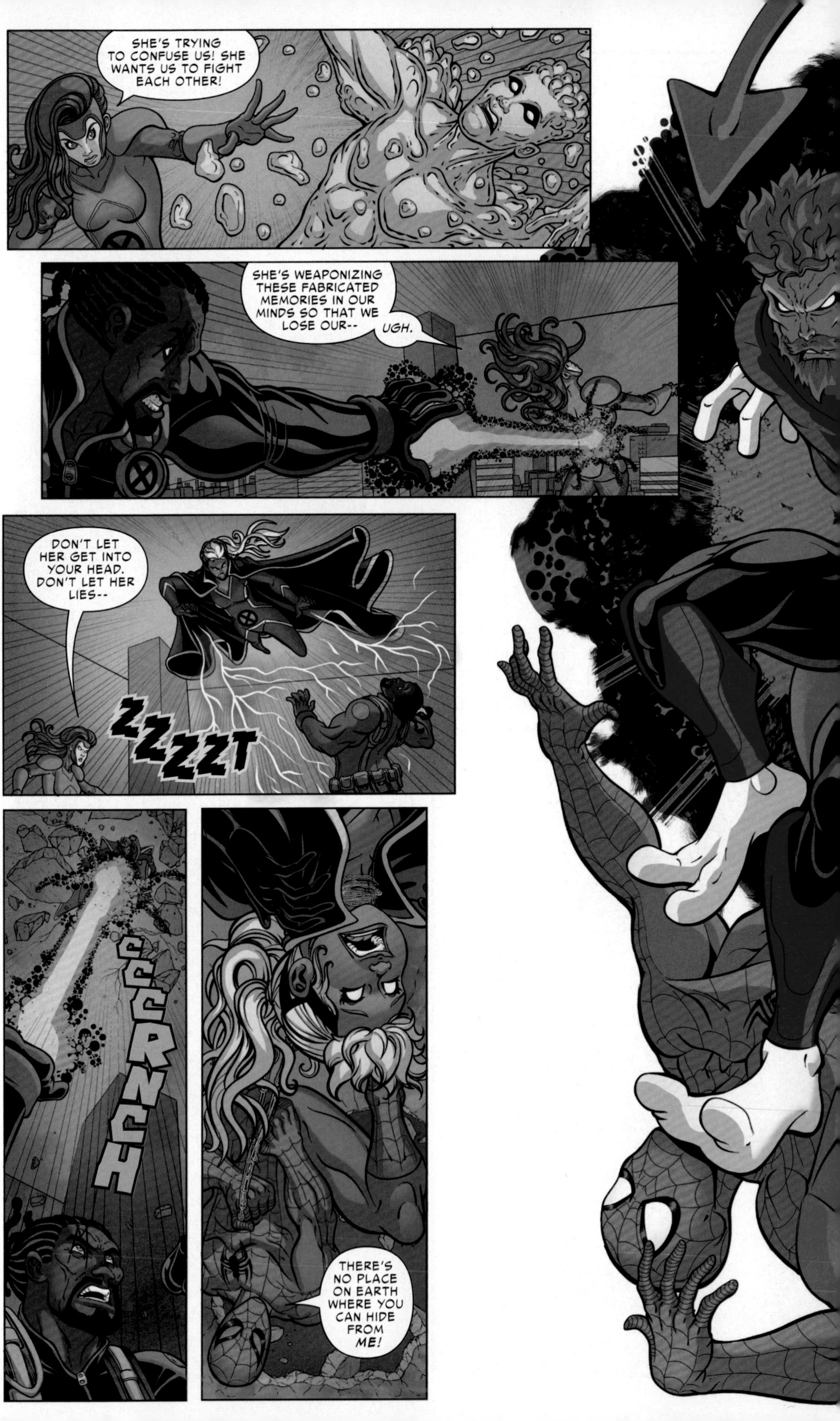
SHE'S TRYING TO CONFUSE US! SHE WANTS US TO FIGHT EACH OTHER!
SHE'S WEAPONIZING THESE FABRICATED MEMORIES IN OUR MINDS SO THAT WE LOSE OUR--
UGH.
DON'T LET HER GET INTO YOUR HEAD. DON'T LET HER LIES--
ZZZZZT
CCCRNCH
THERE'S NO PLACE ON EARTH WHERE YOU CAN HIDE FROM ME!

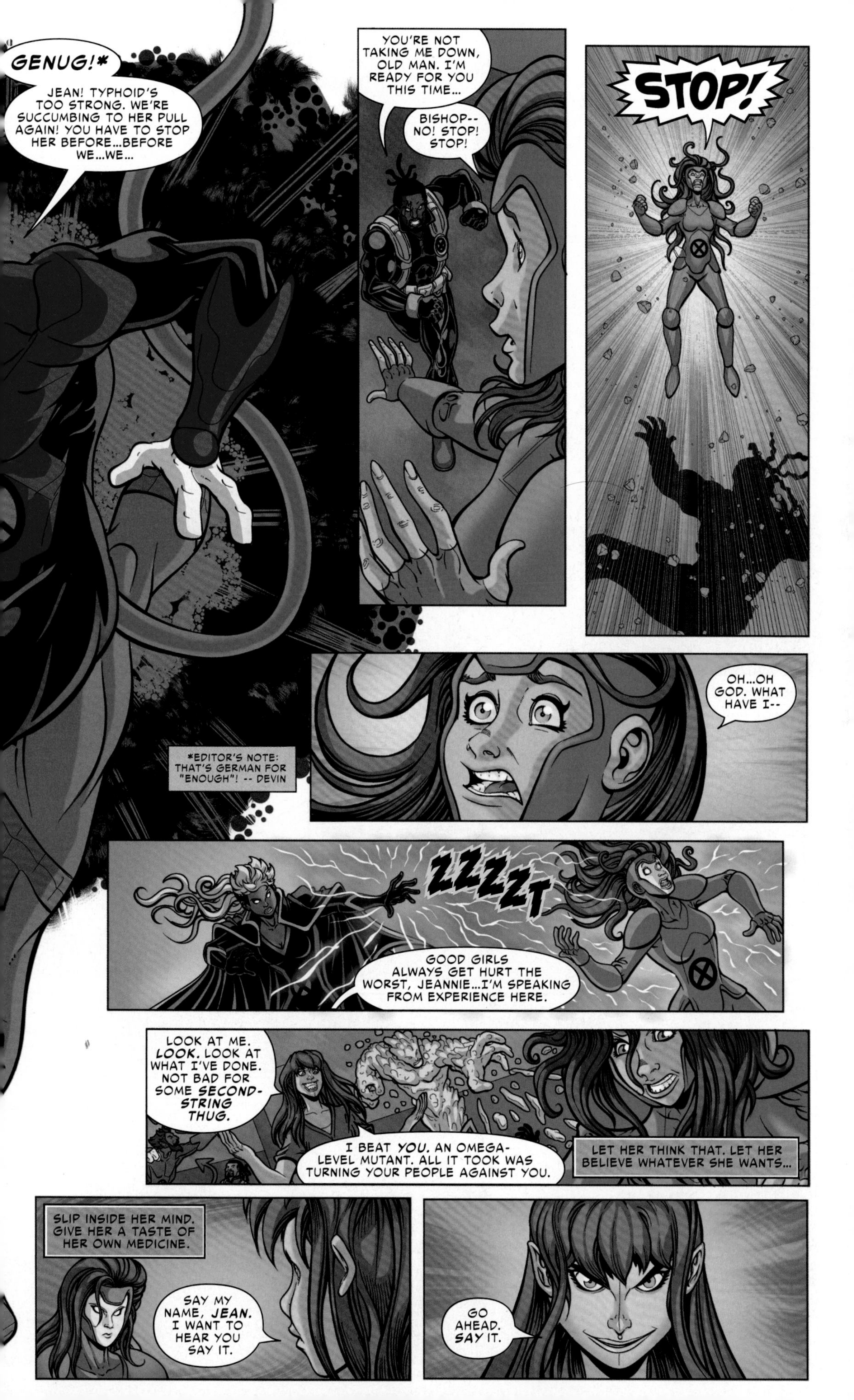

GENUG!*
JEAN! TYPHOID'S TOO STRONG. WE'RE SUCCUMBING TO HER PULL AGAIN! YOU HAVE TO STOP HER BEFORE...BEFORE WE...WE...
YOU'RE NOT TAKING ME DOWN, OLD MAN. I'M READY FOR YOU THIS TIME...
BISHOP-- NO! STOP! STOP!
STOP!
OH...OH GOD. WHAT HAVE I--
*EDITOR'S NOTE: THAT'S GERMAN FOR "ENOUGH"! -- DEVIN
ZZZZZT
GOOD GIRLS ALWAYS GET HURT THE WORST, JEANNIE...I'M SPEAKING FROM EXPERIENCE HERE.
LOOK AT ME. LOOK. LOOK AT WHAT I'VE DONE. NOT BAD FOR SOME SECOND-STRING THUG.
I BEAT YOU. AN OMEGA-LEVEL MUTANT. ALL IT TOOK WAS TURNING YOUR PEOPLE AGAINST YOU.
LET HER THINK THAT. LET HER BELIEVE WHATEVER SHE WANTS...
SLIP INSIDE HER MIND. GIVE HER A TASTE OF HER OWN MEDICINE.
SAY MY NAME, JEAN. I WANT TO HEAR YOU SAY IT.
GO AHEAD. SAY IT.

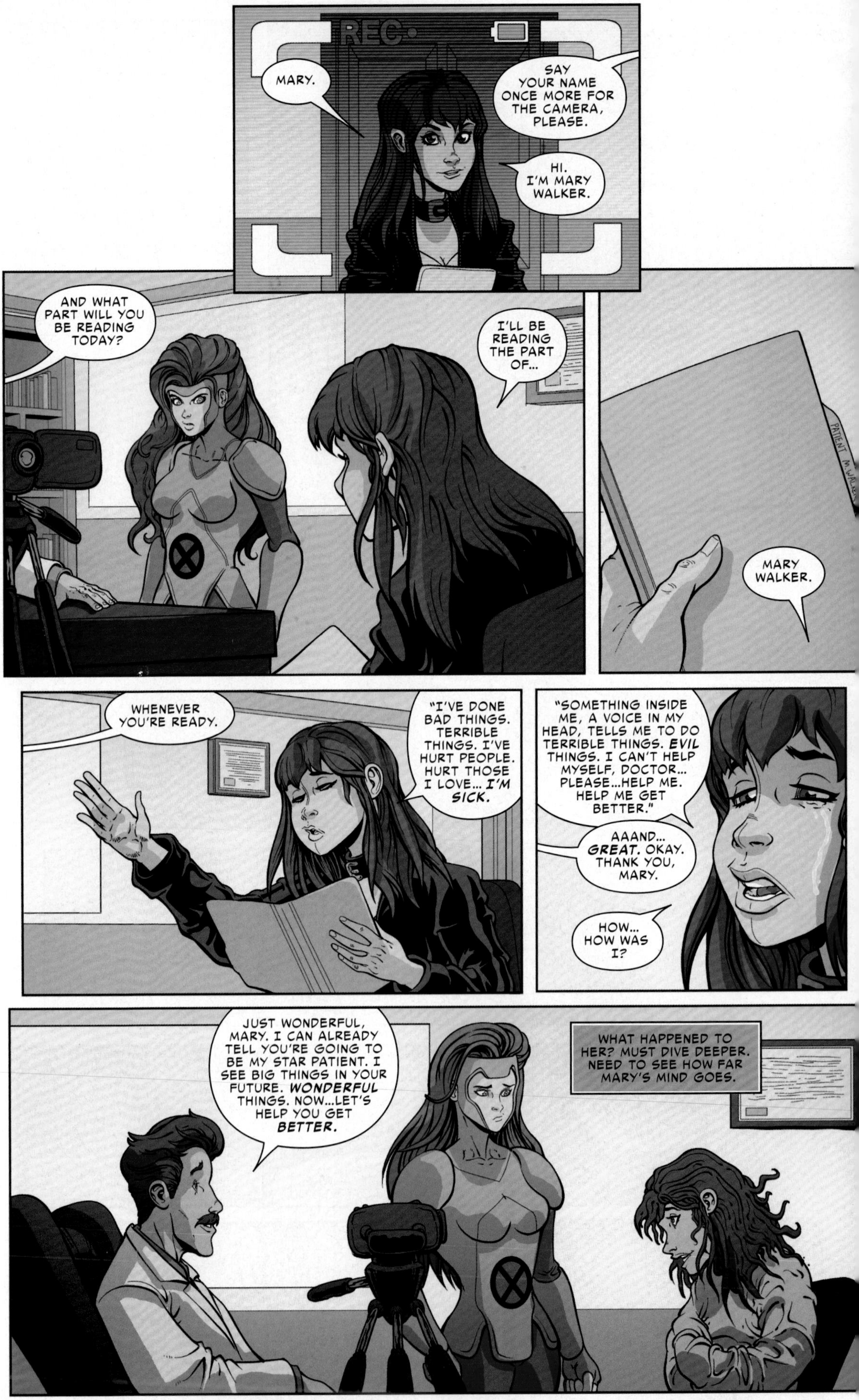

REC
MARY.
SAY YOUR NAME ONCE MORE FOR THE CAMERA, PLEASE.
HI. I'M MARY WALKER.
AND WHAT PART WILL YOU BE READING TODAY?
I'LL BE READING THE PART OF...
PATIENT M. WALKER
MARY WALKER.
WHENEVER YOU'RE READY.
"I'VE DONE BAD THINGS. TERRIBLE THINGS. I'VE HURT PEOPLE. HURT THOSE I LOVE... I'M SICK.
"SOMETHING INSIDE ME, A VOICE IN MY HEAD, TELLS ME TO DO TERRIBLE THINGS. EVIL THINGS. I CAN'T HELP MYSELF, DOCTOR... PLEASE...HELP ME. HELP ME GET BETTER."
AAAND... GREAT. OKAY. THANK YOU, MARY.
HOW... HOW WAS I?
JUST WONDERFUL, MARY. I CAN ALREADY TELL YOU'RE GOING TO BE MY STAR PATIENT. I SEE BIG THINGS IN YOUR FUTURE. WONDERFUL THINGS. NOW...LET'S HELP YOU GET BETTER.
WHAT HAPPENED TO HER? MUST DIVE DEEPER. NEED TO SEE HOW FAR MARY'S MIND GOES.

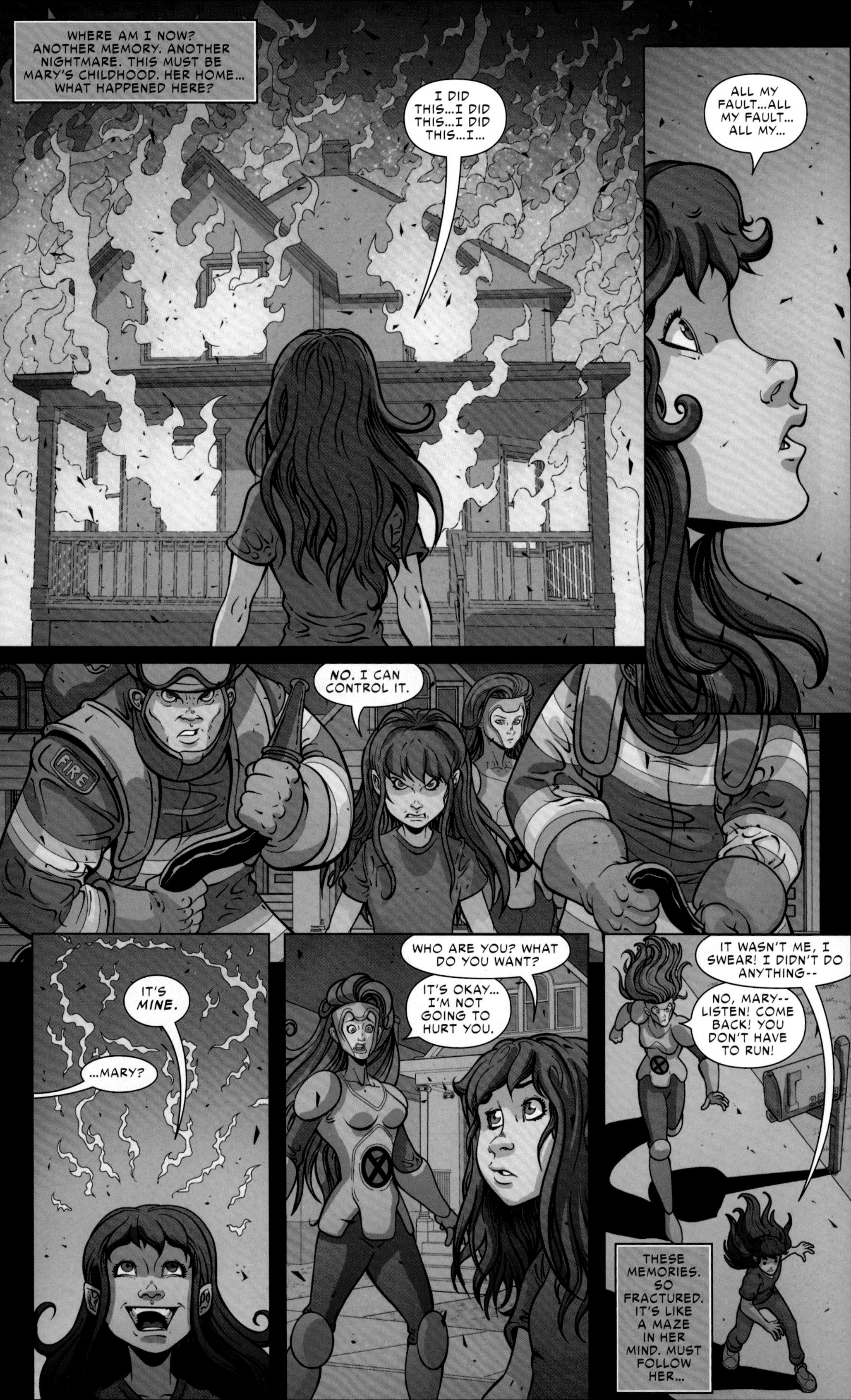

WHERE AM I NOW? ANOTHER MEMORY. ANOTHER NIGHTMARE. THIS MUST BE MARY'S CHILDHOOD. HER HOME... WHAT HAPPENED HERE?
I DID THIS...I DID THIS...I DID THIS...I...
ALL MY FAULT...ALL MY FAULT... ALL MY...
FIRE
NO. I CAN CONTROL IT.
IT'S MINE.
...MARY?
WHO ARE YOU? WHAT DO YOU WANT?
IT'S OKAY... I'M NOT GOING TO HURT YOU.
IT WASN'T ME, I SWEAR! I DIDN'T DO ANYTHING--
NO, MARY-- LISTEN! COME BACK! YOU DON'T HAVE TO RUN!
THESE MEMORIES. SO FRACTURED. IT'S LIKE A MAZE IN HER MIND. MUST FOLLOW HER...

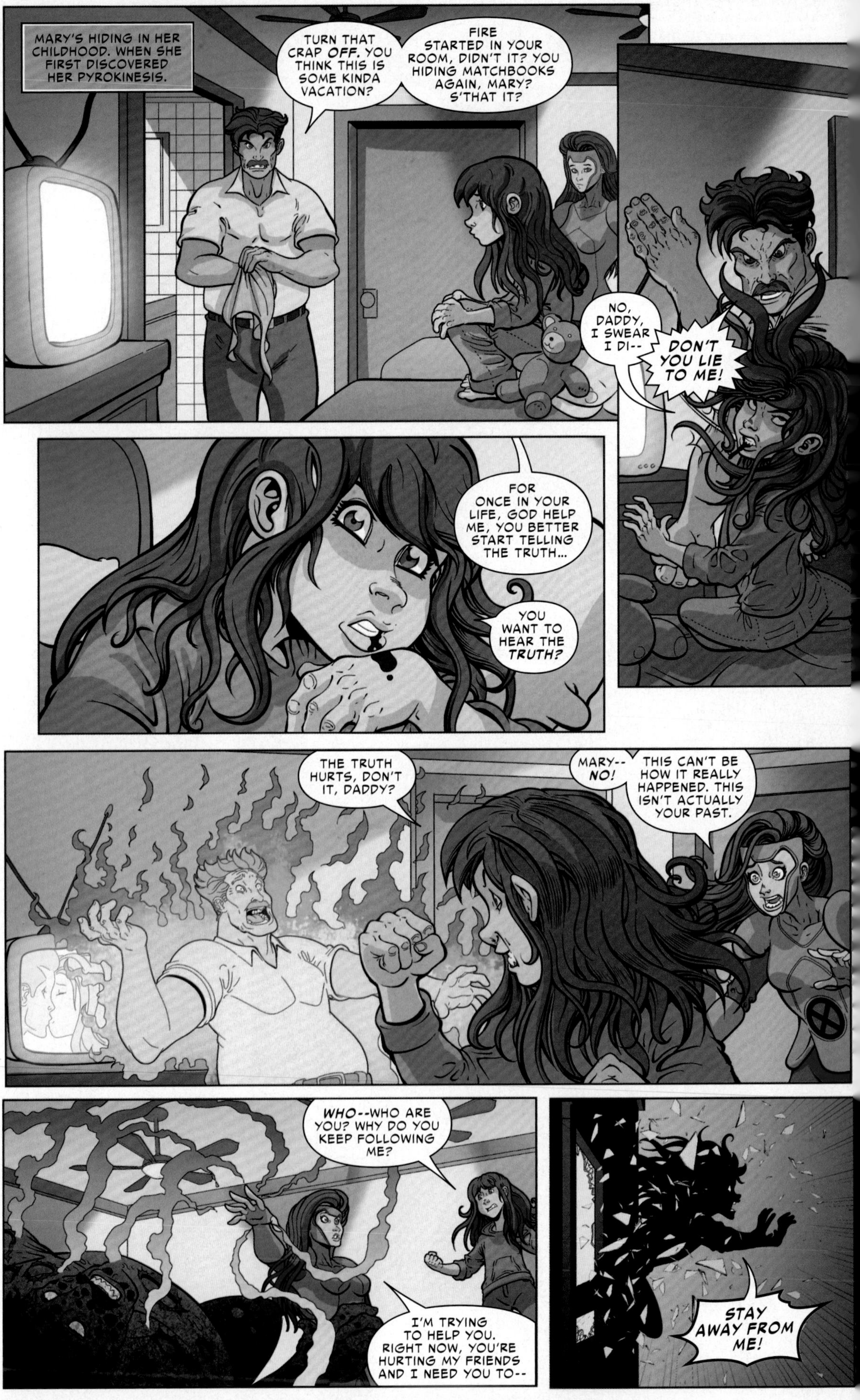
MARY'S HIDING IN HER CHILDHOOD. WHEN SHE FIRST DISCOVERED HER PYROKINESIS.
TURN THAT CRAP OFF. YOU THINK THIS IS SOME KINDA VACATION?
FIRE STARTED IN YOUR ROOM, DIDN'T IT? YOU HIDING MATCHBOOKS AGAIN, MARY? S'THAT IT?
NO, DADDY, I SWEAR I DI--
DON'T YOU LIE TO ME!
FOR ONCE IN YOUR LIFE, GOD HELP ME, YOU BETTER START TELLING THE TRUTH...
YOU WANT TO HEAR THE TRUTH?
THE TRUTH HURTS, DON'T IT, DADDY?
MARY-- NO!
THIS CAN'T BE HOW IT REALLY HAPPENED. THIS ISN'T ACTUALLY YOUR PAST.
WHO--WHO ARE YOU? WHY DO YOU KEEP FOLLOWING ME?
I'M TRYING TO HELP YOU. RIGHT NOW, YOU'RE HURTING MY FRIENDS AND I NEED YOU TO--
STAY AWAY FROM ME!

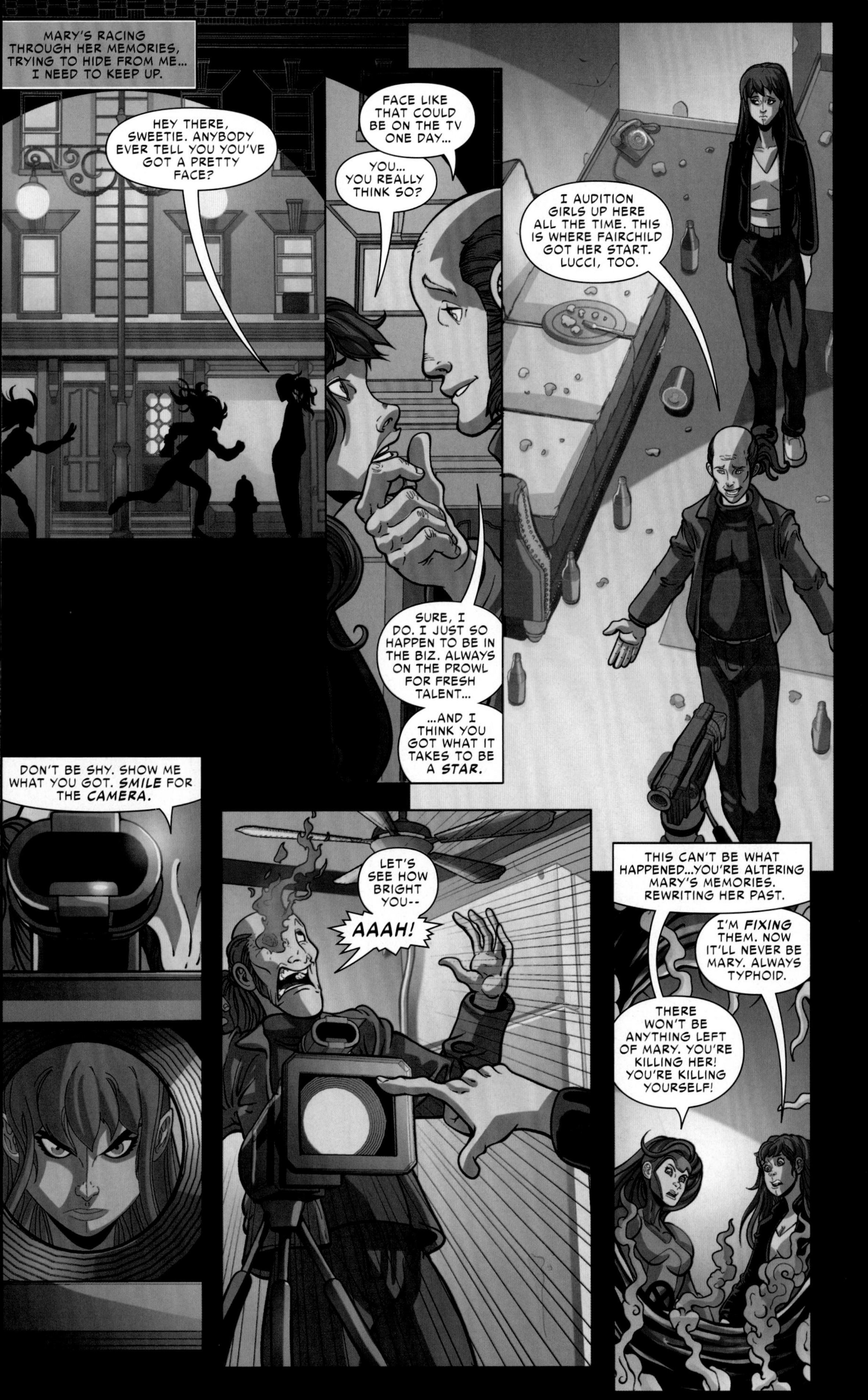

MARY'S RACING THROUGH HER MEMORIES, TRYING TO HIDE FROM ME... I NEED TO KEEP UP.
HEY THERE, SWEETIE. ANYBODY EVER TELL YOU YOU'VE GOT A PRETTY FACE?
FACE LIKE THAT COULD BE ON THE TV ONE DAY...
YOU... YOU REALLY THINK SO?
SURE, I DO. I JUST SO HAPPEN TO BE IN THE BIZ. ALWAYS ON THE PROWL FOR FRESH TALENT...
...AND I THINK YOU GOT WHAT IT TAKES TO BE A STAR.
I AUDITION GIRLS UP HERE ALL THE TIME. THIS IS WHERE FAIRCHILD GOT HER START. LUCCI, TOO.
DON'T BE SHY. SHOW ME WHAT YOU GOT. SMILE FOR THE CAMERA.
LET'S SEE HOW BRIGHT YOU--
AAAH!
THIS CAN'T BE WHAT HAPPENED...YOU'RE ALTERING MARY'S MEMORIES. REWRITING HER PAST.
I'M FIXING THEM. NOW IT'LL NEVER BE MARY. ALWAYS TYPHOID.
THERE WON'T BE ANYTHING LEFT OF MARY. YOU'RE KILLING HER! YOU'RE KILLING YOURSELF!

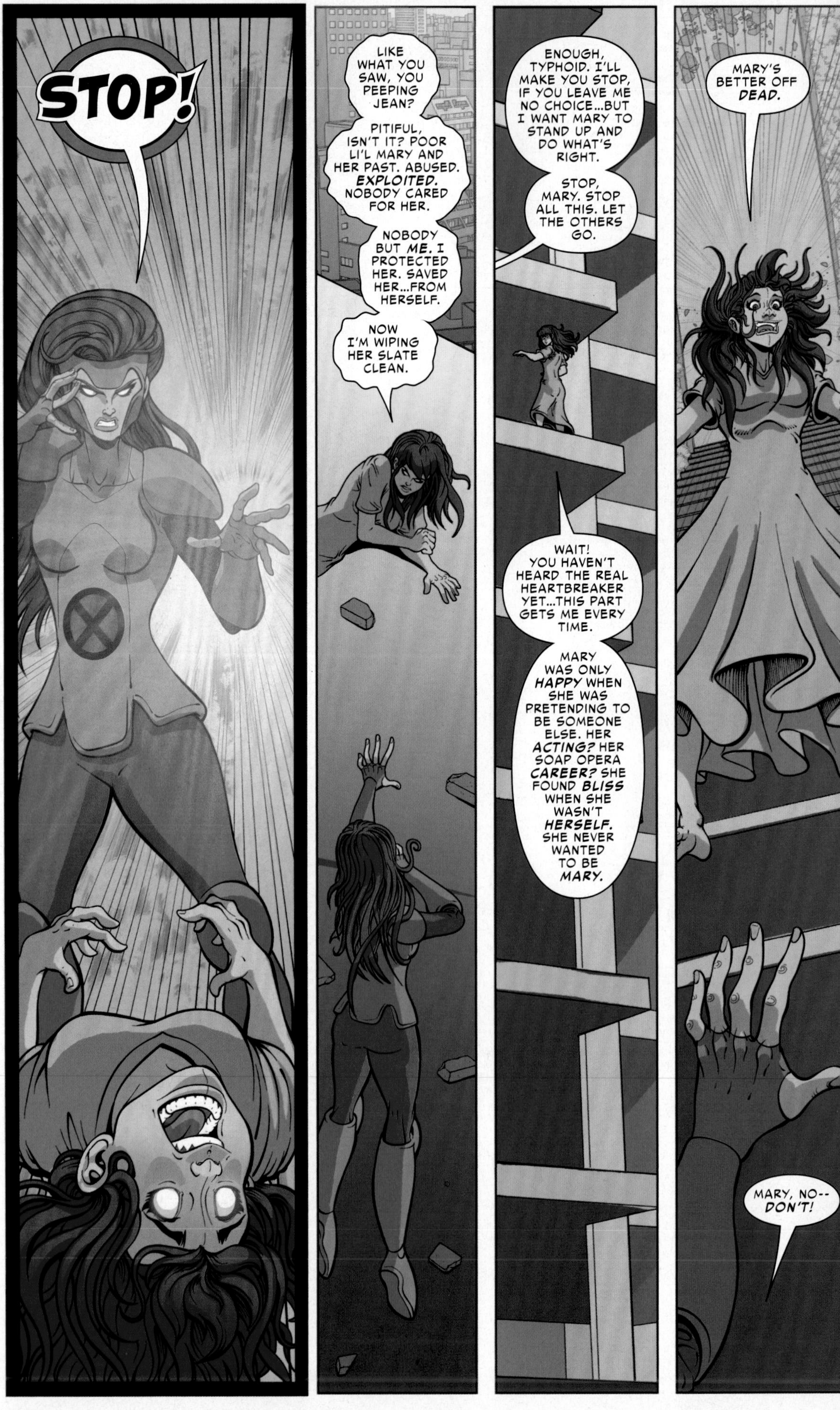
STOP!
LIKE WHAT YOU SAW, YOU PEEPING JEAN?
PITIFUL, ISN'T IT? POOR LI'L MARY AND HER PAST. ABUSED. EXPLOITED. NOBODY CARED FOR HER.
NOBODY BUT ME. I PROTECTED HER. SAVED HER...FROM HERSELF.
NOW I'M WIPING HER SLATE CLEAN.
ENOUGH, TYPHOID. I'LL MAKE YOU STOP, IF YOU LEAVE ME NO CHOICE...BUT I WANT MARY TO STAND UP AND DO WHAT'S RIGHT.
STOP, MARY. STOP ALL THIS. LET THE OTHERS GO.
WAIT! YOU HAVEN'T HEARD THE REAL HEARTBREAKER YET...THIS PART GETS ME EVERY TIME.
MARY WAS ONLY HAPPY WHEN SHE WAS PRETENDING TO BE SOMEONE ELSE. HER ACTING? HER SOAP OPERA CAREER? SHE FOUND BLISS WHEN SHE WASN'T HERSELF. SHE NEVER WANTED TO BE MARY.
MARY'S BETTER OFF DEAD.
MARY, NO--DON'T!

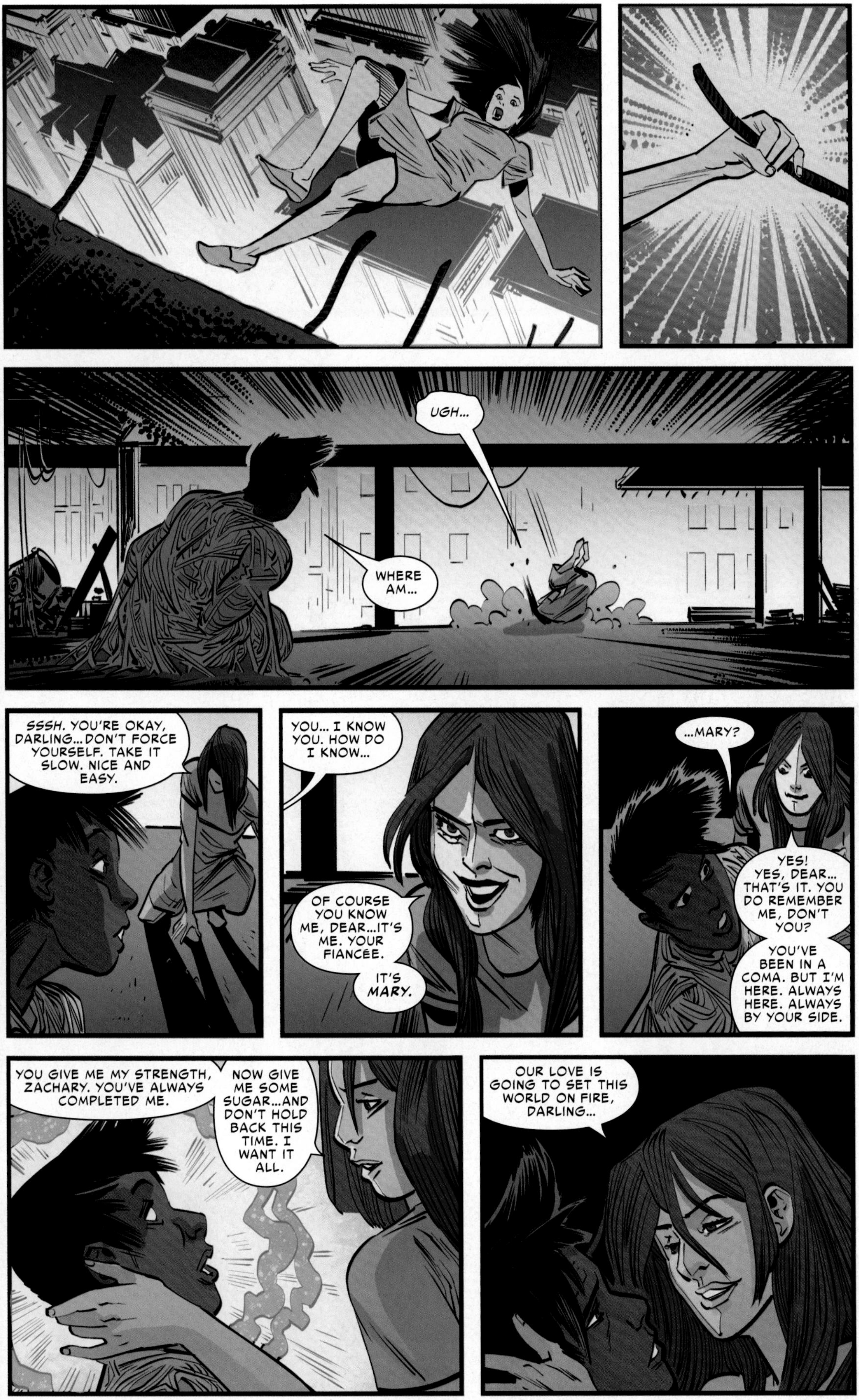
UGH...
WHERE AM...
SSSH. YOU'RE OKAY, DARLING... DON'T FORCE YOURSELF. TAKE IT SLOW. NICE AND EASY.
YOU... I KNOW YOU. HOW DO I KNOW...
OF COURSE YOU KNOW ME, DEAR... IT'S ME. YOUR FIANCÉE.
IT'S MARY.
...MARY?
YES! YES, DEAR... THAT'S IT. YOU DO REMEMBER ME, DON'T YOU?
YOU'VE BEEN IN A COMA. BUT I'M HERE. ALWAYS HERE. ALWAYS BY YOUR SIDE.
YOU GIVE ME MY STRENGTH, ZACHARY. YOU'VE ALWAYS COMPLETED ME.
NOW GIVE ME SOME SUGAR... AND DON'T HOLD BACK THIS TIME. I WANT IT ALL.
OUR LOVE IS GOING TO SET THIS WORLD ON FIRE, DARLING...

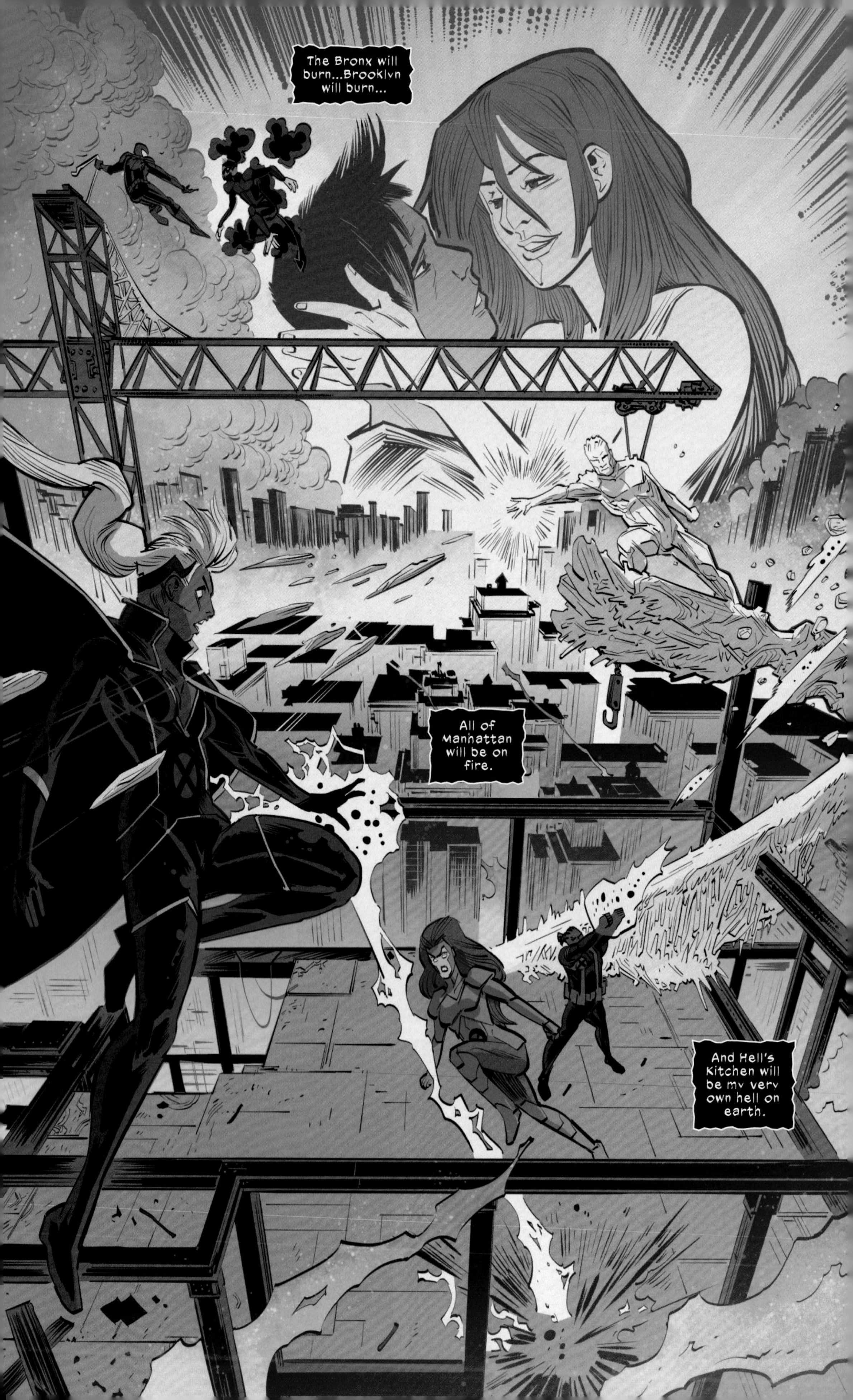
The Bronx will burn...Brooklyn will burn...
All of Manhattan will be on fire.
And Hell's Kitchen will be my very own hell on earth.

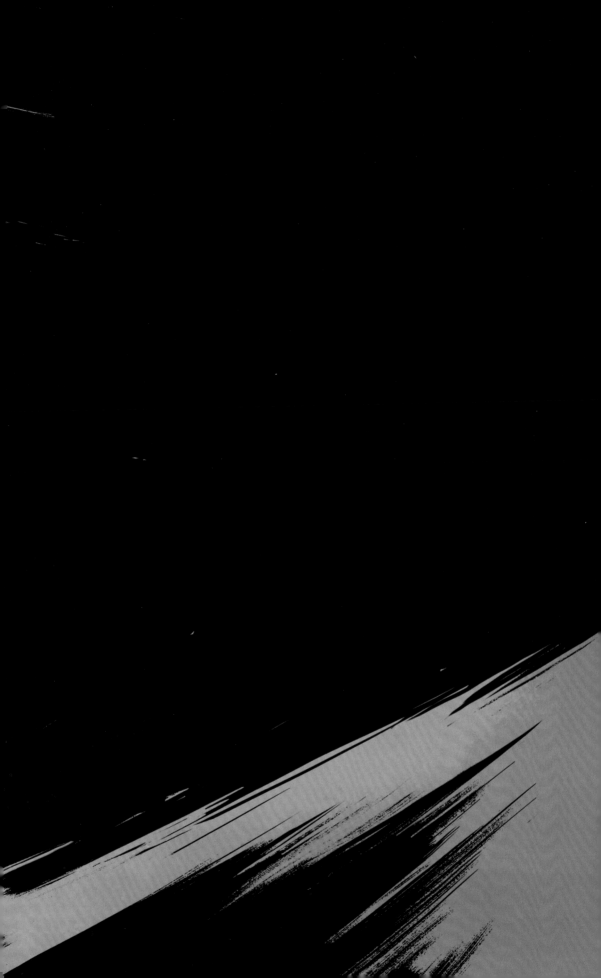

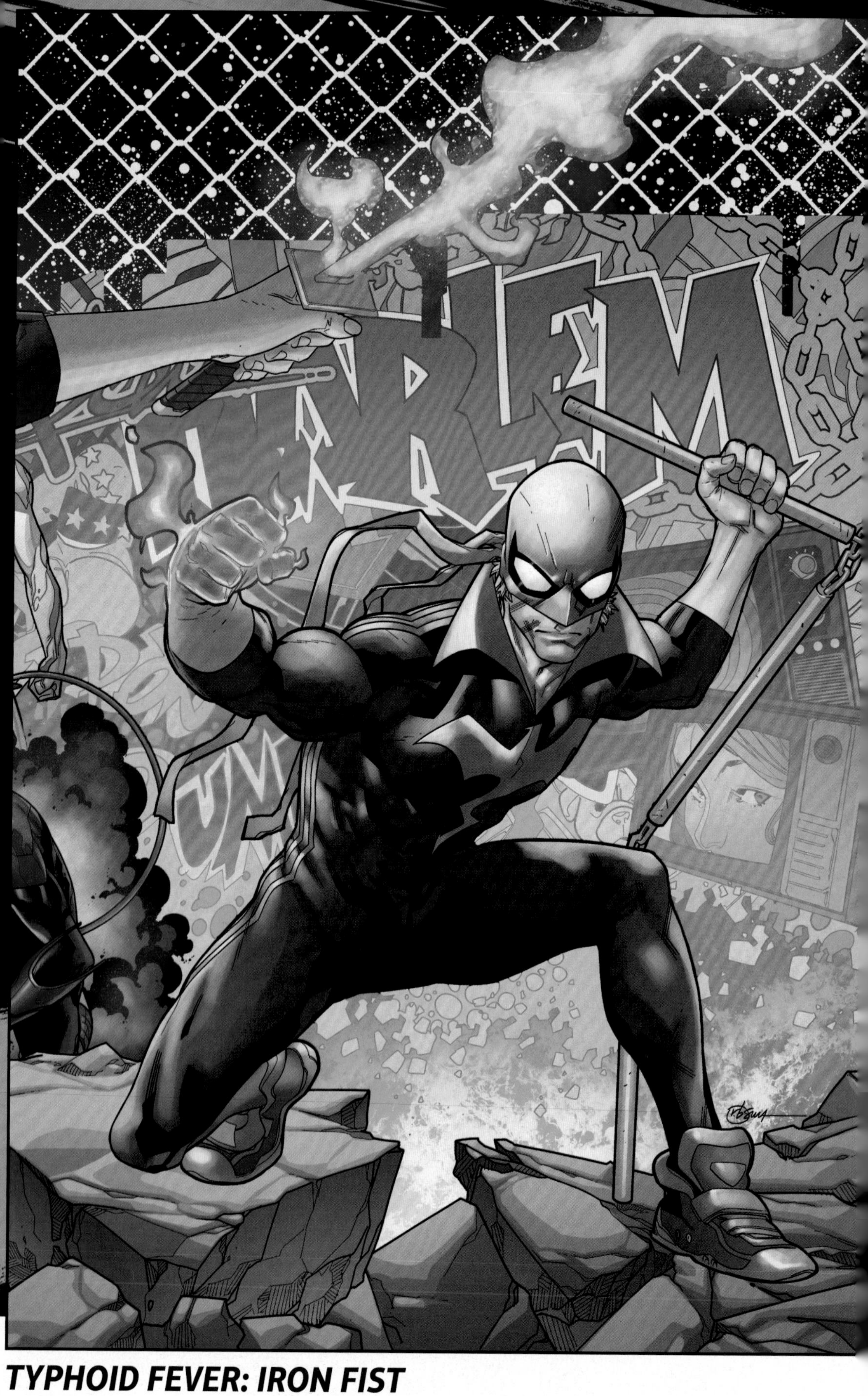

TYPHOID FEVER: IRON FIST

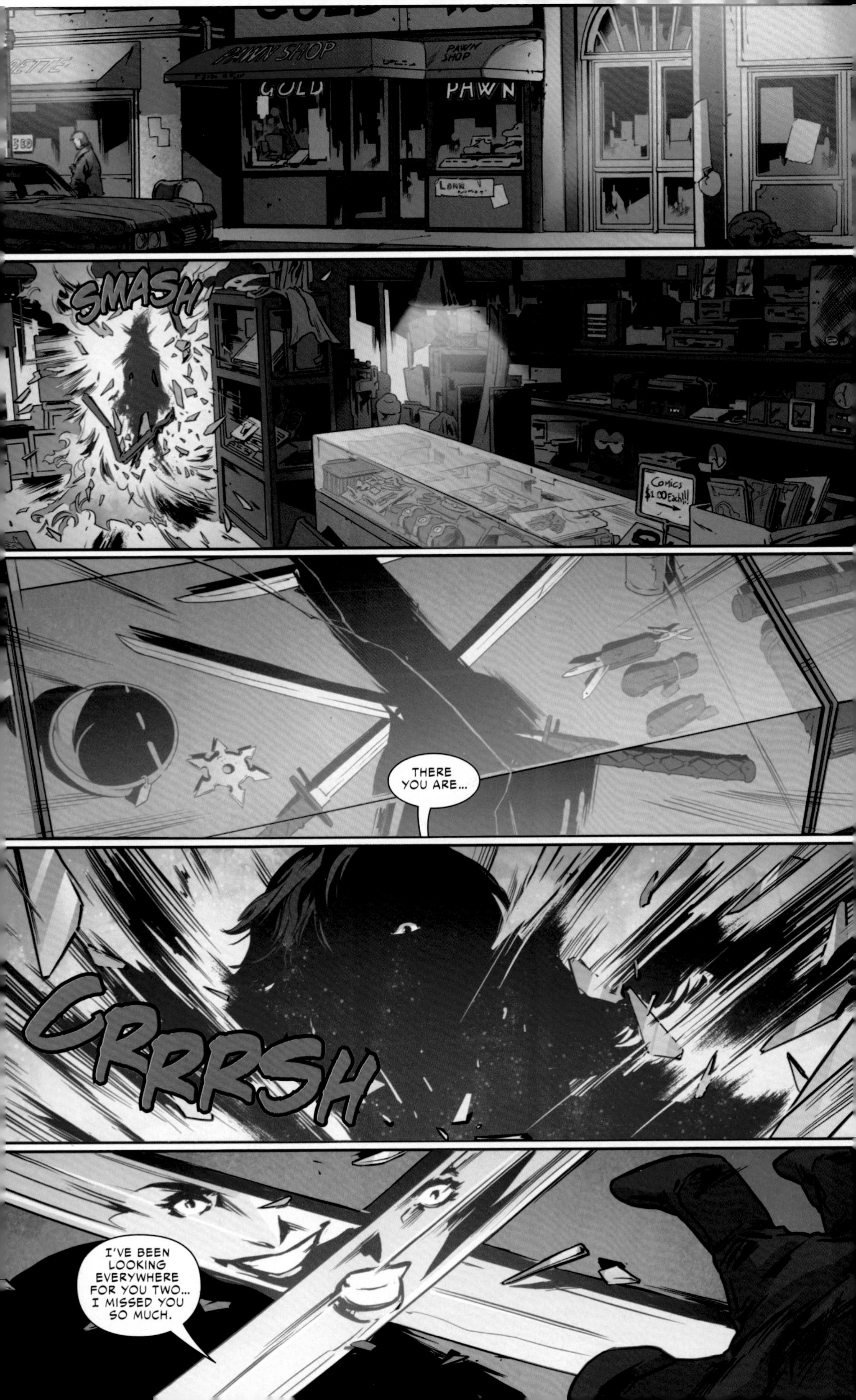
PAWN SHOP
GOLD
PAWN SHOP
PAWN
SMASH
Comics $1.00 Each!!!
THERE YOU ARE...
CRRRSH
I'VE BEEN LOOKING EVERYWHERE FOR YOU TWO... I MISSED YOU SO MUCH.

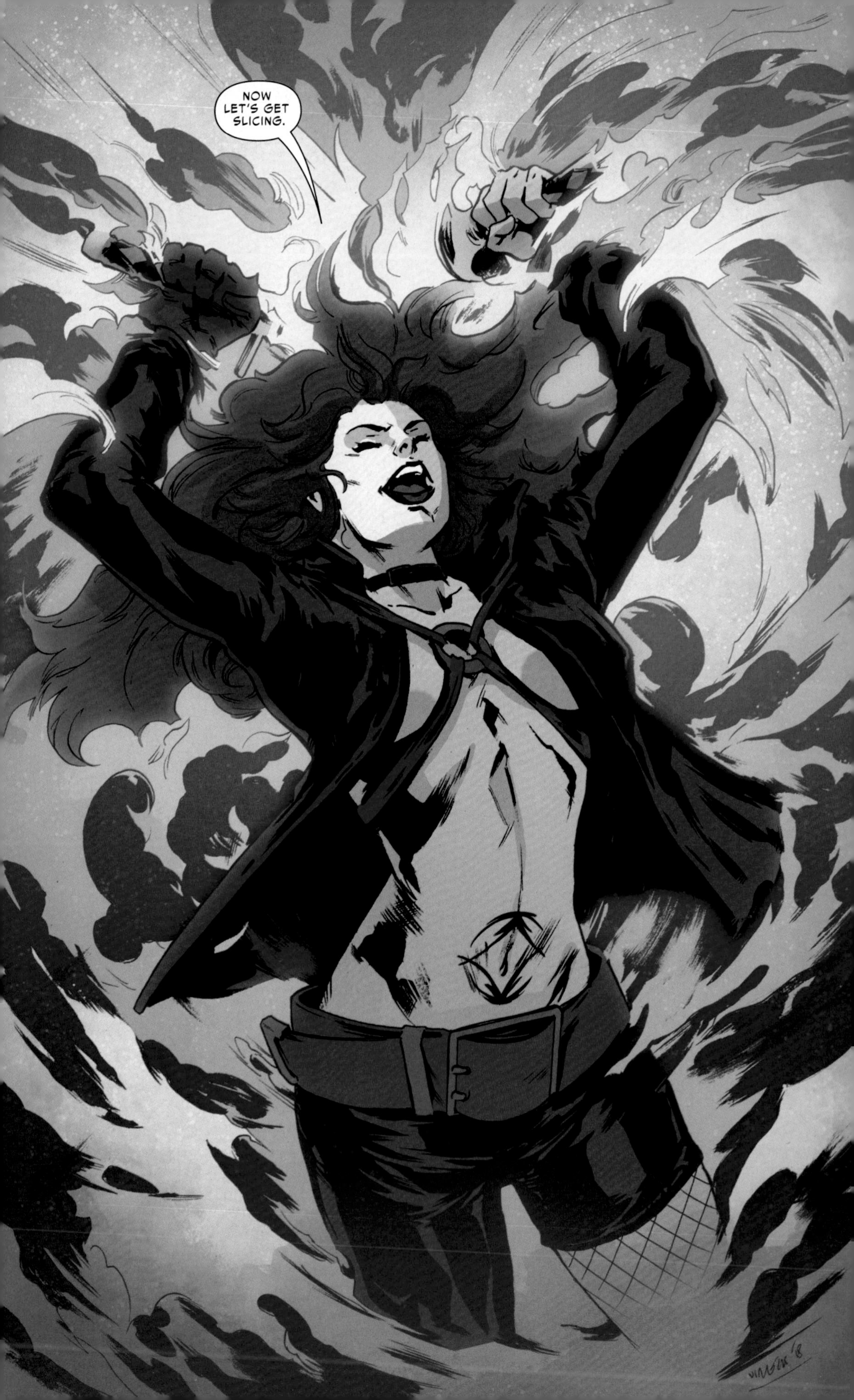
NOW LET'S GET SLICING.

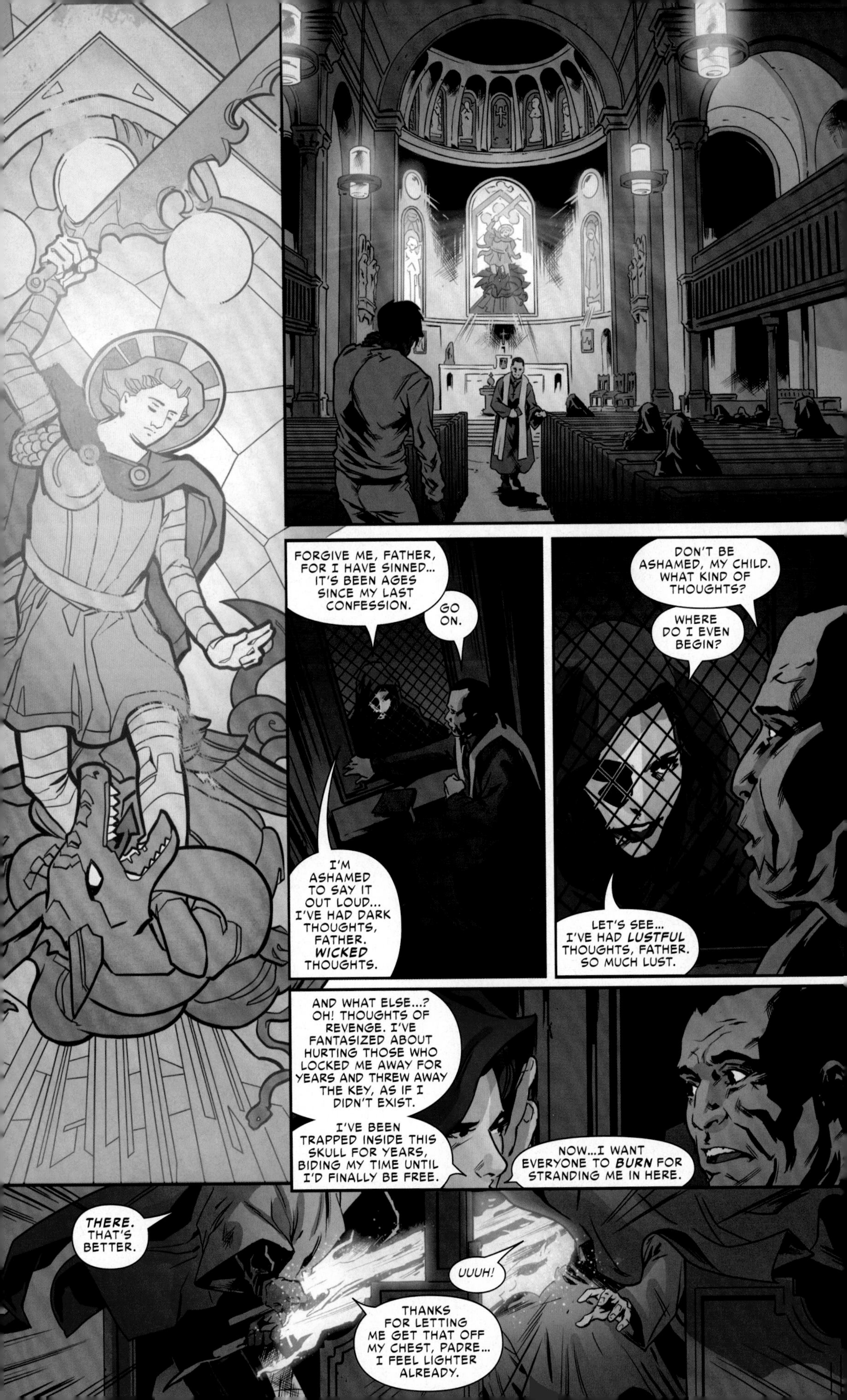
FORGIVE ME, FATHER, FOR I HAVE SINNED... IT'S BEEN AGES SINCE MY LAST CONFESSION.
GO ON.
I'M ASHAMED TO SAY IT OUT LOUD... I'VE HAD DARK THOUGHTS, FATHER. WICKED THOUGHTS.
DON'T BE ASHAMED, MY CHILD. WHAT KIND OF THOUGHTS?
WHERE DO I EVEN BEGIN?
LET'S SEE... I'VE HAD LUSTFUL THOUGHTS, FATHER. SO MUCH LUST.
AND WHAT ELSE...? OH! THOUGHTS OF REVENGE. I'VE FANTASIZED ABOUT HURTING THOSE WHO LOCKED ME AWAY FOR YEARS AND THREW AWAY THE KEY, AS IF I DIDN'T EXIST.
I'VE BEEN TRAPPED INSIDE THIS SKULL FOR YEARS, BIDING MY TIME UNTIL I'D FINALLY BE FREE.
NOW...I WANT EVERYONE TO BURN FOR STRANDING ME IN HERE.
THERE. THAT'S BETTER.
UUUH!
THANKS FOR LETTING ME GET THAT OFF MY CHEST, PADRE... I FEEL LIGHTER ALREADY.

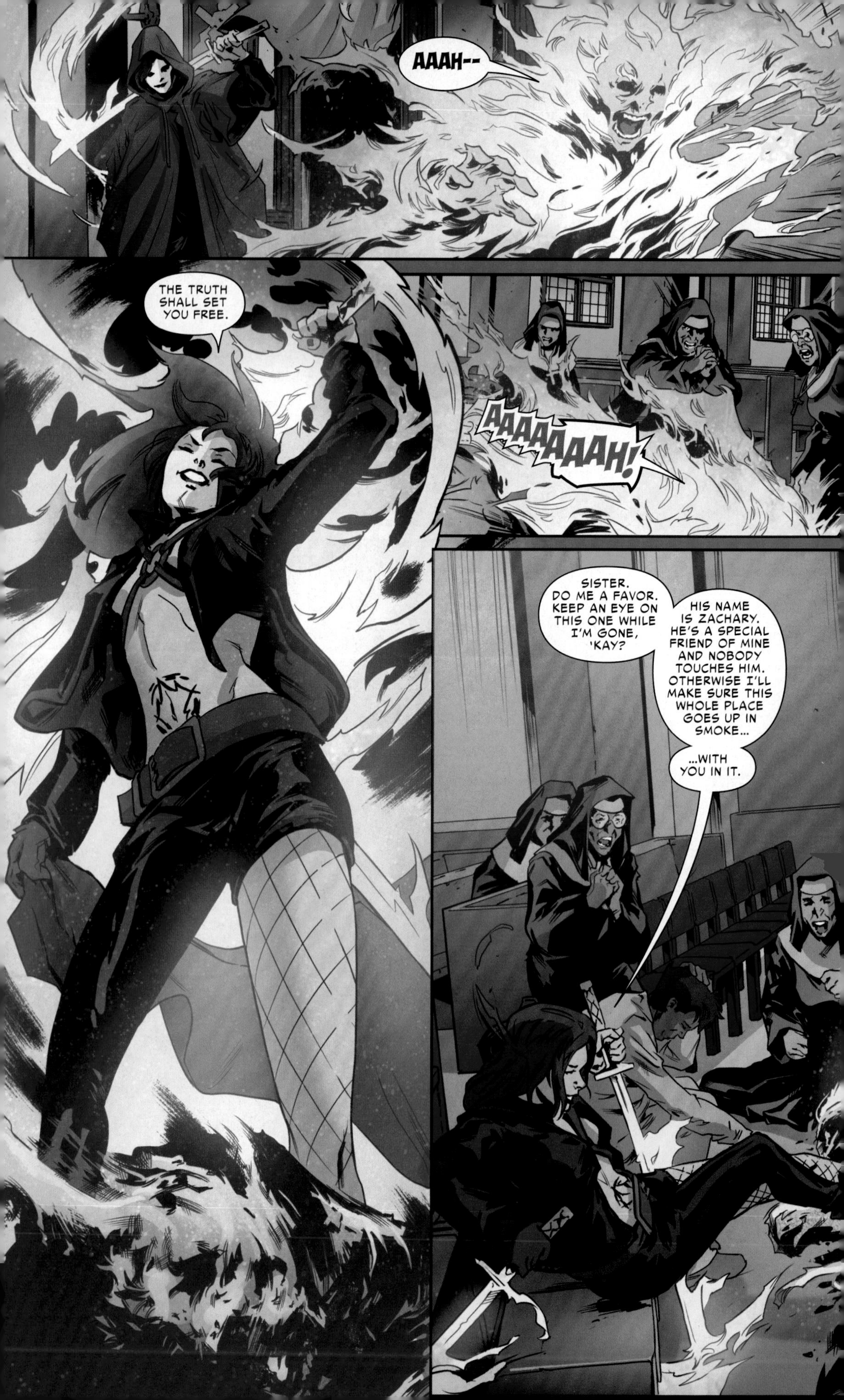
AAAH--
THE TRUTH SHALL SET YOU FREE.
AAAAAAAH!
SISTER. DO ME A FAVOR. KEEP AN EYE ON THIS ONE WHILE I'M GONE, 'KAY?
HIS NAME IS ZACHARY. HE'S A SPECIAL FRIEND OF MINE AND NOBODY TOUCHES HIM. OTHERWISE I'LL MAKE SURE THIS WHOLE PLACE GOES UP IN SMOKE...
...WITH YOU IN IT.

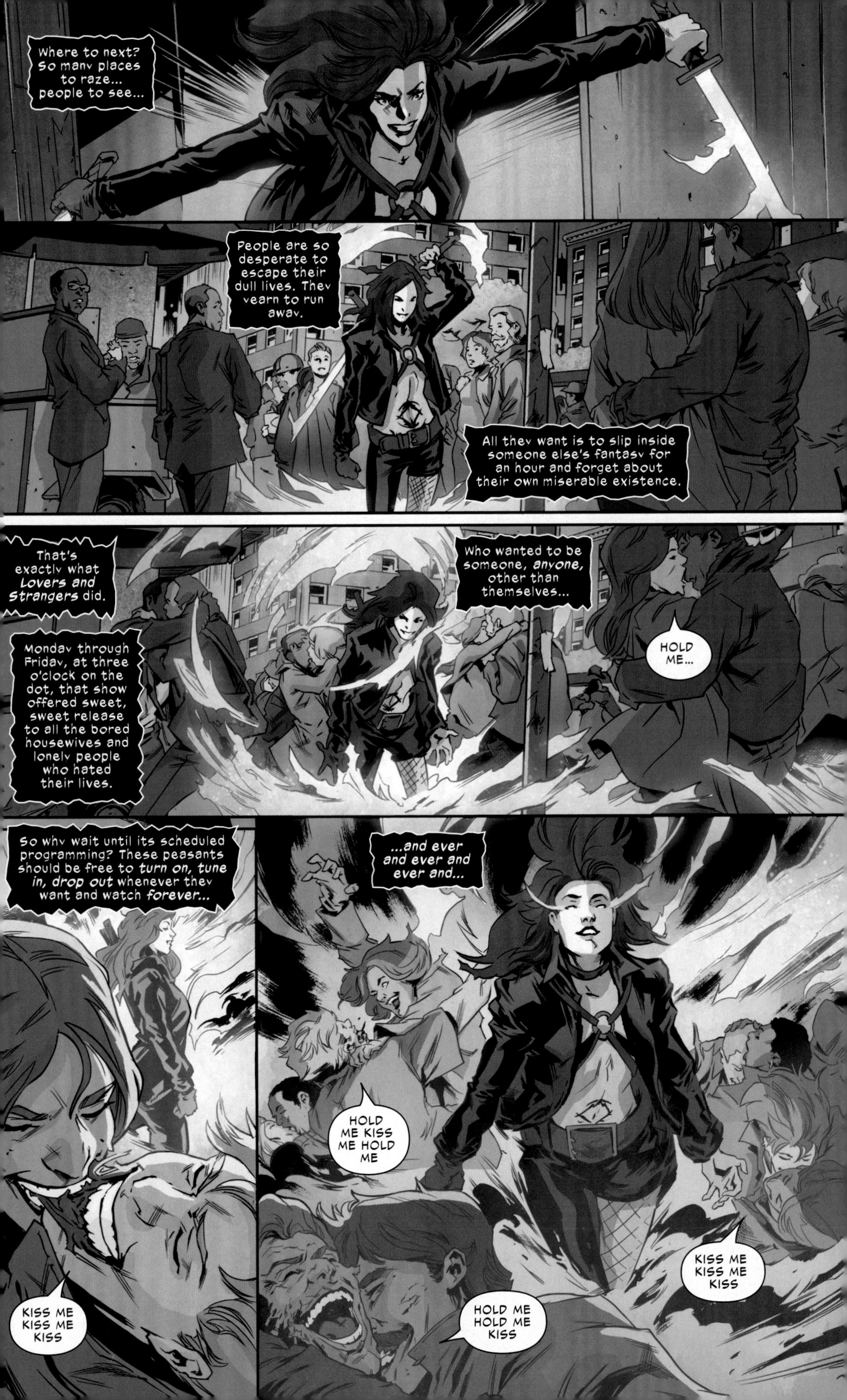
Where to next? So many places to raze... people to see...
People are so desperate to escape their dull lives. They yearn to run away.
All they want is to slip inside someone else's fantasy for an hour and forget about their own miserable existence.
That's exactly what *Lovers and Strangers* did.
Monday through Friday, at three o'clock on the dot, that show offered sweet, sweet release to all the bored housewives and lonely people who hated their lives.
Who wanted to be someone, *anyone*, other than themselves...
HOLD ME...
So why wait until its scheduled programming? These peasants should be free to *turn on, tune in, drop out* whenever they want and watch *forever...*
KISS ME KISS ME KISS
...and ever and ever and ever and...
HOLD ME KISS ME HOLD ME
HOLD ME HOLD ME KISS
KISS ME KISS ME KISS

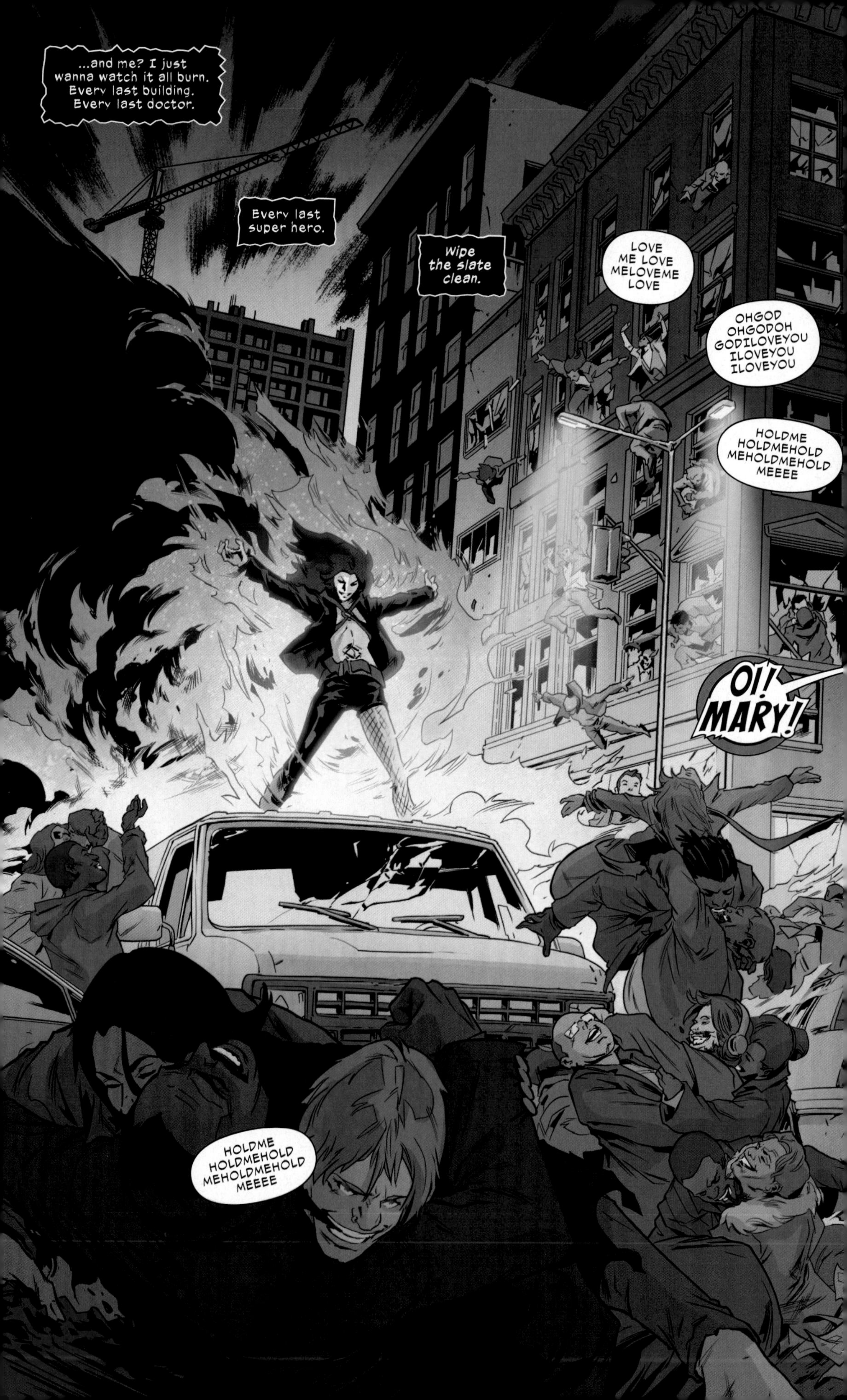

...and me? I just wanna watch it all burn. Every last building. Every last doctor.
Every last super hero.
Wipe the slate clean.
LOVE ME LOVE MELOVEME LOVE
OHGOD OHGODOH GODILOVEYOU ILOVEYOU ILOVEYOU
HOLDME HOLDMEHOLD MEHOLDMEHOLD MEEEE
OI! MARY!
HOLDME HOLDMEHOLD MEHOLDMEHOLD MEEEE

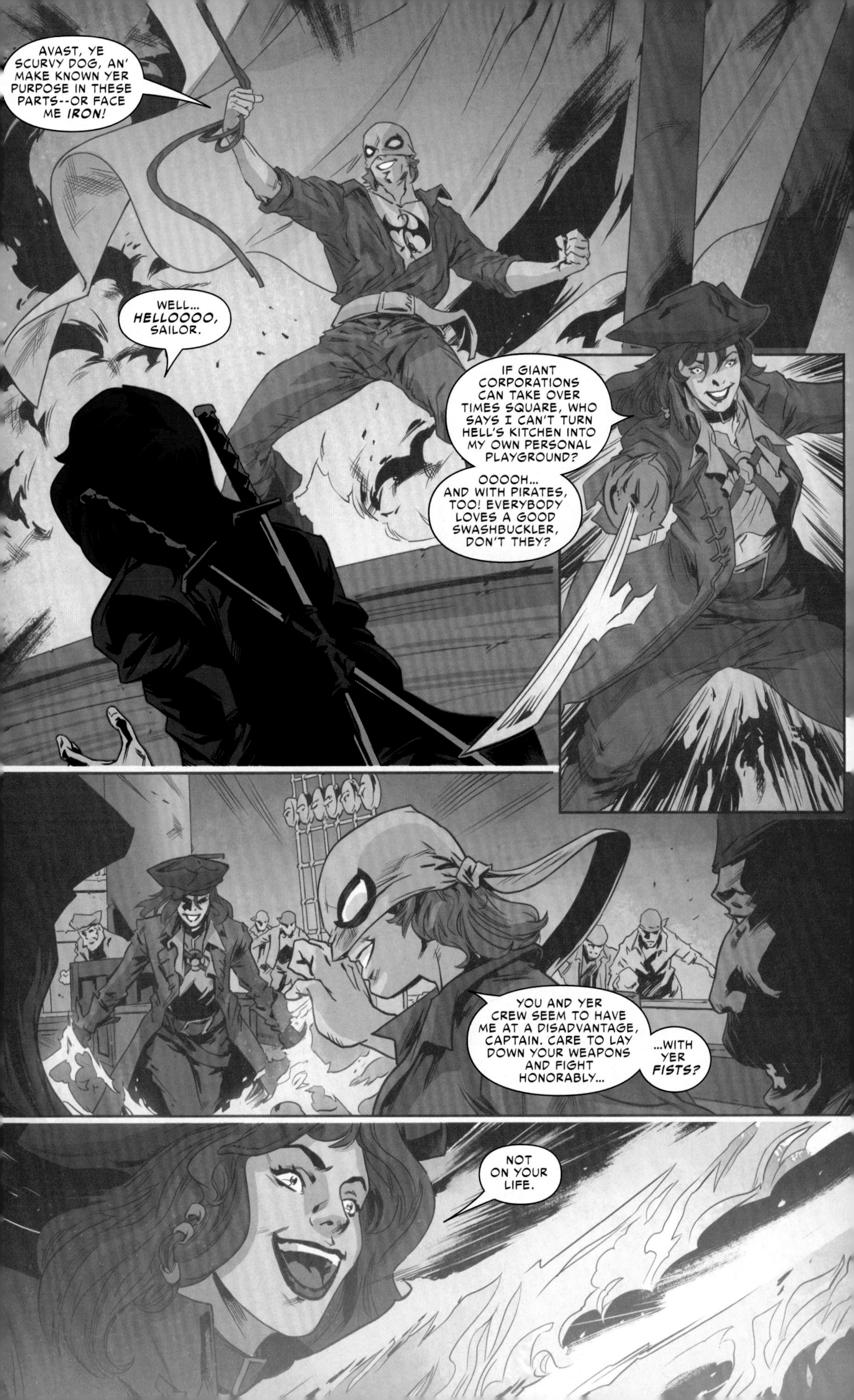
AVAST, YE SCURVY DOG, AN' MAKE KNOWN YER PURPOSE IN THESE PARTS--OR FACE ME IRON!
WELL... HELLOOOO, SAILOR.
IF GIANT CORPORATIONS CAN TAKE OVER TIMES SQUARE, WHO SAYS I CAN'T TURN HELL'S KITCHEN INTO MY OWN PERSONAL PLAYGROUND?
OOOOH... AND WITH PIRATES, TOO! EVERYBODY LOVES A GOOD SWASHBUCKLER, DON'T THEY?
YOU AND YER CREW SEEM TO HAVE ME AT A DISADVANTAGE, CAPTAIN. CARE TO LAY DOWN YOUR WEAPONS AND FIGHT HONORABLY...
...WITH YER FISTS?
NOT ON YOUR LIFE.

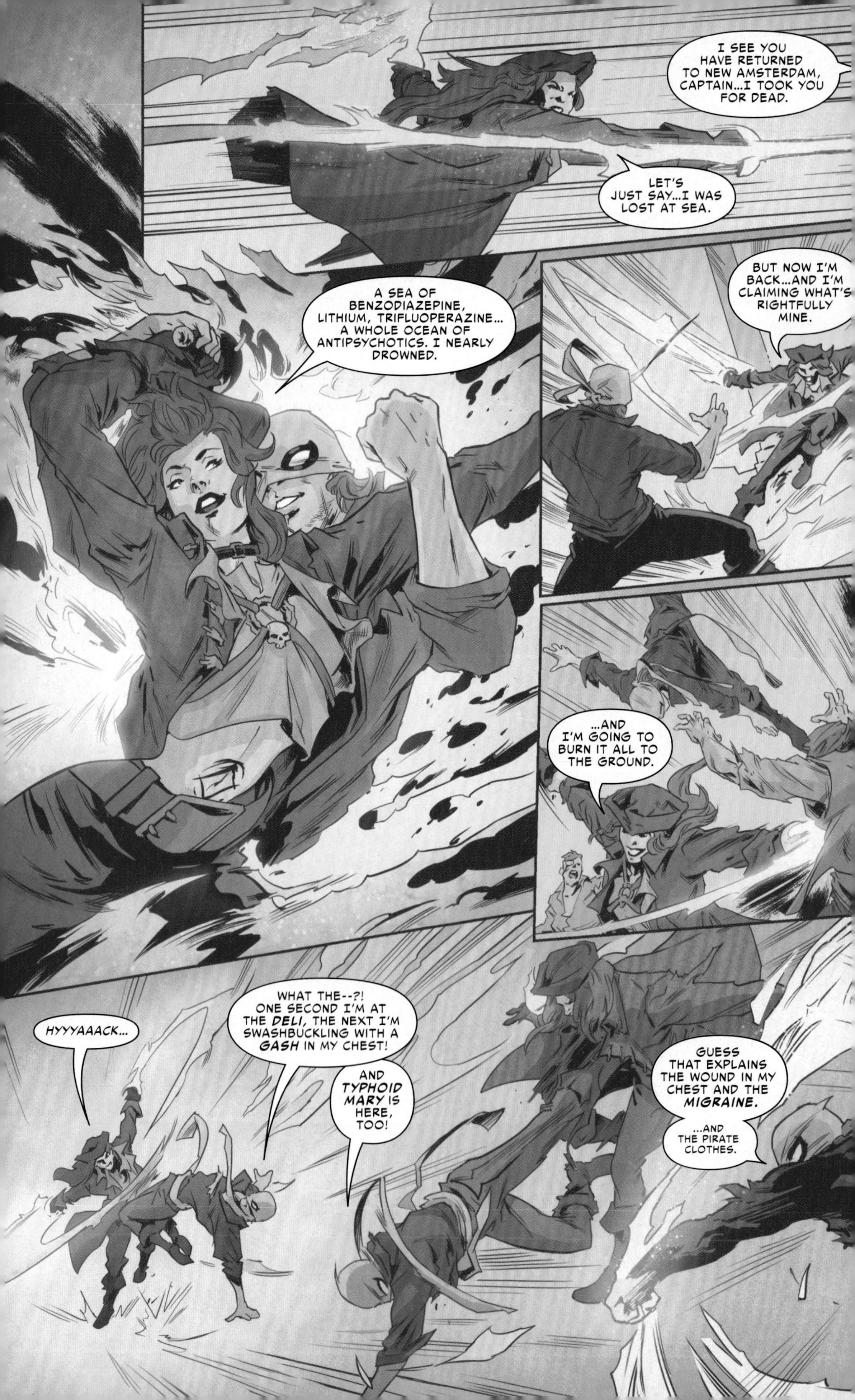
I SEE YOU HAVE RETURNED TO NEW AMSTERDAM, CAPTAIN...I TOOK YOU FOR DEAD.
LET'S JUST SAY...I WAS LOST AT SEA.
A SEA OF BENZODIAZEPINE, LITHIUM, TRIFLUOPERAZINE... A WHOLE OCEAN OF ANTIPSYCHOTICS. I NEARLY DROWNED.
BUT NOW I'M BACK...AND I'M CLAIMING WHAT'S RIGHTFULLY MINE.
...AND I'M GOING TO BURN IT ALL TO THE GROUND.
HYYYAAACK...
WHAT THE--?! ONE SECOND I'M AT THE DELI, THE NEXT I'M SWASHBUCKLING WITH A GASH IN MY CHEST!
AND TYPHOID MARY IS HERE, TOO!
GUESS THAT EXPLAINS THE WOUND IN MY CHEST AND THE MIGRAINE.
...AND THE PIRATE CLOTHES.

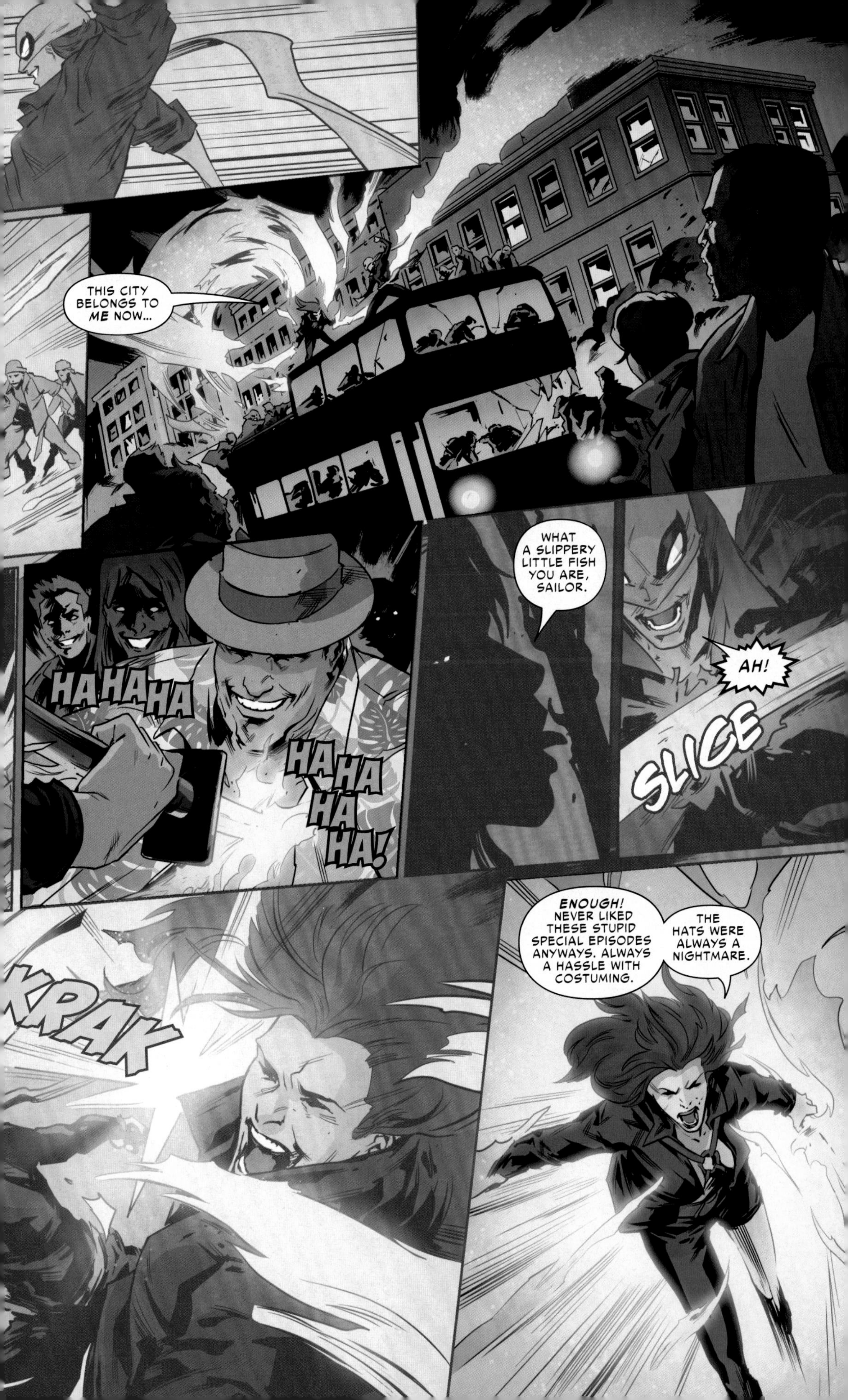
THIS CITY BELONGS TO *ME* NOW...
HA HA HA HA
HA HA HA HA HA!
WHAT A SLIPPERY LITTLE FISH YOU ARE, SAILOR.
AH!
SLICE
KRAK
ENOUGH! NEVER LIKED THESE STUPID SPECIAL EPISODES ANYWAYS. ALWAYS A HASSLE WITH COSTUMING.
THE HATS WERE ALWAYS A NIGHTMARE.

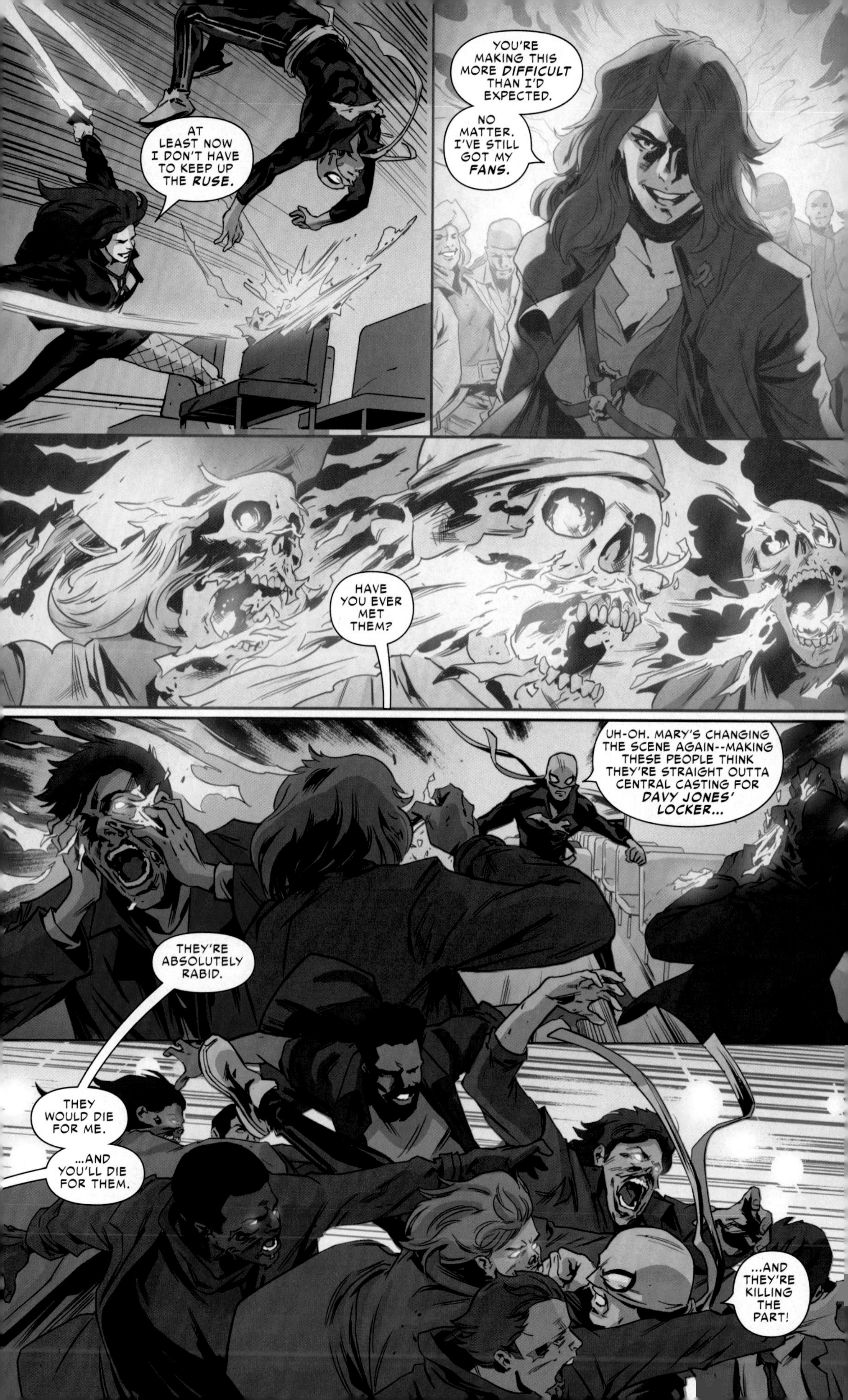
AT LEAST NOW I DON'T HAVE TO KEEP UP THE RUSE.
YOU'RE MAKING THIS MORE DIFFICULT THAN I'D EXPECTED.
NO MATTER. I'VE STILL GOT MY FANS.
HAVE YOU EVER MET THEM?
UH-OH. MARY'S CHANGING THE SCENE AGAIN--MAKING THESE PEOPLE THINK THEY'RE STRAIGHT OUTTA CENTRAL CASTING FOR DAVY JONES' LOCKER...
THEY'RE ABSOLUTELY RABID.
THEY WOULD DIE FOR ME.
...AND YOU'LL DIE FOR THEM.
...AND THEY'RE KILLING THE PART!

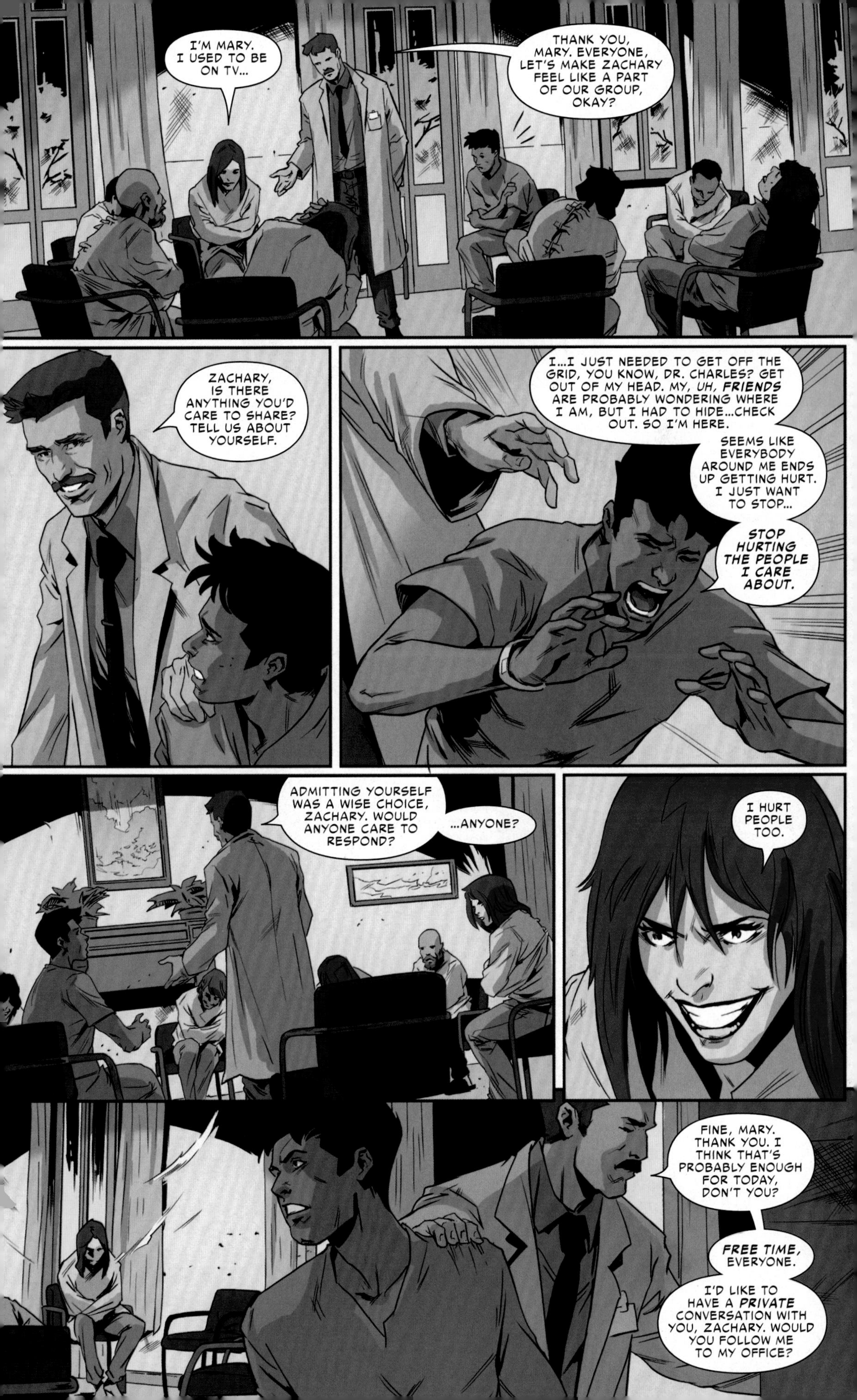
I'M MARY. I USED TO BE ON TV...
THANK YOU, MARY. EVERYONE, LET'S MAKE ZACHARY FEEL LIKE A PART OF OUR GROUP, OKAY?
ZACHARY, IS THERE ANYTHING YOU'D CARE TO SHARE? TELL US ABOUT YOURSELF.
I...I JUST NEEDED TO GET OFF THE GRID, YOU KNOW, DR. CHARLES? GET OUT OF MY HEAD. MY, UH, FRIENDS ARE PROBABLY WONDERING WHERE I AM, BUT I HAD TO HIDE...CHECK OUT. SO I'M HERE.
SEEMS LIKE EVERYBODY AROUND ME ENDS UP GETTING HURT. I JUST WANT TO STOP...
STOP HURTING THE PEOPLE I CARE ABOUT.
ADMITTING YOURSELF WAS A WISE CHOICE, ZACHARY. WOULD ANYONE CARE TO RESPOND?
...ANYONE?
I HURT PEOPLE TOO.
FINE, MARY. THANK YOU. I THINK THAT'S PROBABLY ENOUGH FOR TODAY, DON'T YOU?
FREE TIME, EVERYONE.
I'D LIKE TO HAVE A PRIVATE CONVERSATION WITH YOU, ZACHARY. WOULD YOU FOLLOW ME TO MY OFFICE?

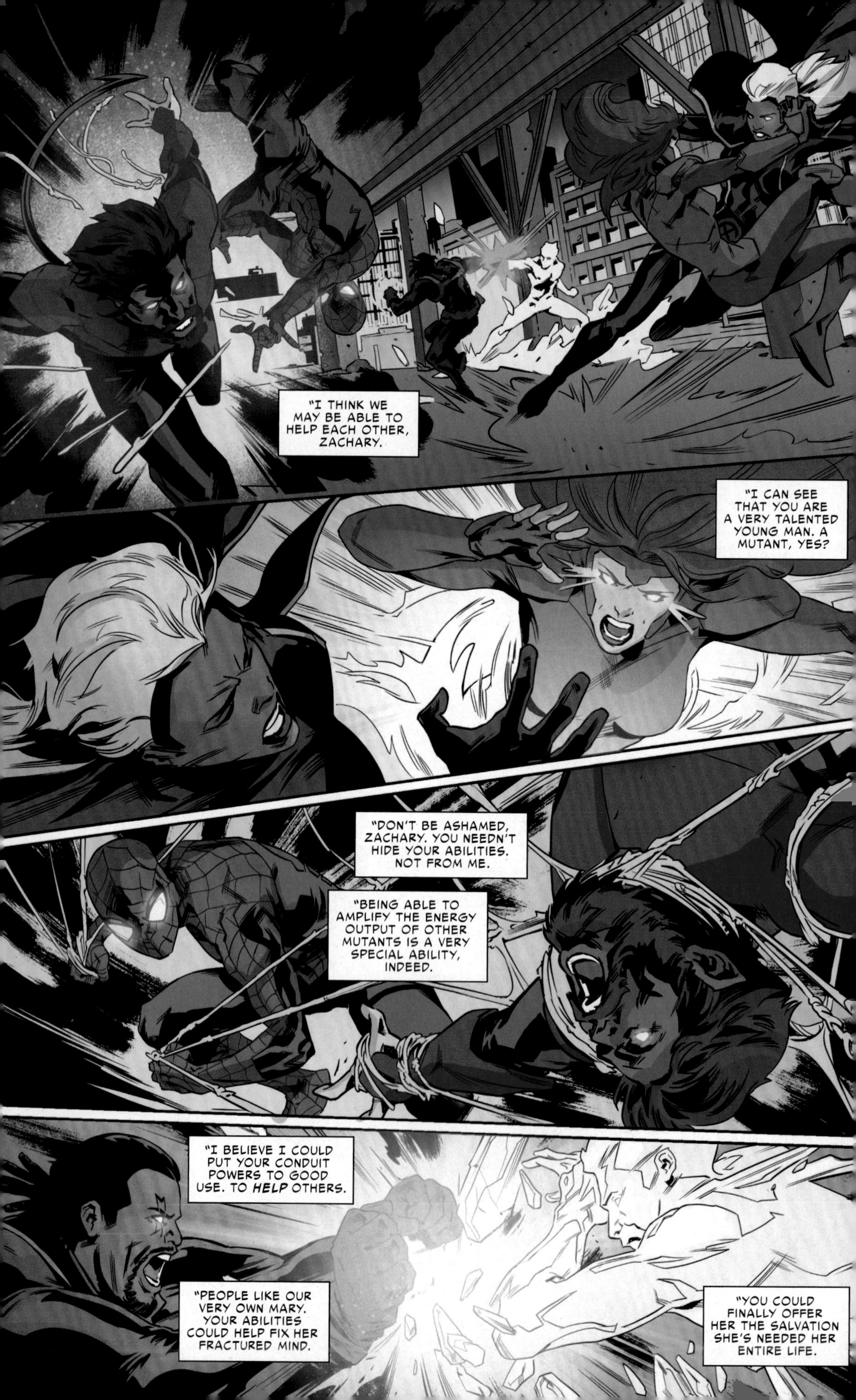
"I THINK WE MAY BE ABLE TO HELP EACH OTHER, ZACHARY.
"I CAN SEE THAT YOU ARE A VERY TALENTED YOUNG MAN. A MUTANT, YES?
"DON'T BE ASHAMED, ZACHARY. YOU NEEDN'T HIDE YOUR ABILITIES. NOT FROM ME.
"BEING ABLE TO AMPLIFY THE ENERGY OUTPUT OF OTHER MUTANTS IS A VERY SPECIAL ABILITY, INDEED.
"I BELIEVE I COULD PUT YOUR CONDUIT POWERS TO GOOD USE. TO *HELP* OTHERS.
"PEOPLE LIKE OUR VERY OWN MARY. YOUR ABILITIES COULD HELP FIX HER FRACTURED MIND.
"YOU COULD FINALLY OFFER HER THE SALVATION SHE'S NEEDED HER ENTIRE LIFE.

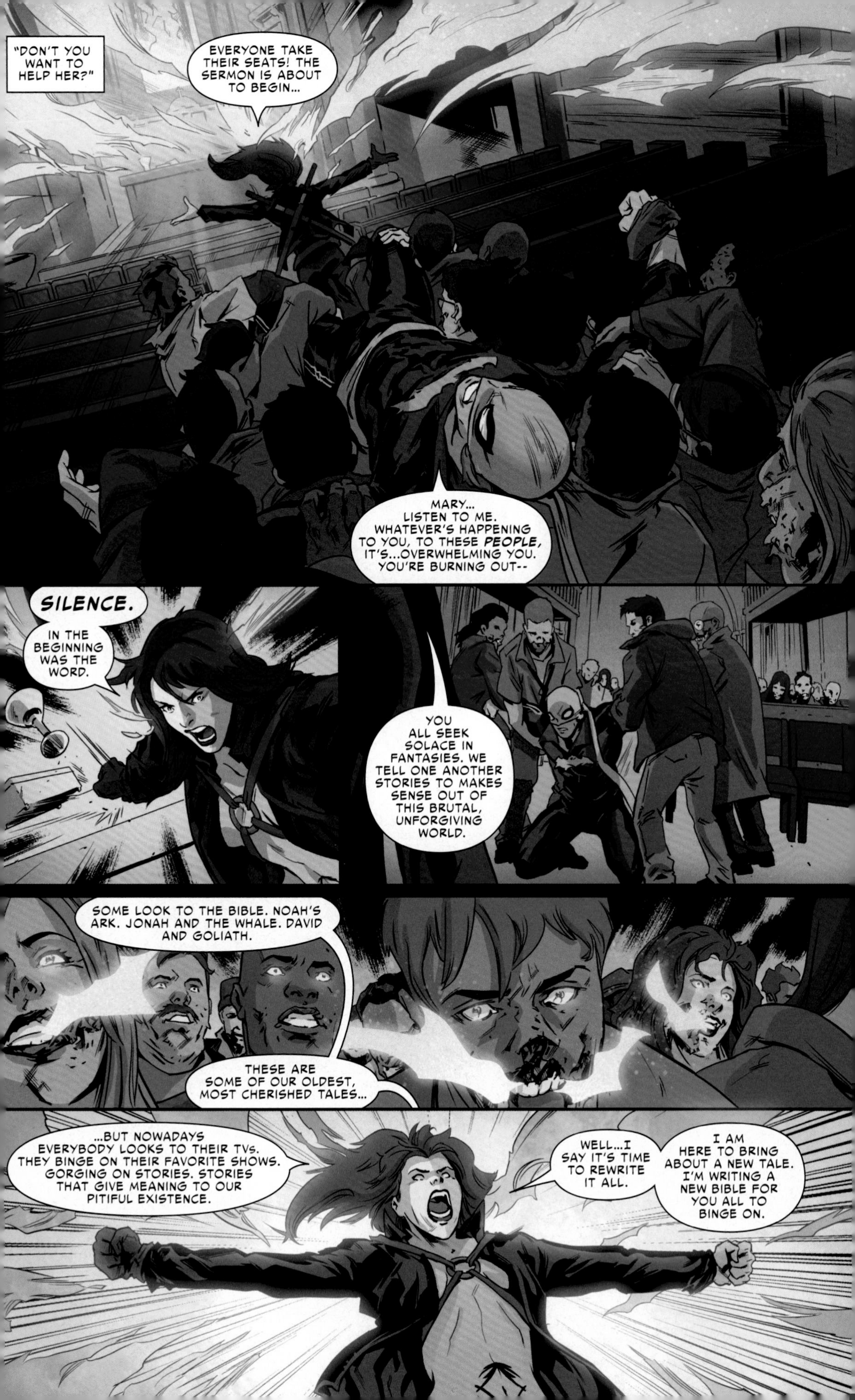
"DON'T YOU WANT TO HELP HER?"
EVERYONE TAKE THEIR SEATS! THE SERMON IS ABOUT TO BEGIN...
MARY... LISTEN TO ME. WHATEVER'S HAPPENING TO YOU, TO THESE PEOPLE, IT'S...OVERWHELMING YOU. YOU'RE BURNING OUT--
SILENCE.
IN THE BEGINNING WAS THE WORD.
YOU ALL SEEK SOLACE IN FANTASIES. WE TELL ONE ANOTHER STORIES TO MAKES SENSE OUT OF THIS BRUTAL, UNFORGIVING WORLD.
SOME LOOK TO THE BIBLE. NOAH'S ARK. JONAH AND THE WHALE. DAVID AND GOLIATH.
THESE ARE SOME OF OUR OLDEST, MOST CHERISHED TALES...
...BUT NOWADAYS EVERYBODY LOOKS TO THEIR TVs. THEY BINGE ON THEIR FAVORITE SHOWS. GORGING ON STORIES. STORIES THAT GIVE MEANING TO OUR PITIFUL EXISTENCE.
WELL...I SAY IT'S TIME TO REWRITE IT ALL.
I AM HERE TO BRING ABOUT A NEW TALE. I'M WRITING A NEW BIBLE FOR YOU ALL TO BINGE ON.

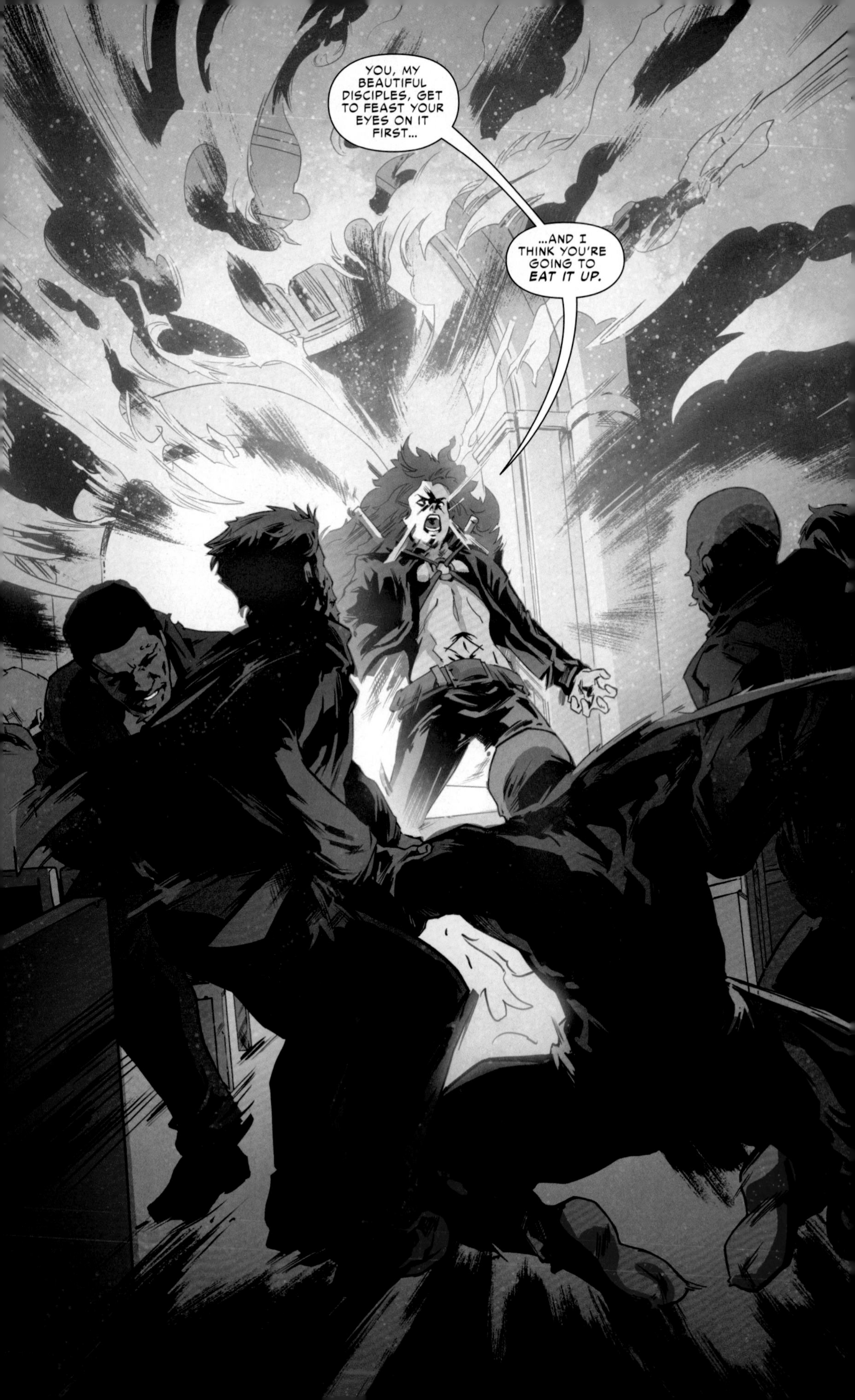
YOU, MY BEAUTIFUL DISCIPLES, GET TO FEAST YOUR EYES ON IT FIRST...
...AND I THINK YOU'RE GOING TO *EAT IT UP.*

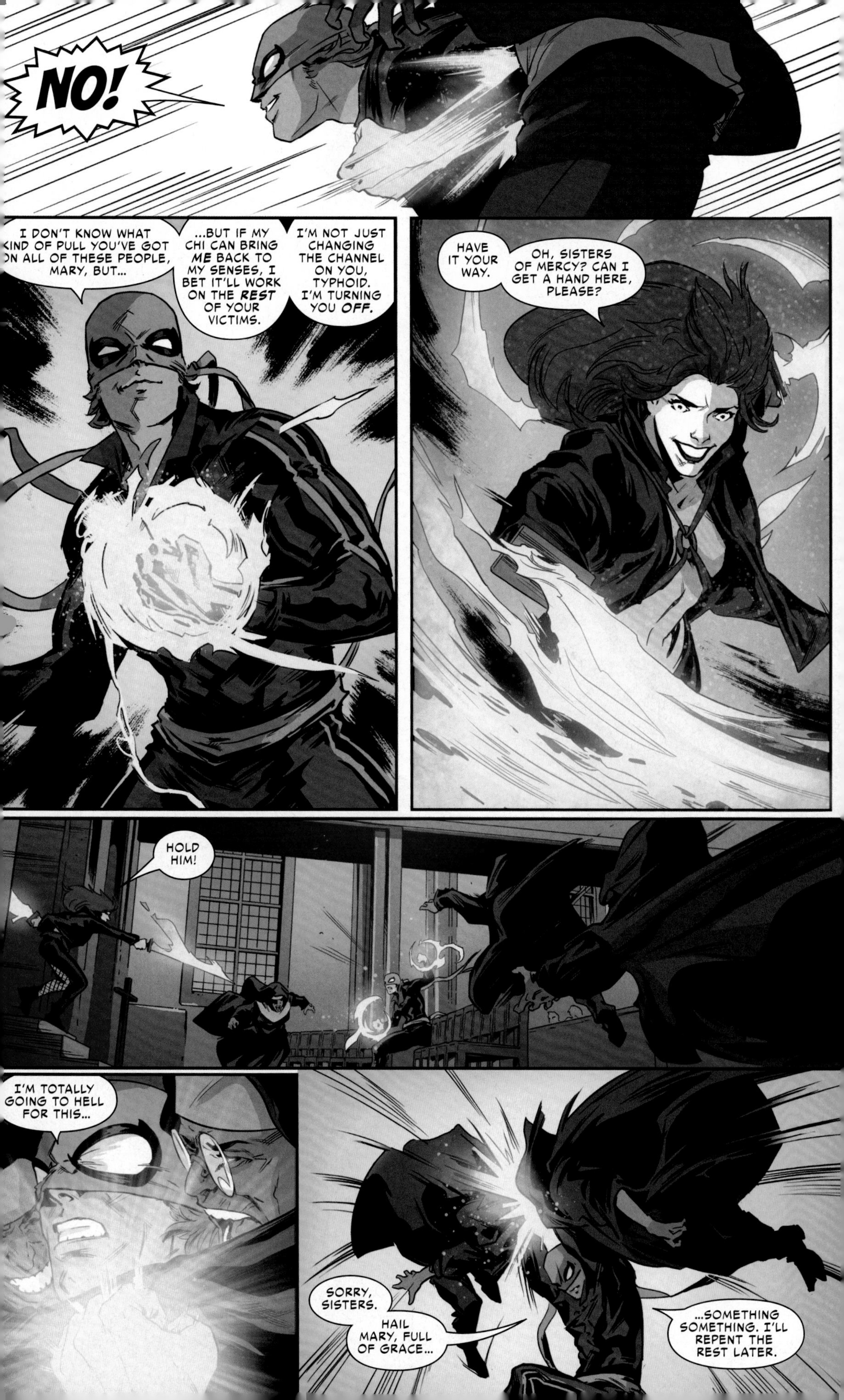
NO!
I DON'T KNOW WHAT KIND OF PULL YOU'VE GOT ON ALL OF THESE PEOPLE, MARY, BUT...
...BUT IF MY CHI CAN BRING ME BACK TO MY SENSES, I BET IT'LL WORK ON THE REST OF YOUR VICTIMS.
I'M NOT JUST CHANGING THE CHANNEL ON YOU, TYPHOID. I'M TURNING YOU OFF.
HAVE IT YOUR WAY.
OH, SISTERS OF MERCY? CAN I GET A HAND HERE, PLEASE?
HOLD HIM!
I'M TOTALLY GOING TO HELL FOR THIS...
SORRY, SISTERS.
HAIL MARY, FULL OF GRACE...
...SOMETHING SOMETHING. I'LL REPENT THE REST LATER.

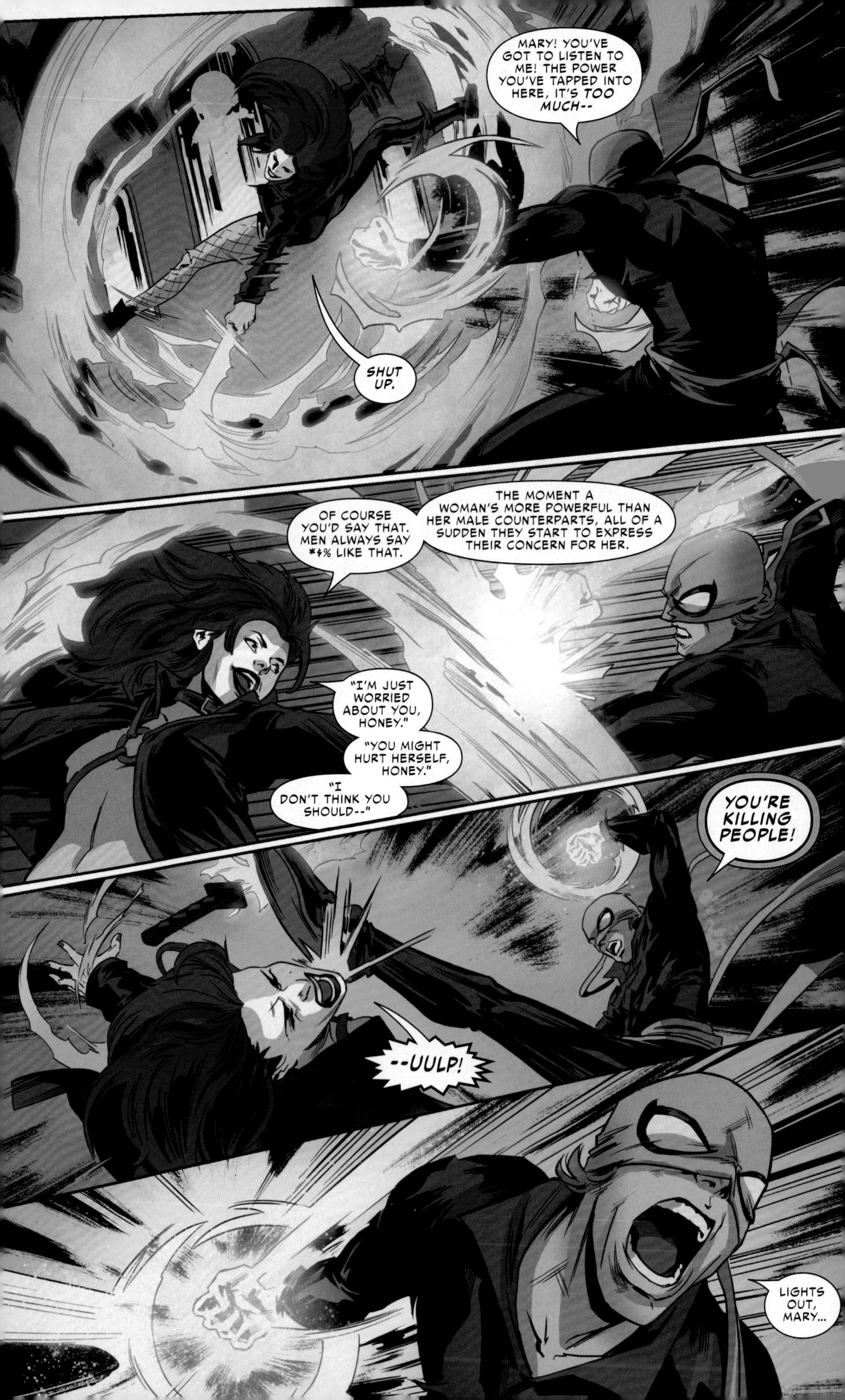
MARY! YOU'VE GOT TO LISTEN TO ME! THE POWER YOU'VE TAPPED INTO HERE, IT'S TOO MUCH--
SHUT UP.
OF COURSE YOU'D SAY THAT. MEN ALWAYS SAY *$% LIKE THAT.
THE MOMENT A WOMAN'S MORE POWERFUL THAN HER MALE COUNTERPARTS, ALL OF A SUDDEN THEY START TO EXPRESS THEIR CONCERN FOR HER.
"I'M JUST WORRIED ABOUT YOU, HONEY."
"YOU MIGHT HURT HERSELF, HONEY."
"I DON'T THINK YOU SHOULD--"
YOU'RE KILLING PEOPLE!
--UULP!
LIGHTS OUT, MARY...

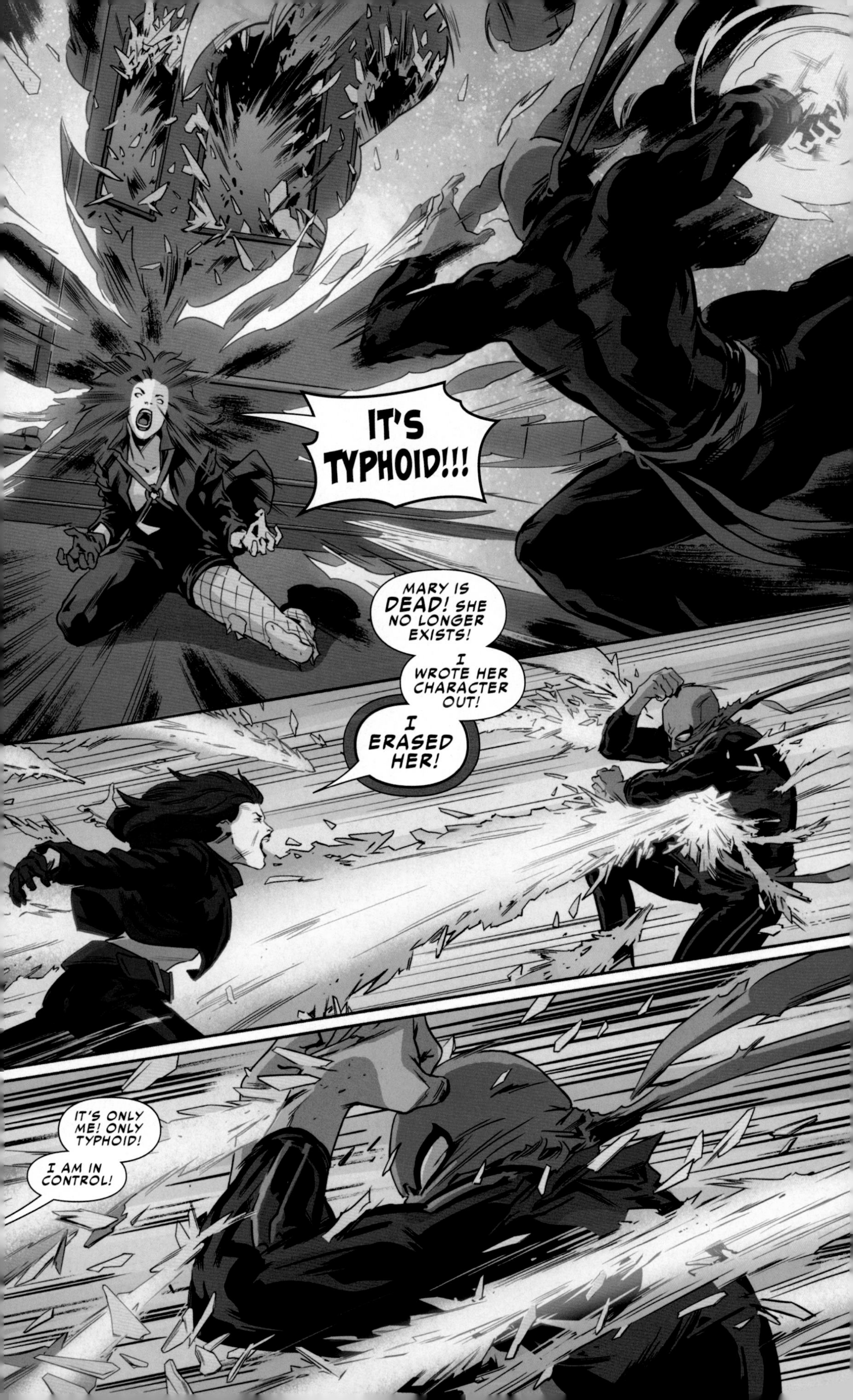
IT'S TYPHOID!!!
MARY IS DEAD! SHE NO LONGER EXISTS!
I WROTE HER CHARACTER OUT!
I ERASED HER!
IT'S ONLY ME! ONLY TYPHOID!
I AM IN CONTROL!

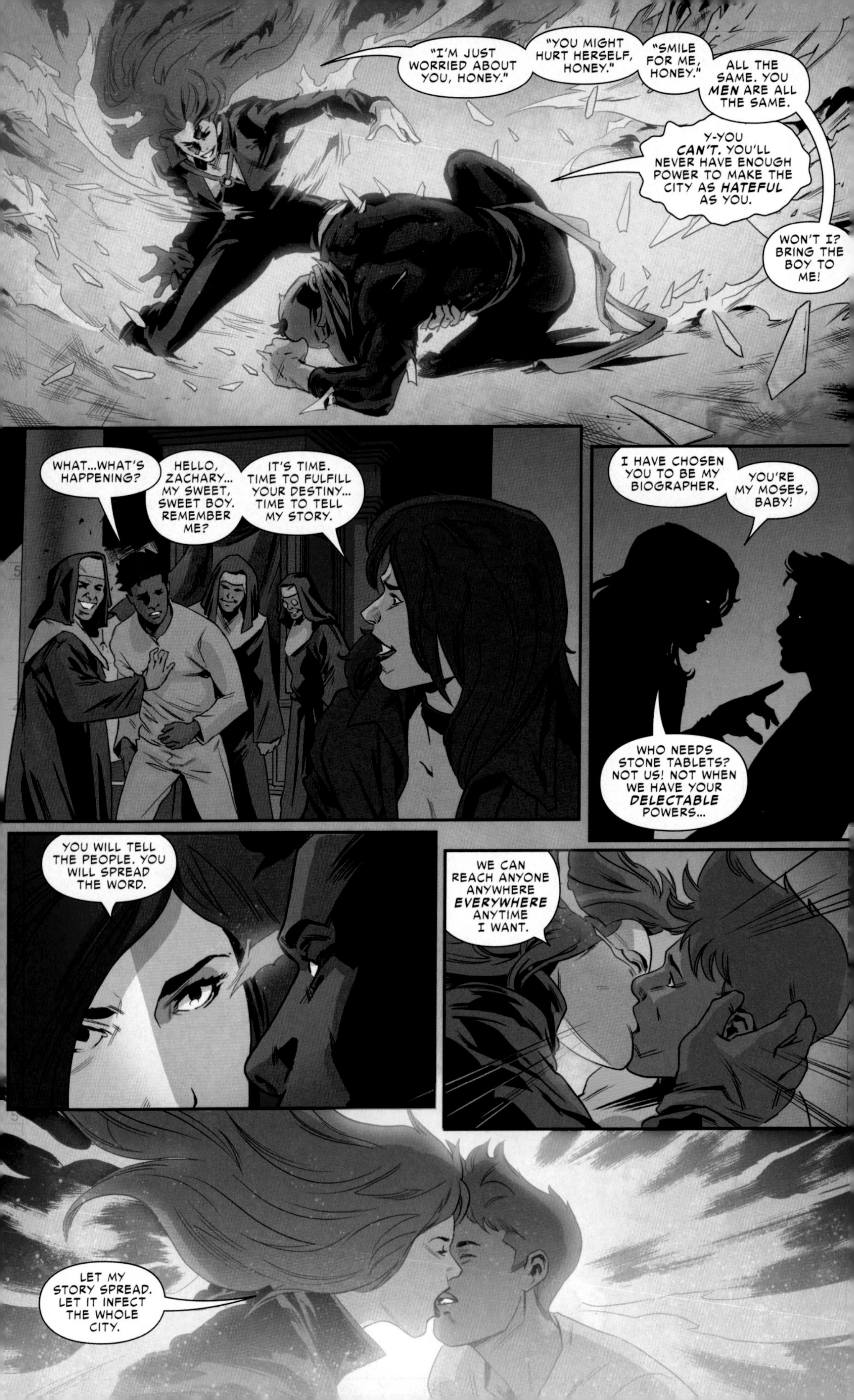
"I'M JUST WORRIED ABOUT YOU, HONEY."
"YOU MIGHT HURT HERSELF, HONEY."
"SMILE FOR ME, HONEY."
ALL THE SAME. YOU MEN ARE ALL THE SAME.
Y-YOU CAN'T. YOU'LL NEVER HAVE ENOUGH POWER TO MAKE THE CITY AS HATEFUL AS YOU.
WON'T I? BRING THE BOY TO ME!
WHAT...WHAT'S HAPPENING?
HELLO, ZACHARY... MY SWEET, SWEET BOY. REMEMBER ME?
IT'S TIME. TIME TO FULFILL YOUR DESTINY... TIME TO TELL MY STORY.
I HAVE CHOSEN YOU TO BE MY BIOGRAPHER.
YOU'RE MY MOSES, BABY!
WHO NEEDS STONE TABLETS? NOT US! NOT WHEN WE HAVE YOUR DELECTABLE POWERS...
YOU WILL TELL THE PEOPLE. YOU WILL SPREAD THE WORD.
WE CAN REACH ANYONE ANYWHERE EVERYWHERE ANYTIME I WANT.
LET MY STORY SPREAD. LET IT INFECT THE WHOLE CITY.

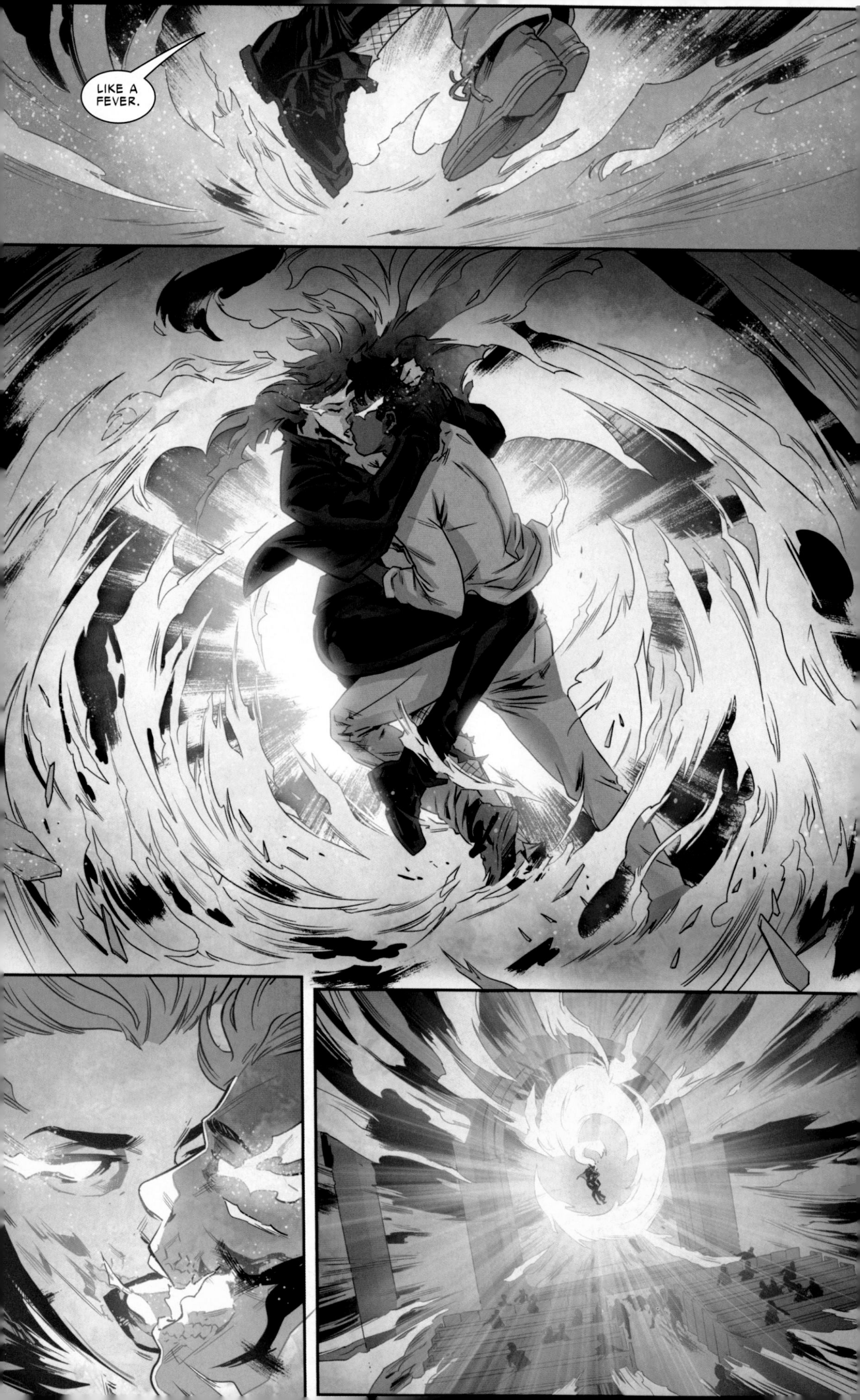
LIKE A FEVER.

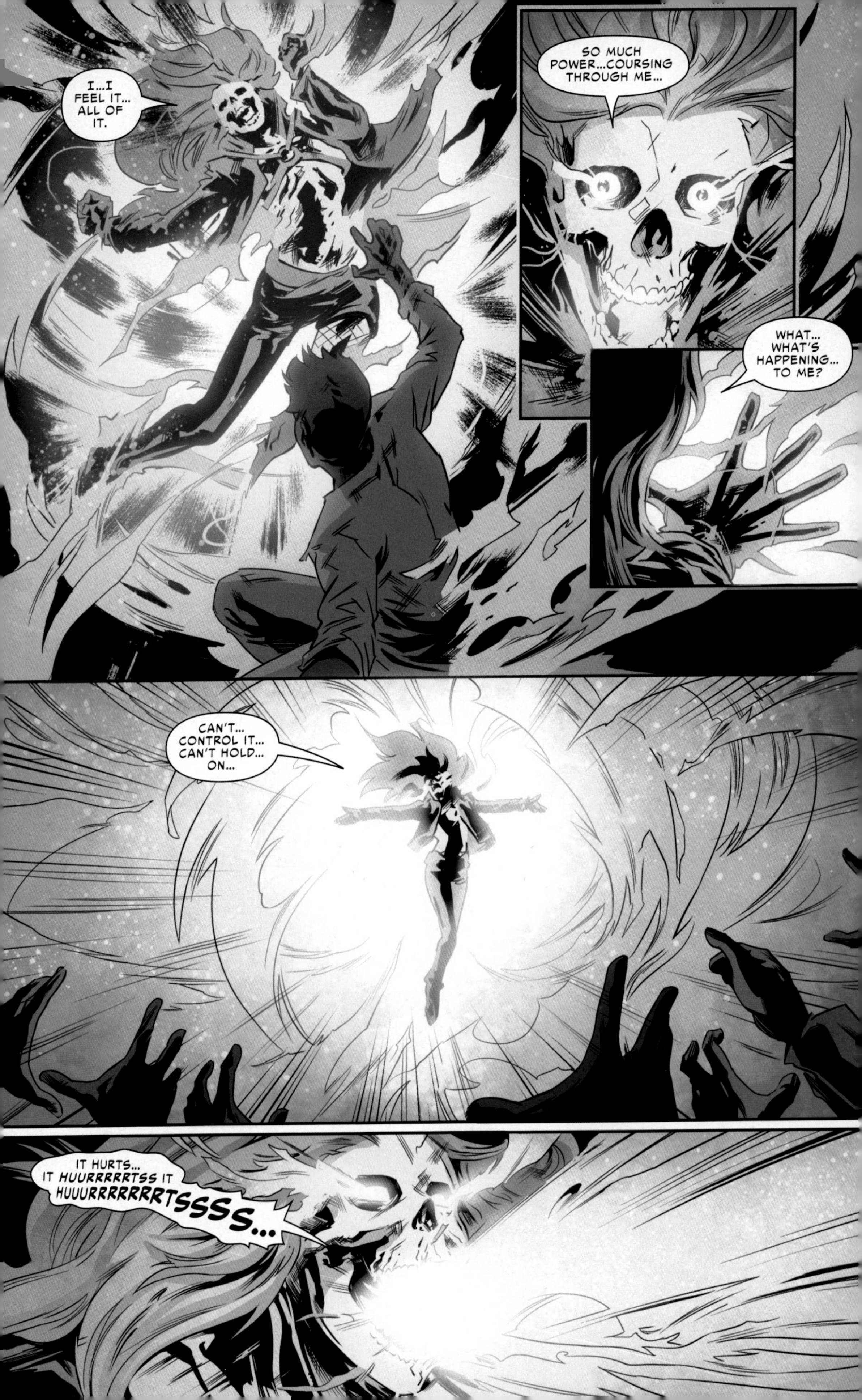
I...I FEEL IT... ALL OF IT.
SO MUCH POWER...COURSING THROUGH ME...
WHAT... WHAT'S HAPPENING... TO ME?
CAN'T... CONTROL IT... CAN'T HOLD... ON...
IT HURTS... IT HUURRRRRTSS IT HUUURRRRRRRTSSSS...

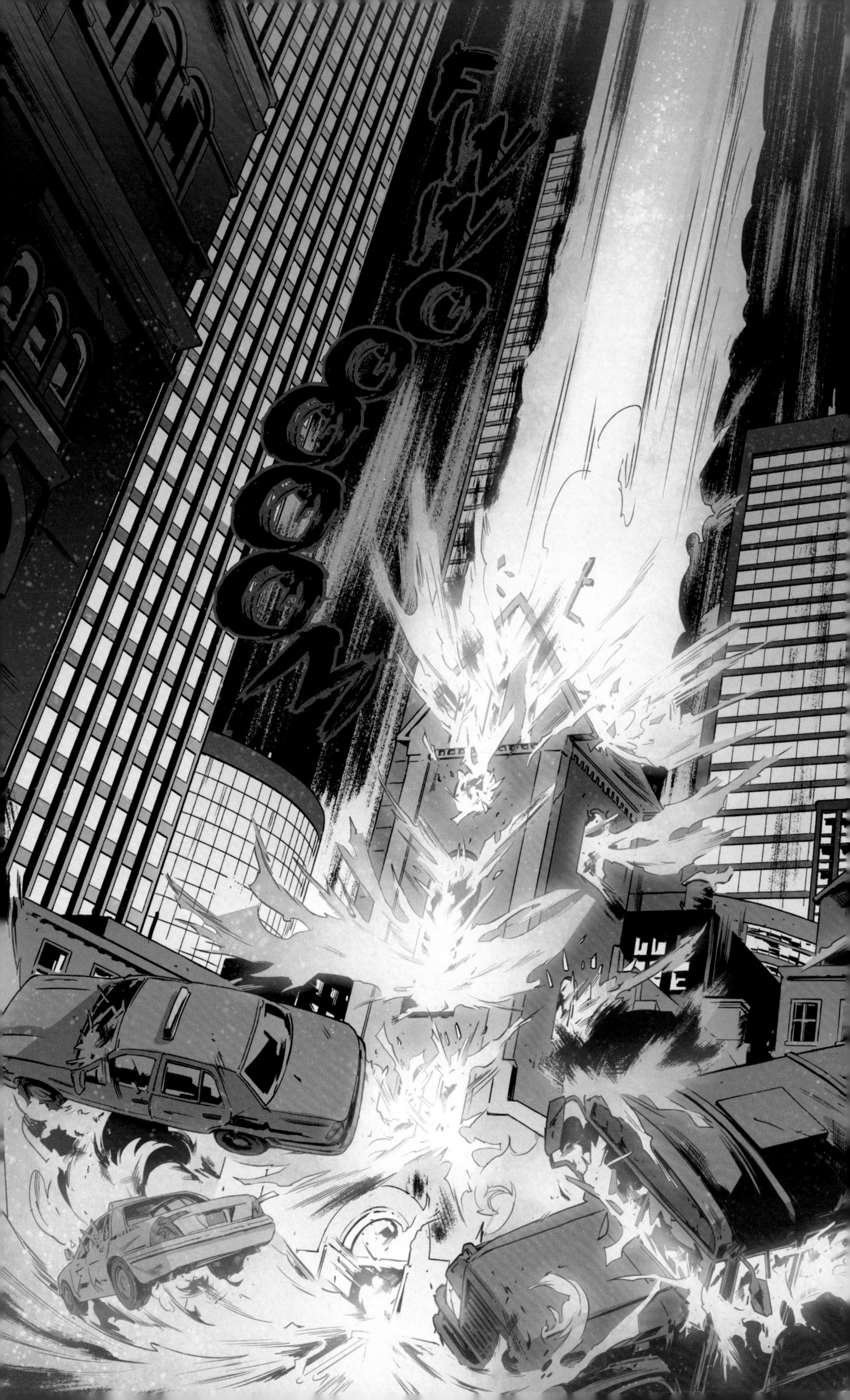
FWOOOOOM

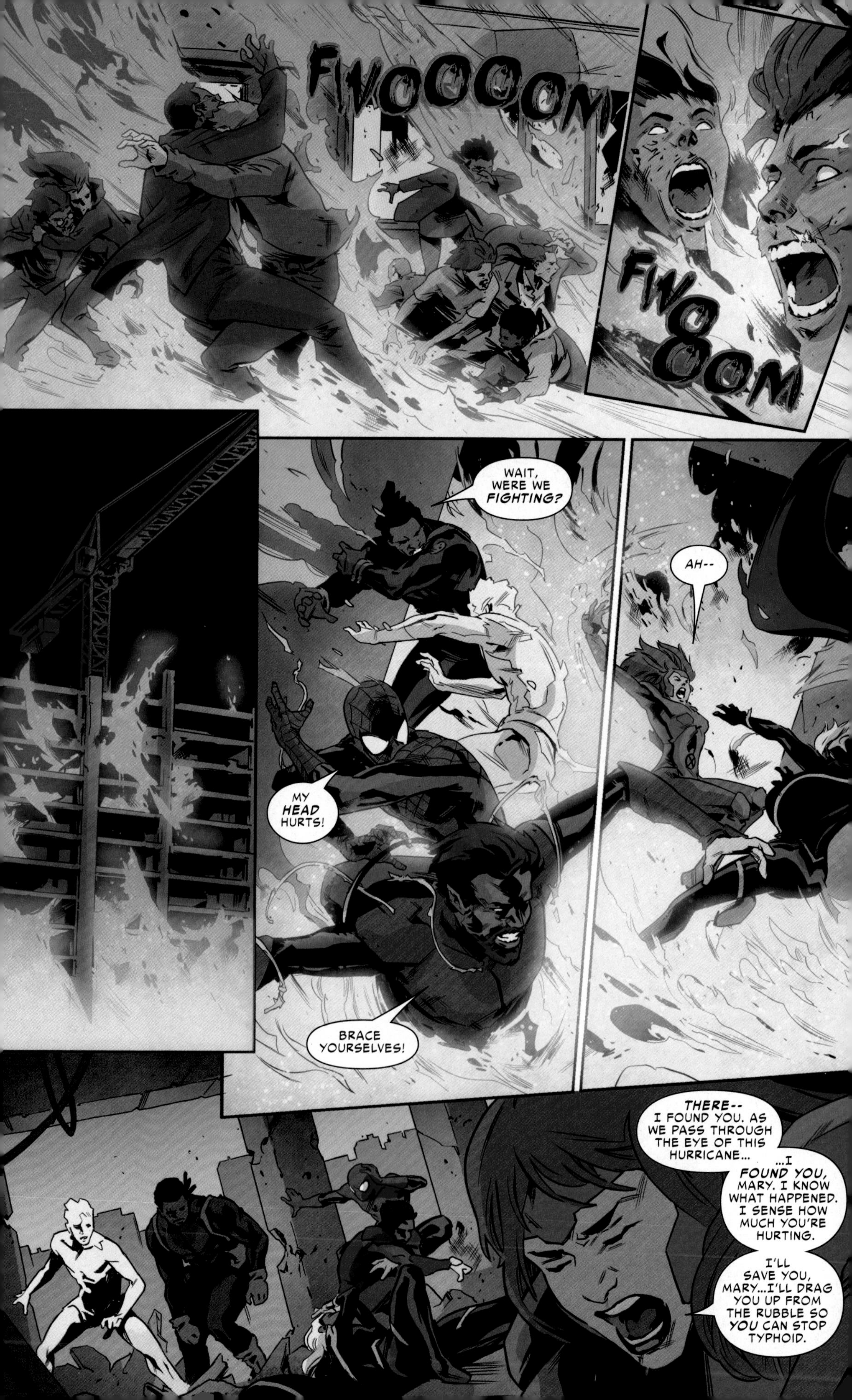
FWOOOOOM
FWOOOM
WAIT, WERE WE FIGHTING?
MY HEAD HURTS!
BRACE YOURSELVES!
AH--
THERE-- I FOUND YOU. AS WE PASS THROUGH THE EYE OF THIS HURRICANE...
...I FOUND YOU, MARY. I KNOW WHAT HAPPENED. I SENSE HOW MUCH YOU'RE HURTING.
I'LL SAVE YOU, MARY...I'LL DRAG YOU UP FROM THE RUBBLE SO YOU CAN STOP TYPHOID.

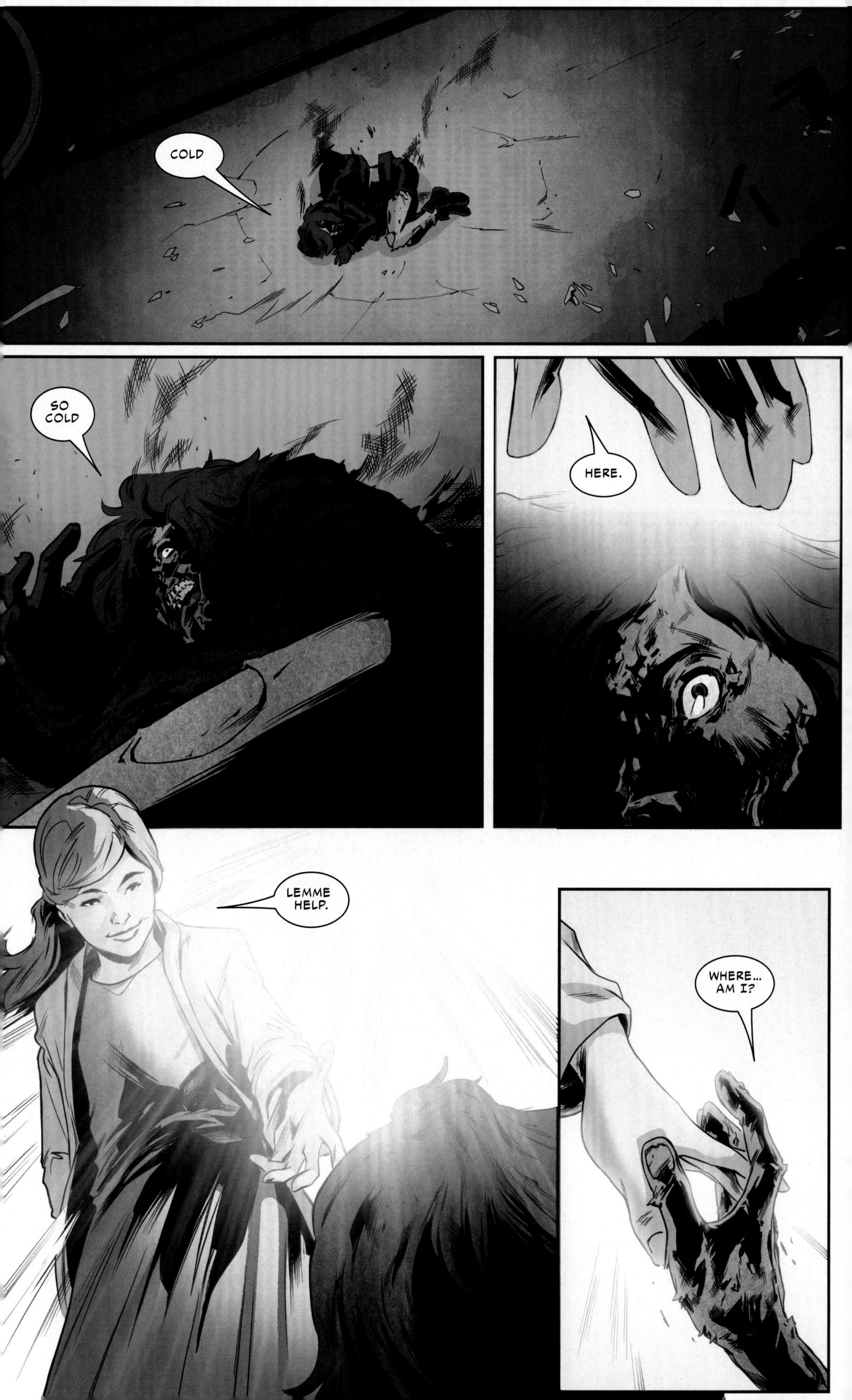
COLD
SO COLD
HERE.
LEMME HELP.
WHERE... AM I?

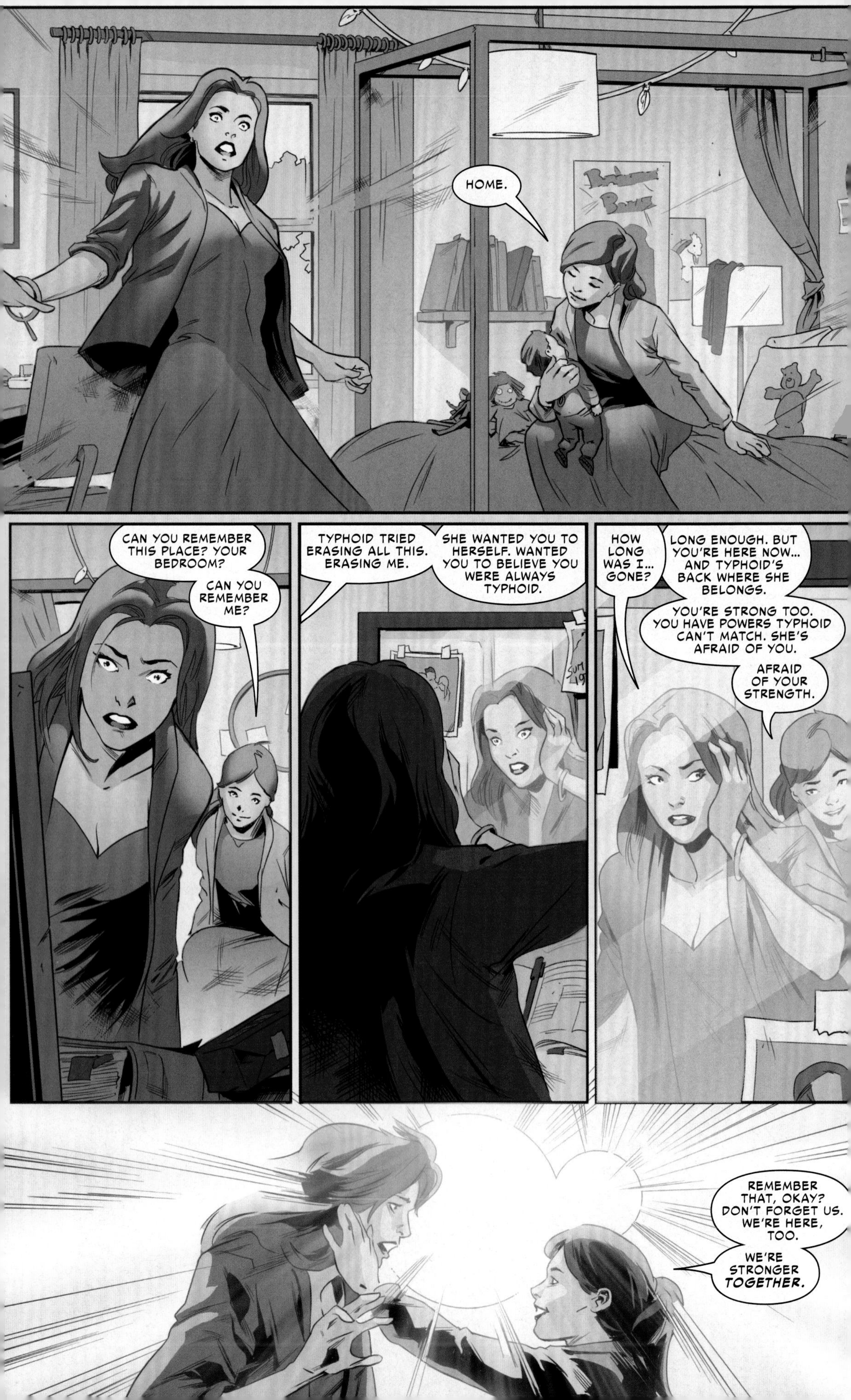
HOME.
CAN YOU REMEMBER THIS PLACE? YOUR BEDROOM?
CAN YOU REMEMBER ME?
TYPHOID TRIED ERASING ALL THIS. ERASING ME.
SHE WANTED YOU TO HERSELF. WANTED YOU TO BELIEVE YOU WERE ALWAYS TYPHOID.
HOW LONG WAS I... GONE?
LONG ENOUGH. BUT YOU'RE HERE NOW... AND TYPHOID'S BACK WHERE SHE BELONGS.
YOU'RE STRONG TOO. YOU HAVE POWERS TYPHOID CAN'T MATCH. SHE'S AFRAID OF YOU.
AFRAID OF YOUR STRENGTH.
REMEMBER THAT, OKAY? DON'T FORGET US. WE'RE HERE, TOO.
WE'RE STRONGER *TOGETHER*.

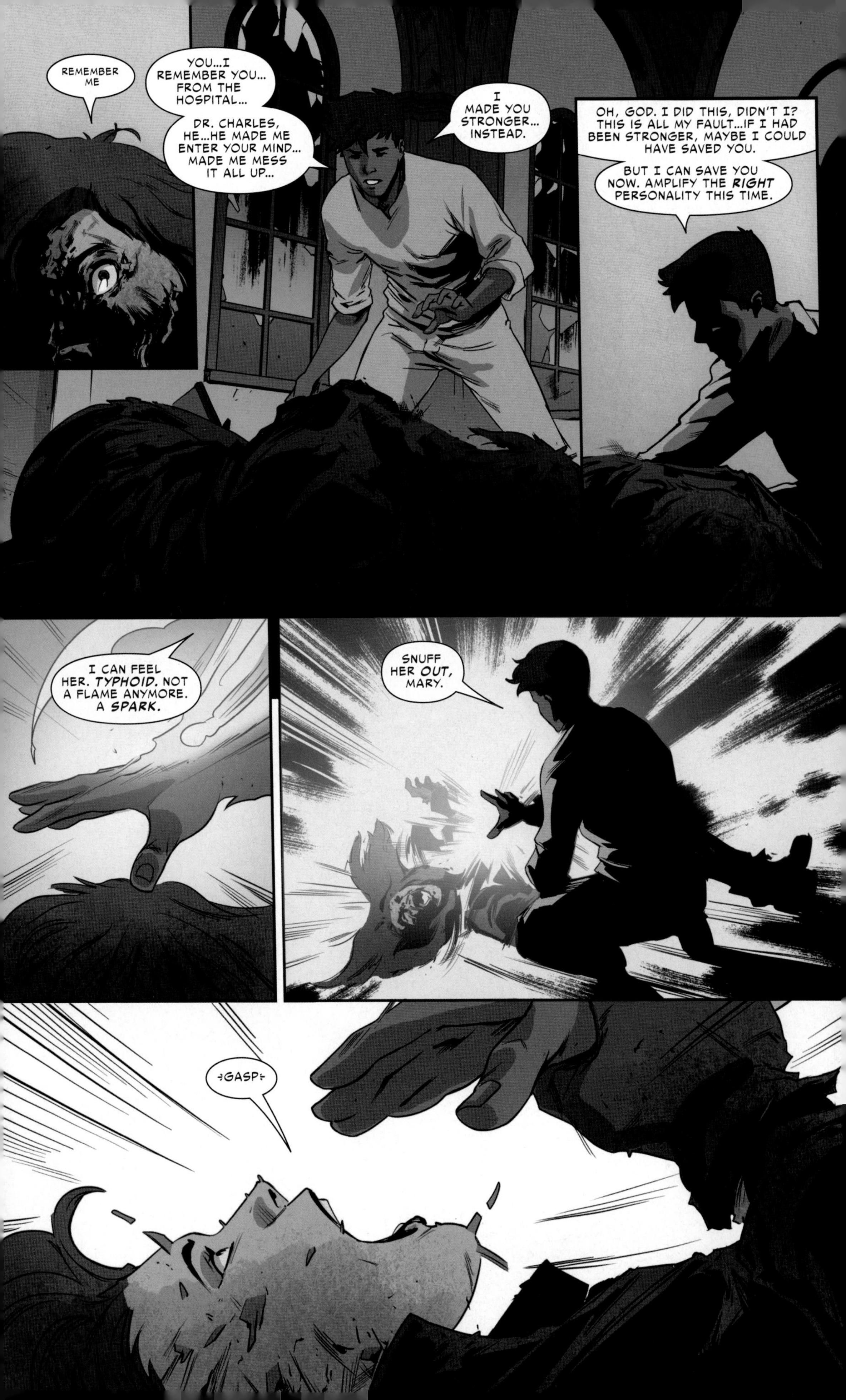
REMEMBER ME
YOU...I REMEMBER YOU... FROM THE HOSPITAL...
DR. CHARLES, HE...HE MADE ME ENTER YOUR MIND... MADE ME MESS IT ALL UP...
I MADE YOU STRONGER... INSTEAD.
OH, GOD. I DID THIS, DIDN'T I? THIS IS ALL MY FAULT...IF I HAD BEEN STRONGER, MAYBE I COULD HAVE SAVED YOU.
BUT I CAN SAVE YOU NOW. AMPLIFY THE *RIGHT* PERSONALITY THIS TIME.
I CAN FEEL HER. *TYPHOID.* NOT A FLAME ANYMORE. A *SPARK.*
SNUFF HER *OUT,* MARY.
GASP

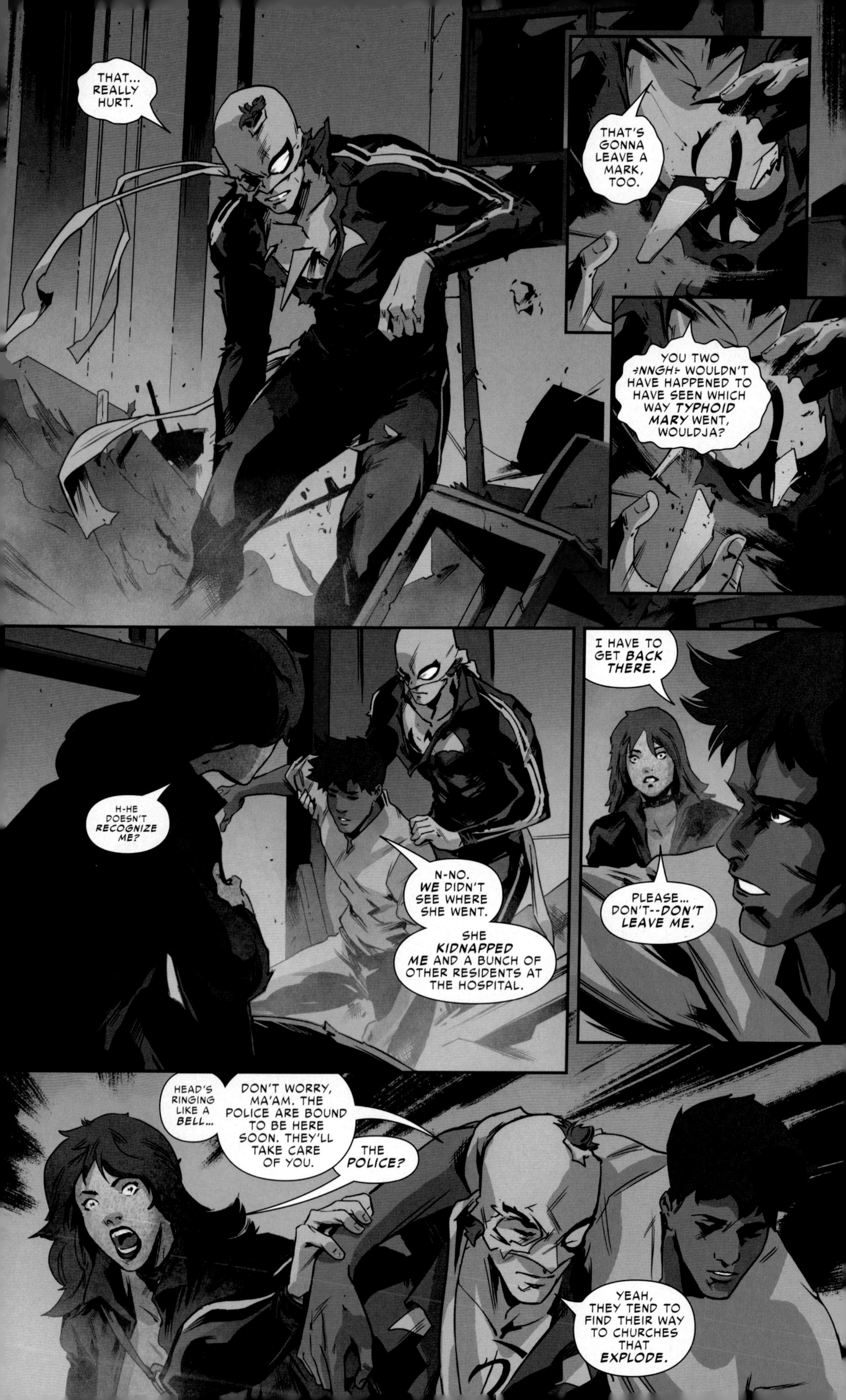

THAT... REALLY HURT.
THAT'S GONNA LEAVE A MARK, TOO.
YOU TWO -NNGH- WOULDN'T HAVE HAPPENED TO HAVE SEEN WHICH WAY TYPHOID MARY WENT, WOULDJA?
H-HE DOESN'T RECOGNIZE ME?
N-NO. WE DIDN'T SEE WHERE SHE WENT.
SHE KIDNAPPED ME AND A BUNCH OF OTHER RESIDENTS AT THE HOSPITAL.
I HAVE TO GET BACK THERE.
PLEASE... DON'T--DON'T LEAVE ME.
HEAD'S RINGING LIKE A BELL...
DON'T WORRY, MA'AM. THE POLICE ARE BOUND TO BE HERE SOON. THEY'LL TAKE CARE OF YOU.
THE POLICE?
YEAH, THEY TEND TO FIND THEIR WAY TO CHURCHES THAT EXPLODE.

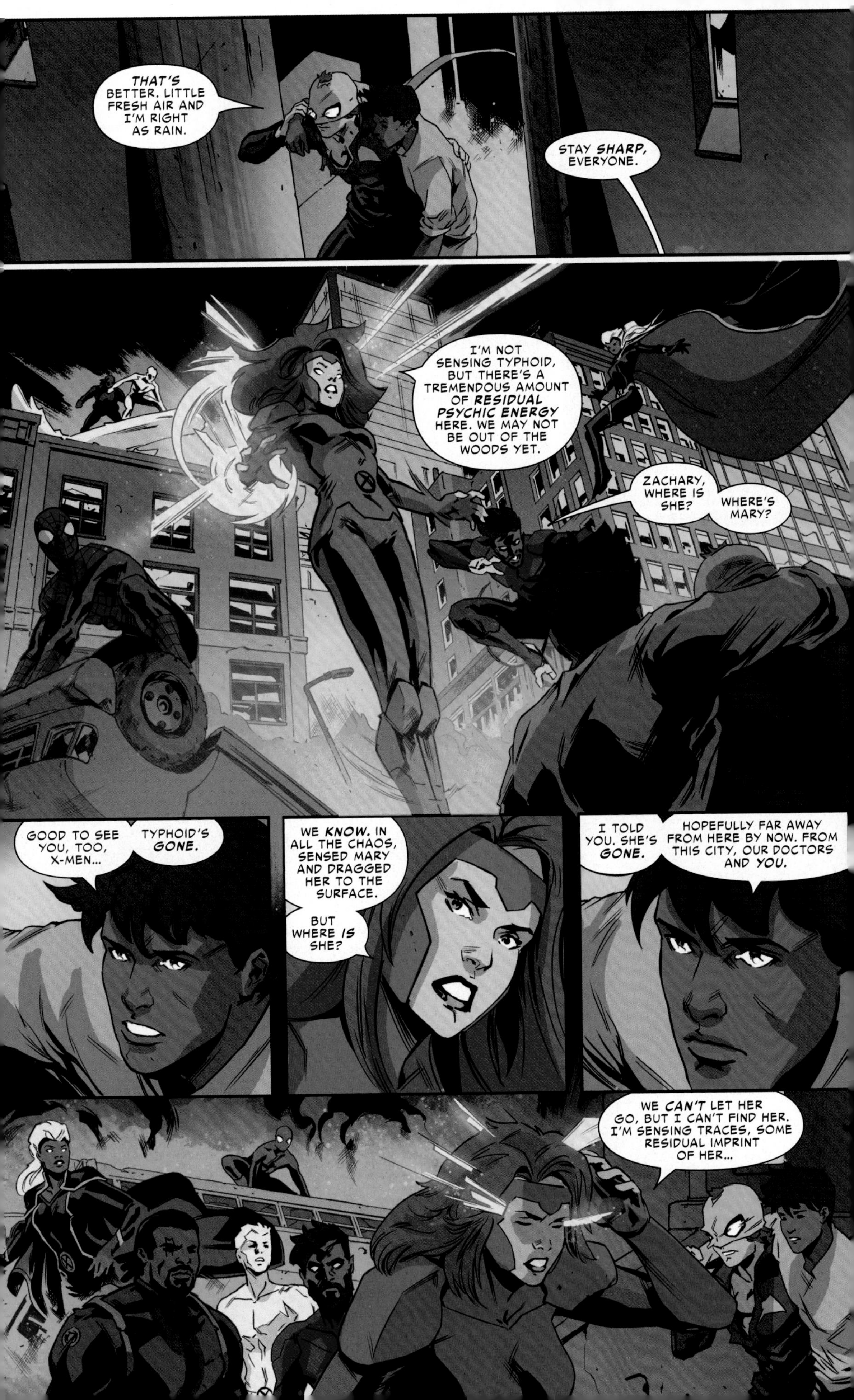

THAT'S BETTER. LITTLE FRESH AIR AND I'M RIGHT AS RAIN.
STAY SHARP, EVERYONE.
I'M NOT SENSING TYPHOID, BUT THERE'S A TREMENDOUS AMOUNT OF RESIDUAL PSYCHIC ENERGY HERE. WE MAY NOT BE OUT OF THE WOODS YET.
ZACHARY, WHERE IS SHE?
WHERE'S MARY?
GOOD TO SEE YOU, TOO, X-MEN...
TYPHOID'S GONE.
WE KNOW. IN ALL THE CHAOS, SENSED MARY AND DRAGGED HER TO THE SURFACE.
BUT WHERE IS SHE?
I TOLD YOU. SHE'S GONE.
HOPEFULLY FAR AWAY FROM HERE BY NOW. FROM THIS CITY, OUR DOCTORS AND YOU.
WE CAN'T LET HER GO, BUT I CAN'T FIND HER. I'M SENSING TRACES, SOME RESIDUAL IMPRINT OF HER...

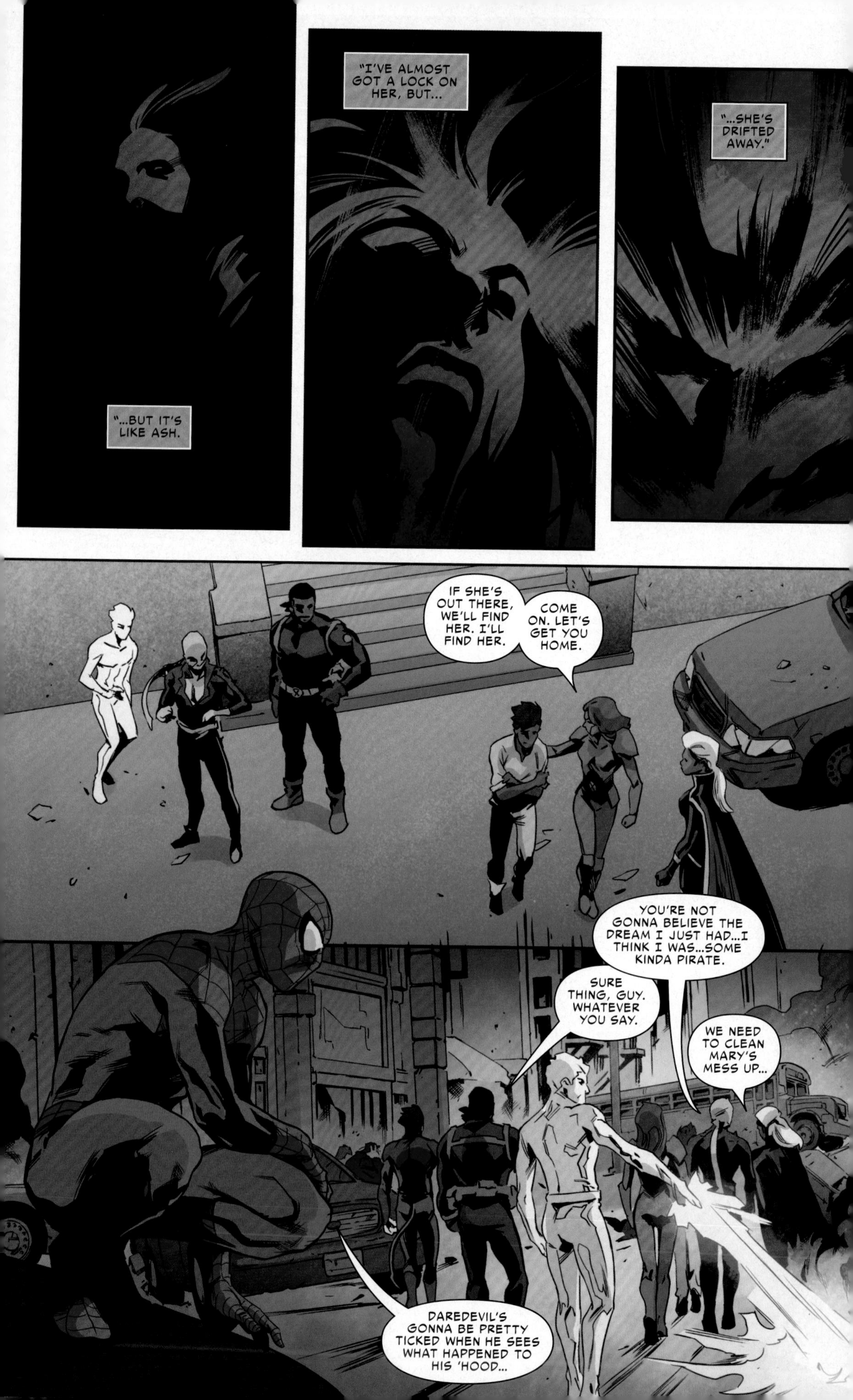

"...BUT IT'S LIKE ASH.
"I'VE ALMOST GOT A LOCK ON HER, BUT...
"...SHE'S DRIFTED AWAY."
IF SHE'S OUT THERE, WE'LL FIND HER. I'LL FIND HER.
COME ON. LET'S GET YOU HOME.
YOU'RE NOT GONNA BELIEVE THE DREAM I JUST HAD...I THINK I WAS...SOME KINDA PIRATE.
SURE THING, GUY. WHATEVER YOU SAY.
WE NEED TO CLEAN MARY'S MESS UP...
DAREDEVIL'S GONNA BE PRETTY TICKED WHEN HE SEES WHAT HAPPENED TO HIS 'HOOD...

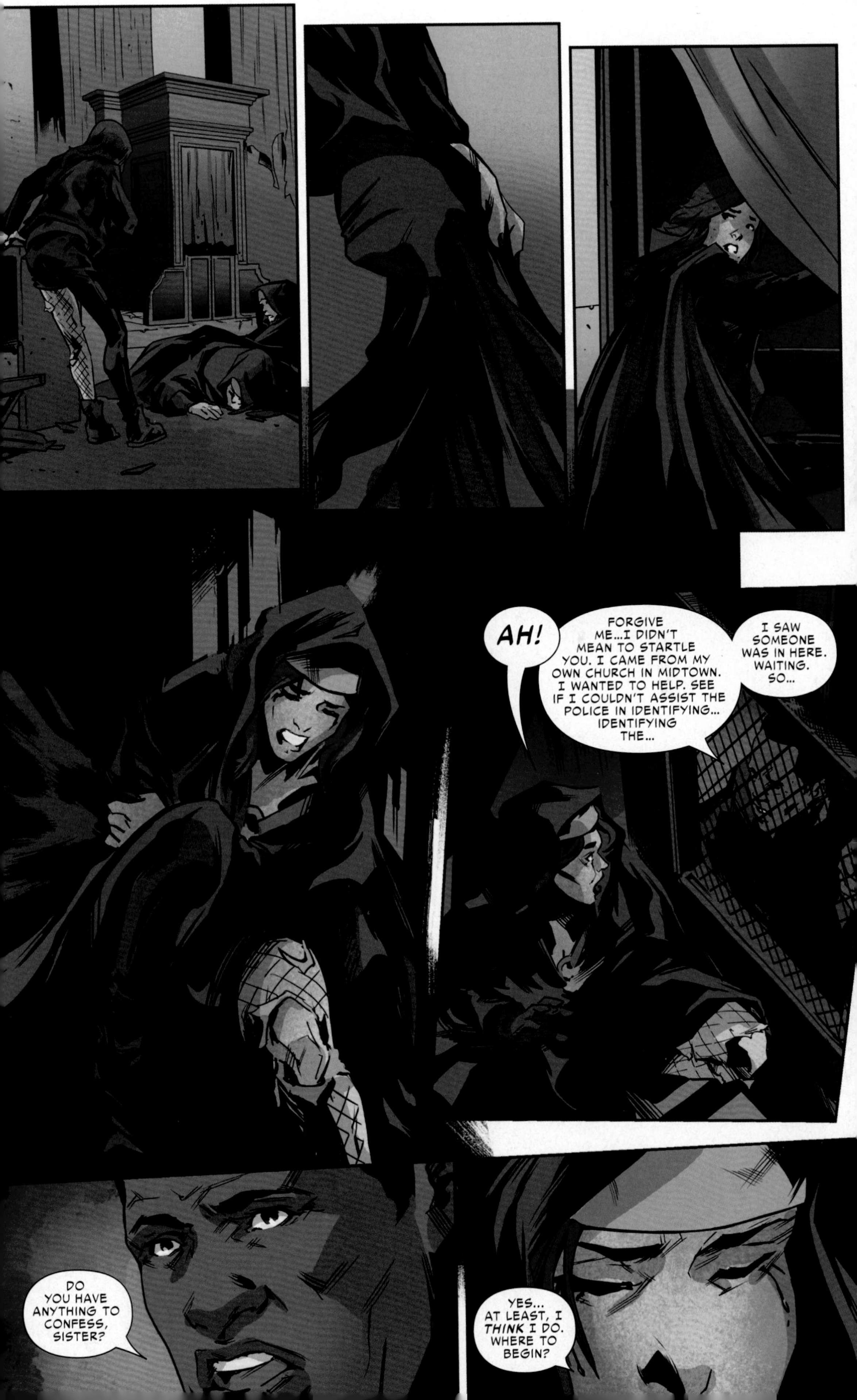
AH!
FORGIVE ME...I DIDN'T MEAN TO STARTLE YOU. I CAME FROM MY OWN CHURCH IN MIDTOWN. I WANTED TO HELP. SEE IF I COULDN'T ASSIST THE POLICE IN IDENTIFYING... IDENTIFYING THE...
I SAW SOMEONE WAS IN HERE. WAITING. SO...
DO YOU HAVE ANYTHING TO CONFESS, SISTER?
YES... AT LEAST, I *THINK* I DO. WHERE TO BEGIN?

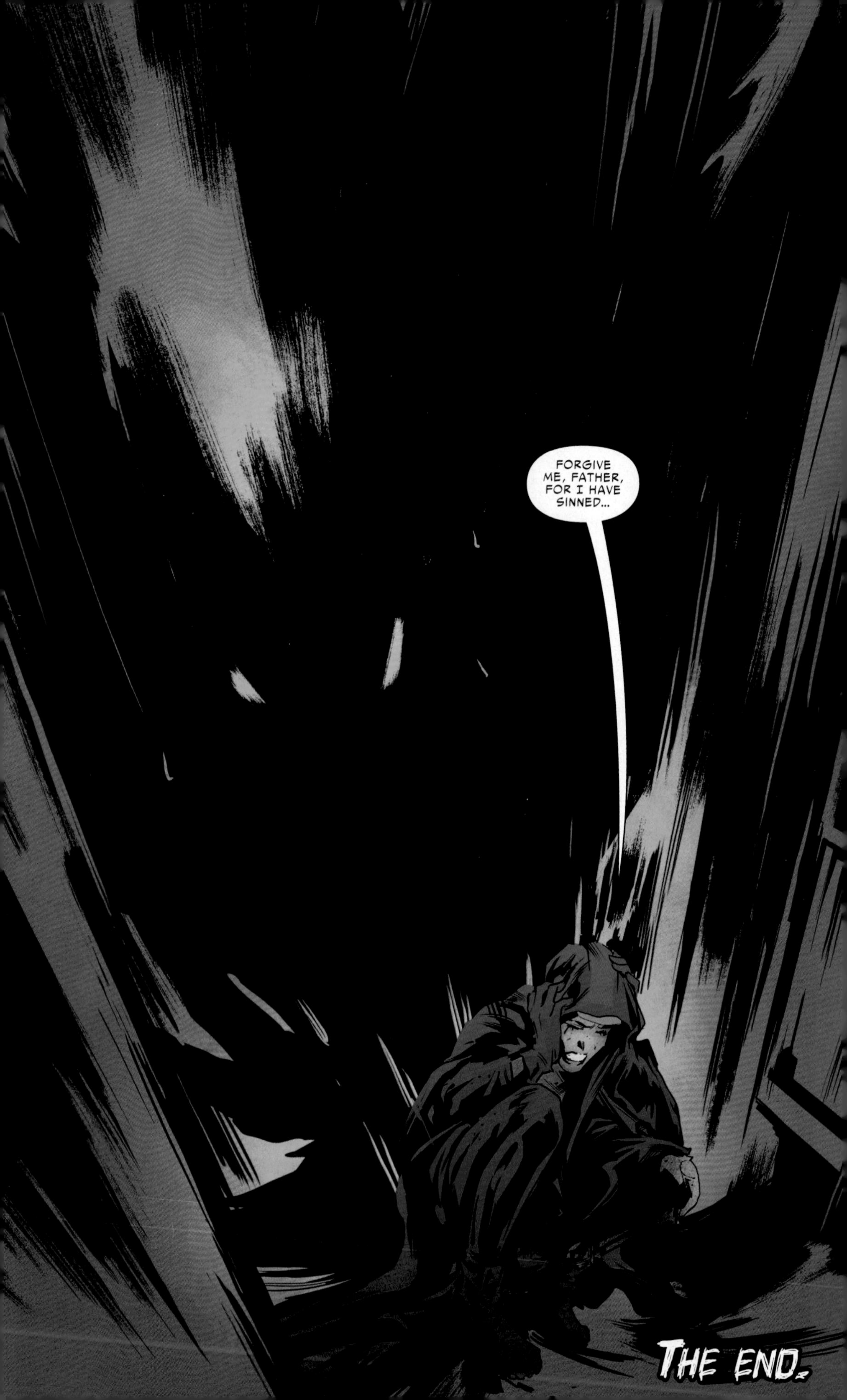
FORGIVE ME, FATHER, FOR I HAVE SINNED...
THE END.

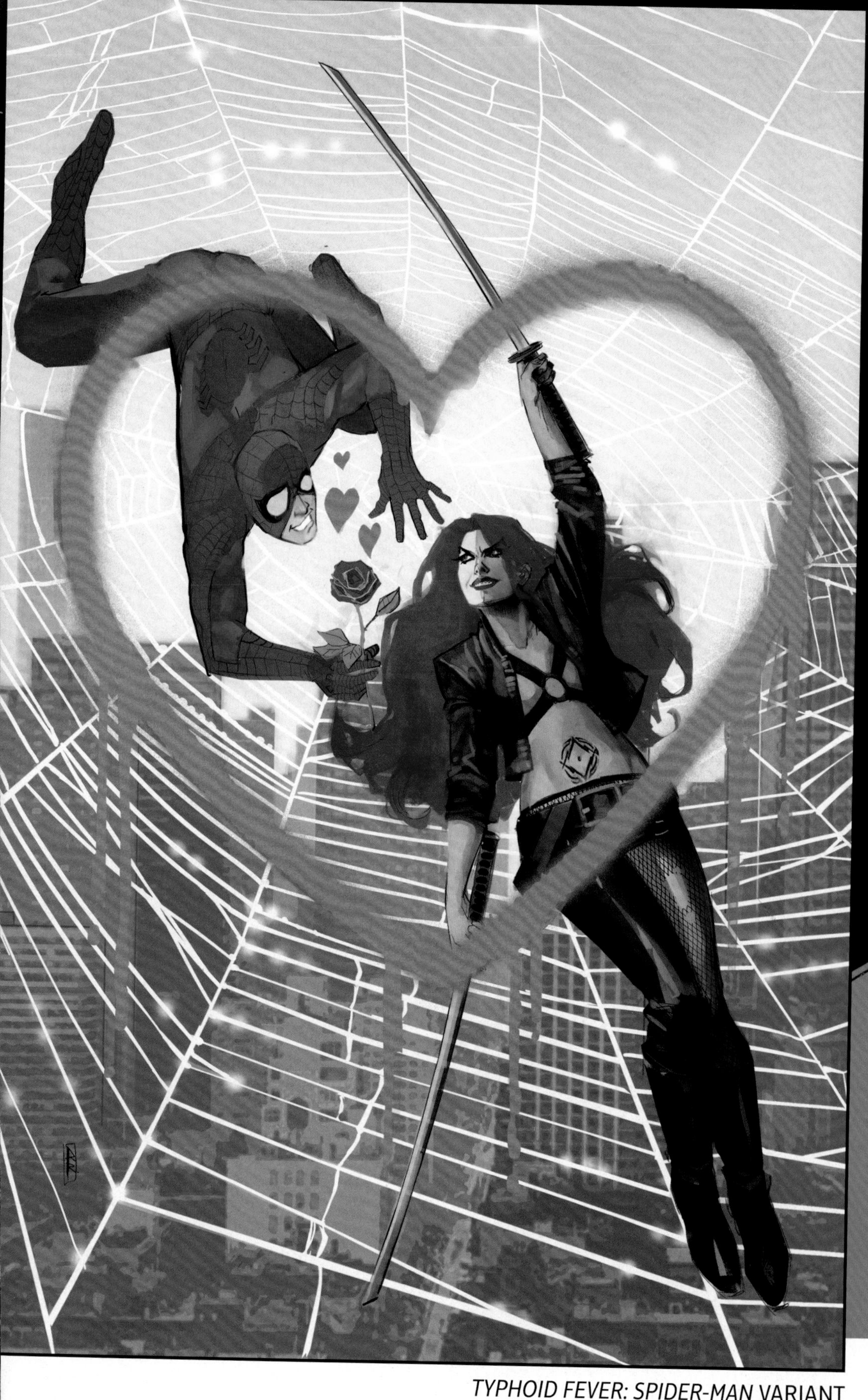

TYPHOID FEVER: SPIDER-MAN VARIANT
BY **ROD REIS**

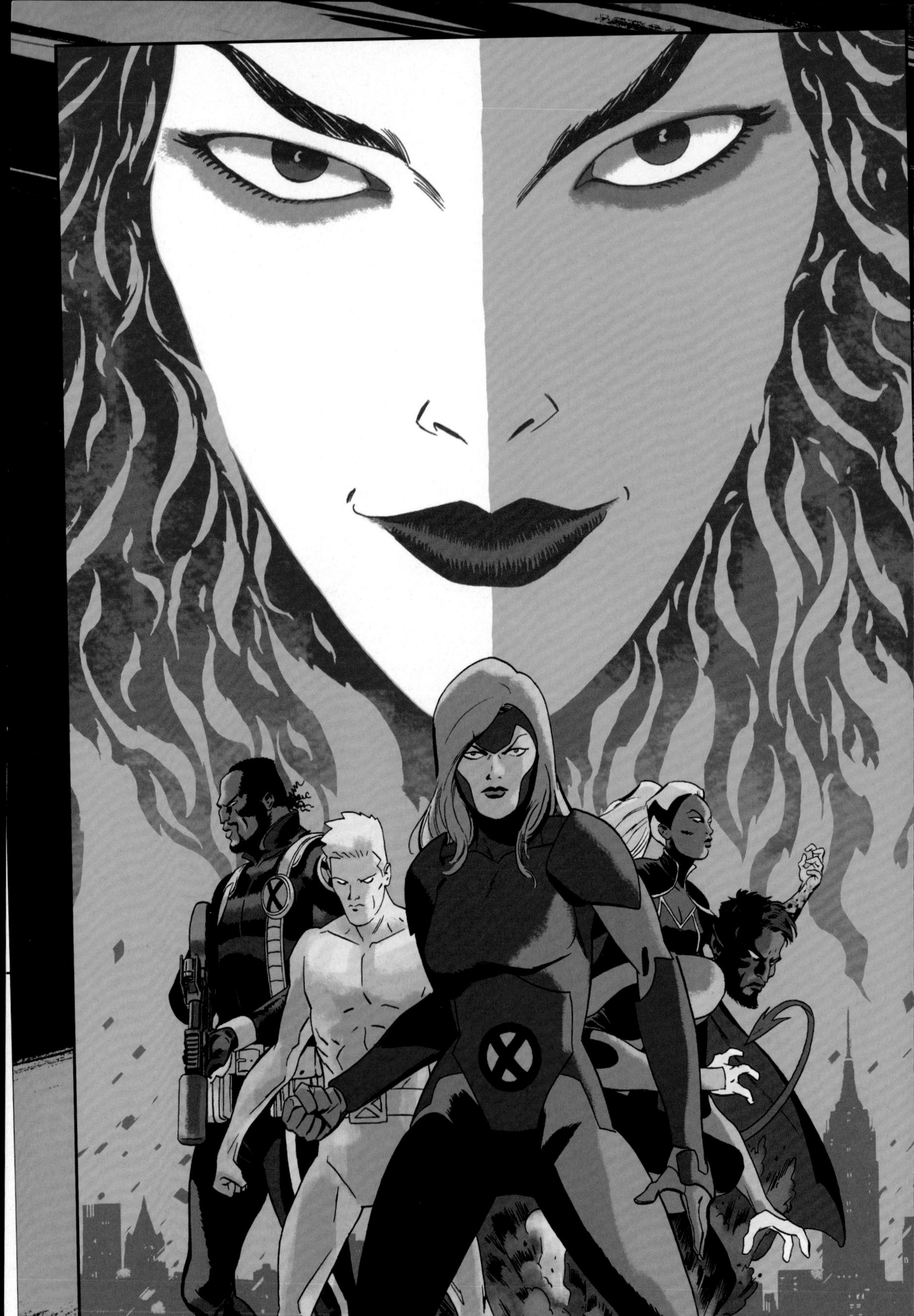

TYPHOID FEVER: X-MEN VARIANT
BY **MARCOS MARTIN**

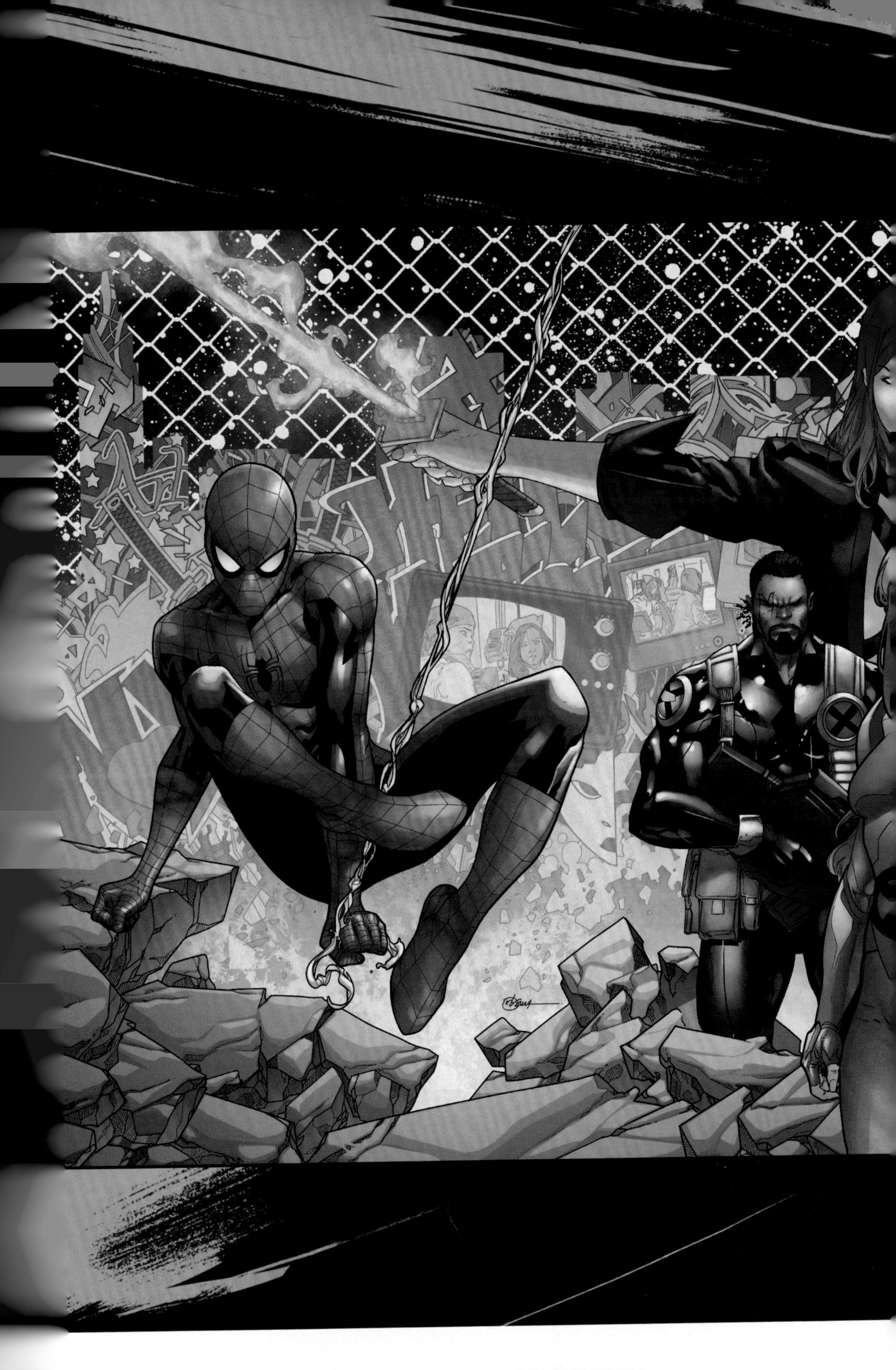

CONNECTING COVERS BY **R.B. SILVA & CHRIS SOTOMAYOR**

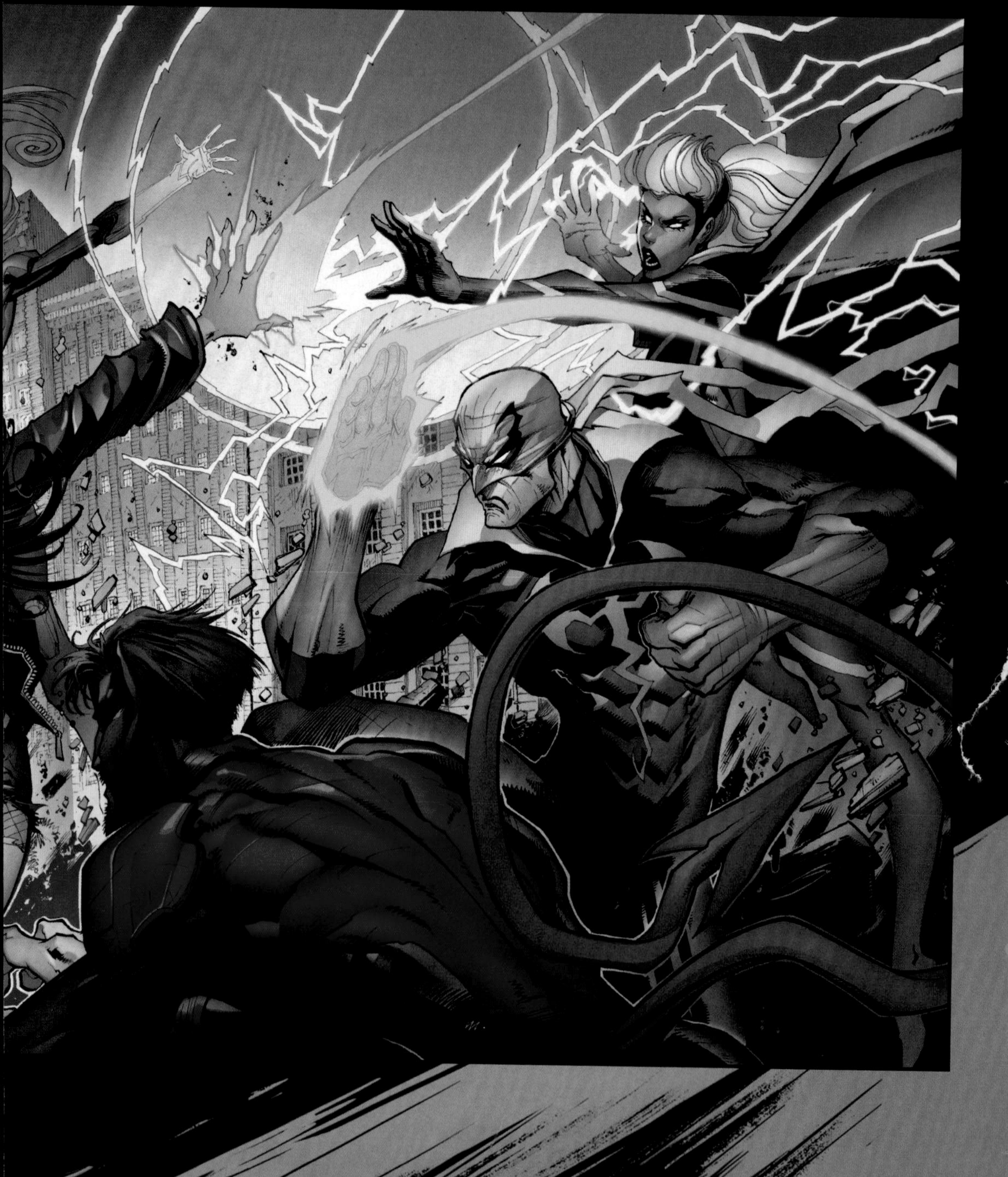

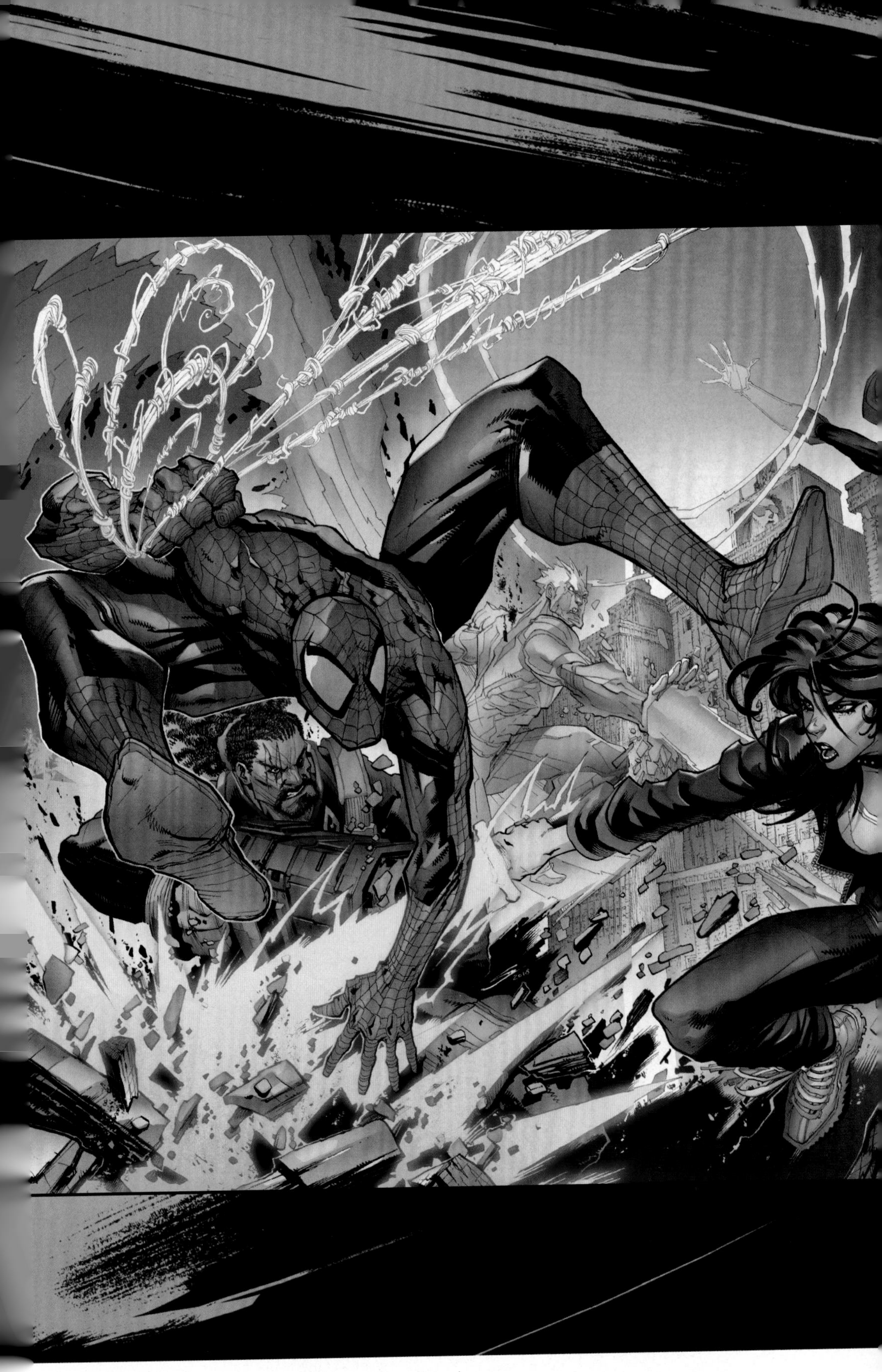

CONNECTING VARIANTS BY **GERARDO SANDOVAL & ERICK ARCINIEGA**

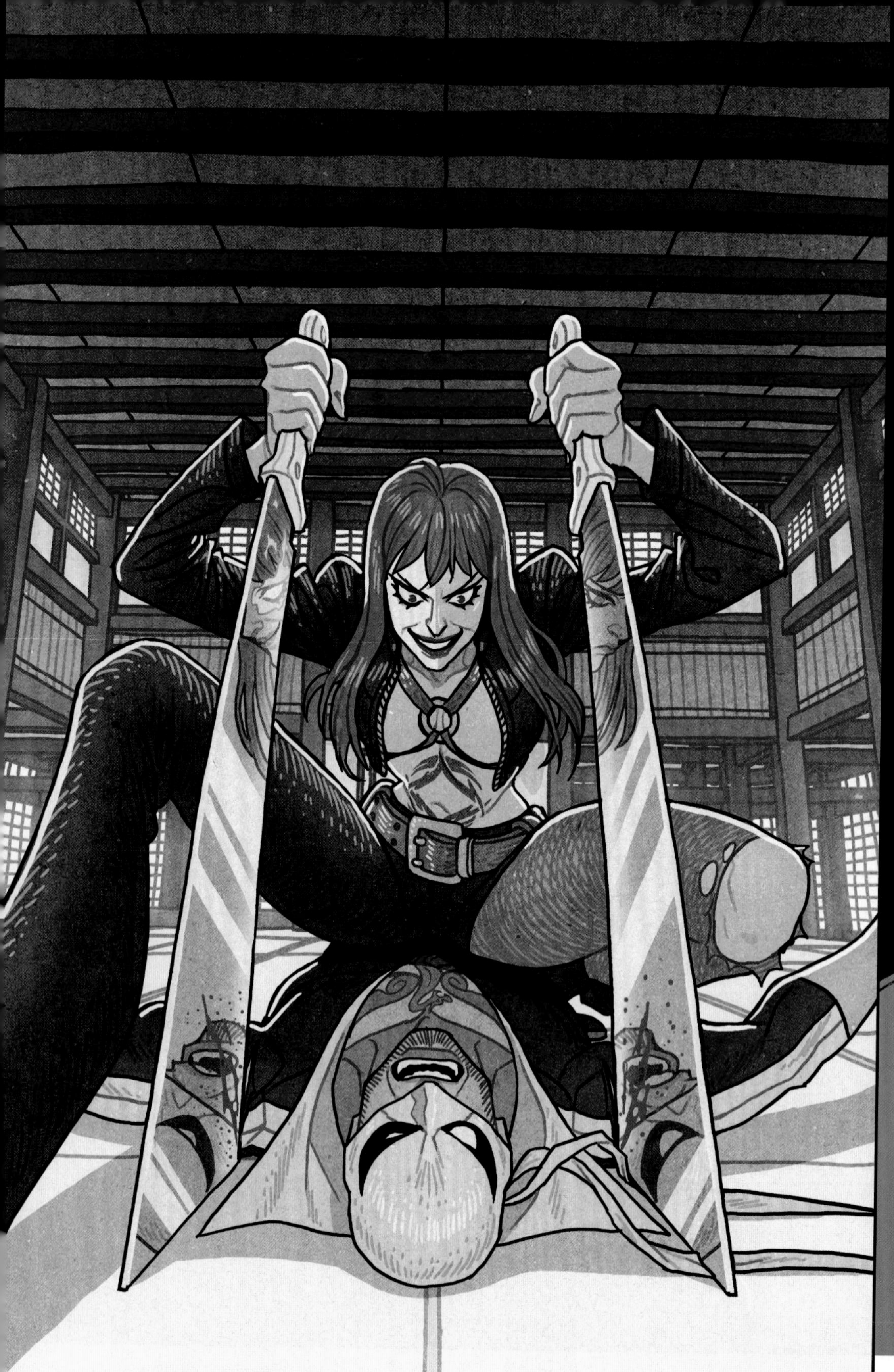

TYPHOID FEVER: IRON FIST VARIANT
BY **AFU CHAN**

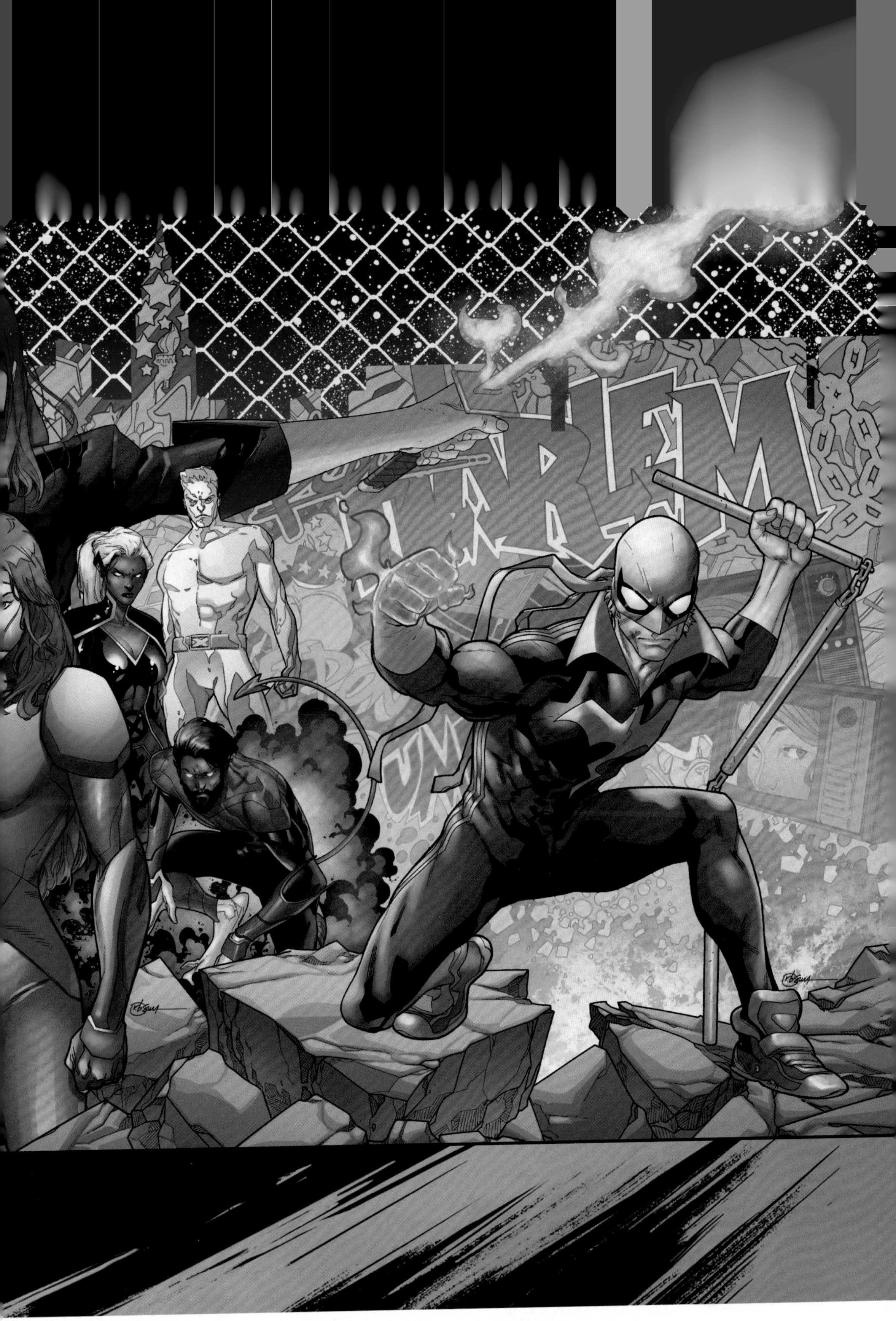

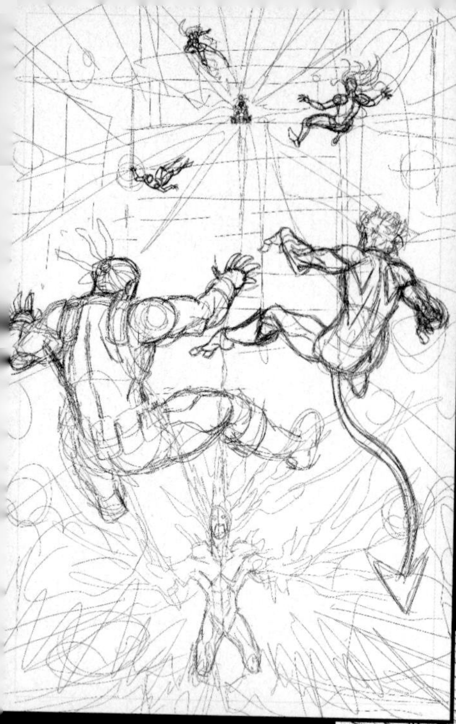

INKS

LAYOUTS

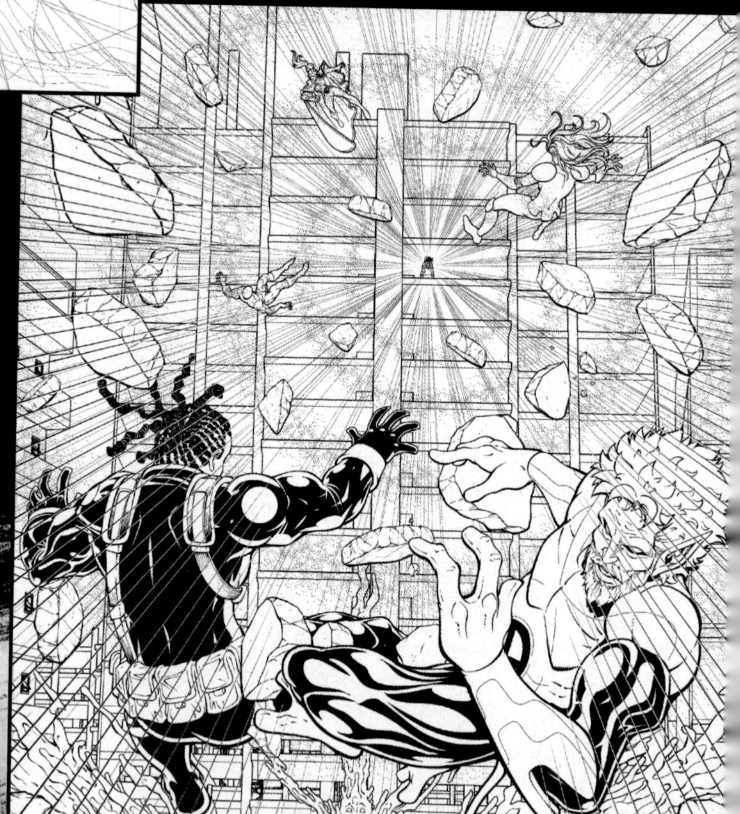

TYPHOID FEVER: X-MEN PAGE 12
ART PROCESS BY **WILL ROBSON**

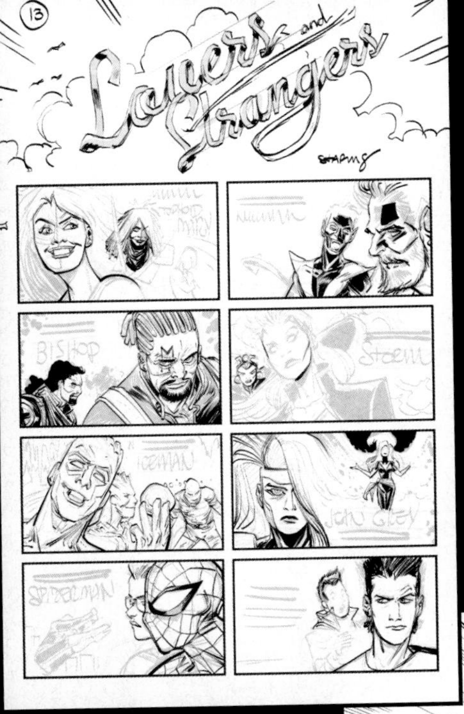
13
Lovers and Strangers
Starring
Bishop
Storm
Iceman
Jean Grey

LAYOUTS

INKS

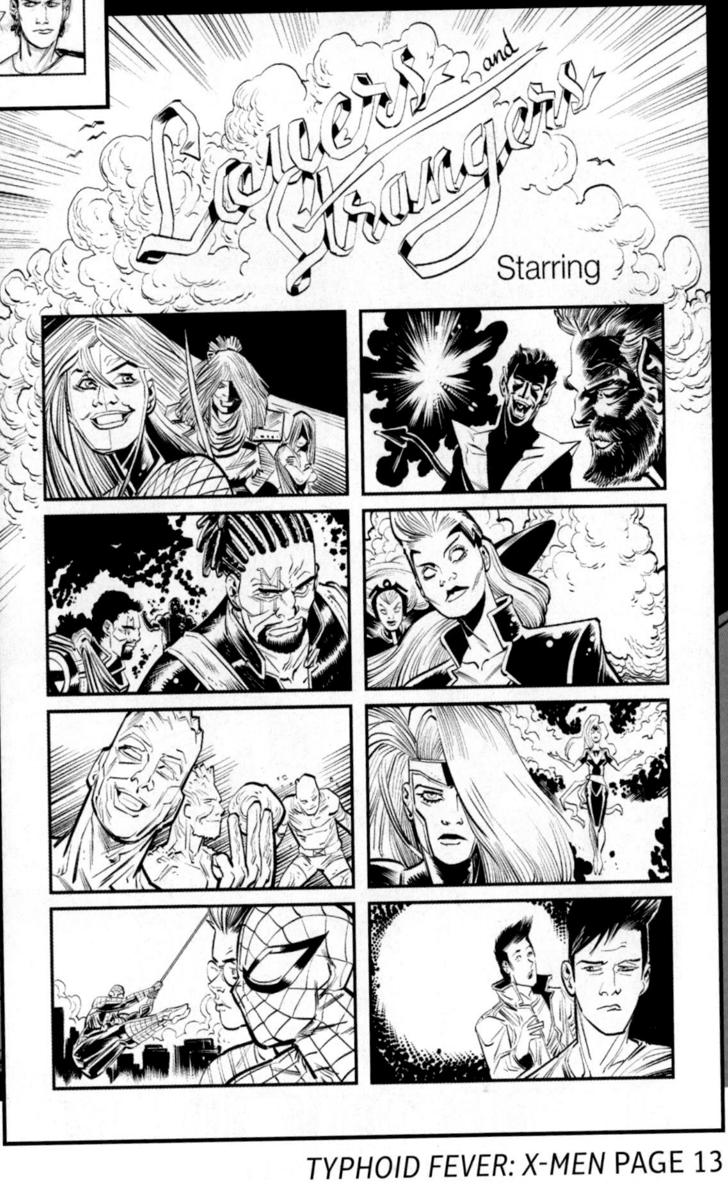
Lovers and Strangers
Starring

TYPHOID FEVER: X-MEN PAGE 13
ART PROCESS BY **DANILO S. BEYRUTH**

LAYOUTS

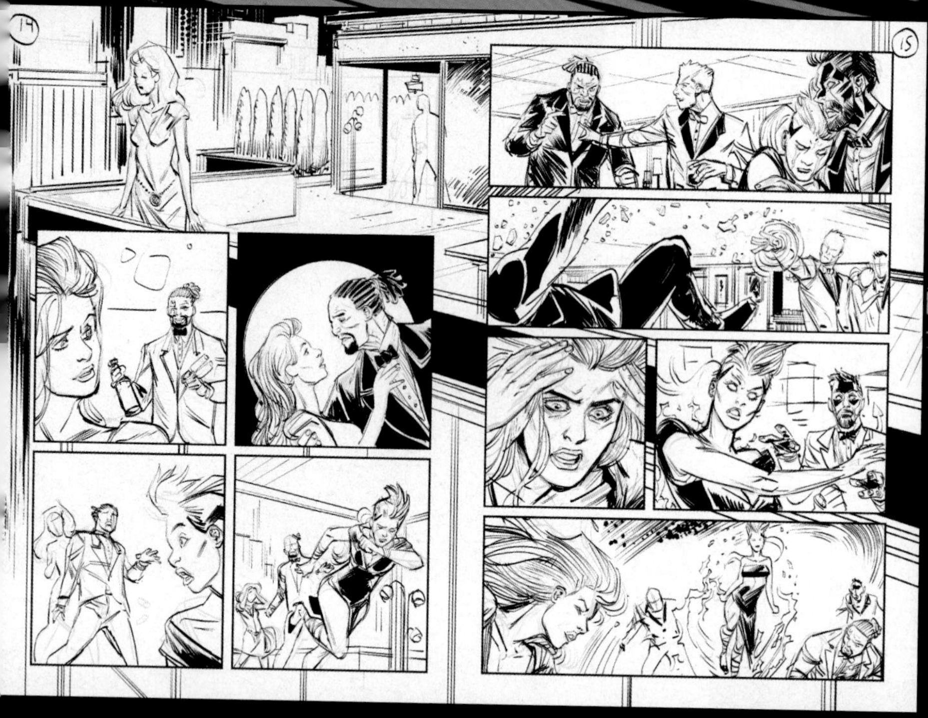

14
15

NKS

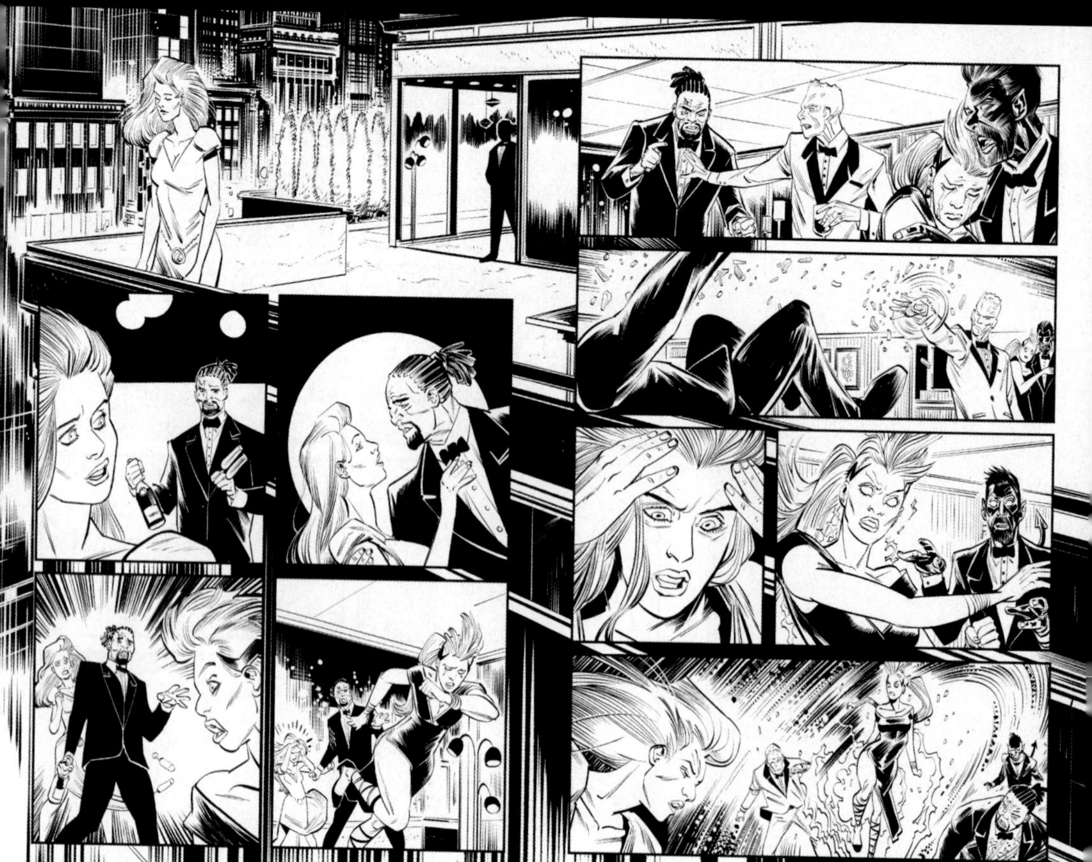

TYPHOID FEVER: X-MEN PAGES 14-15
ART PROCESS BY **DANILO S. BEYRUTH**

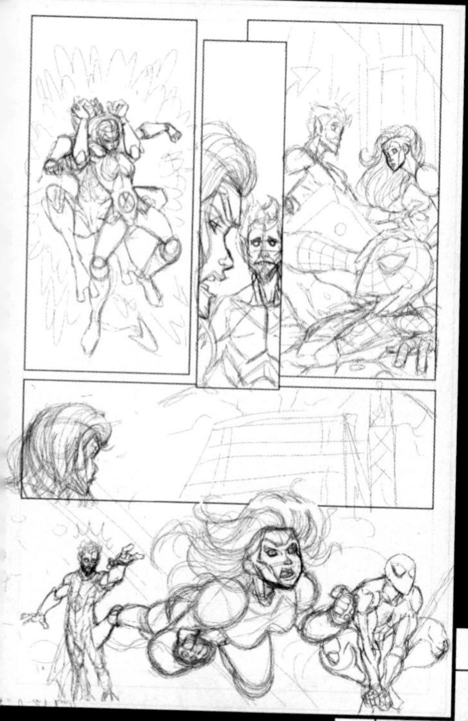

LAYOUTS

INKS

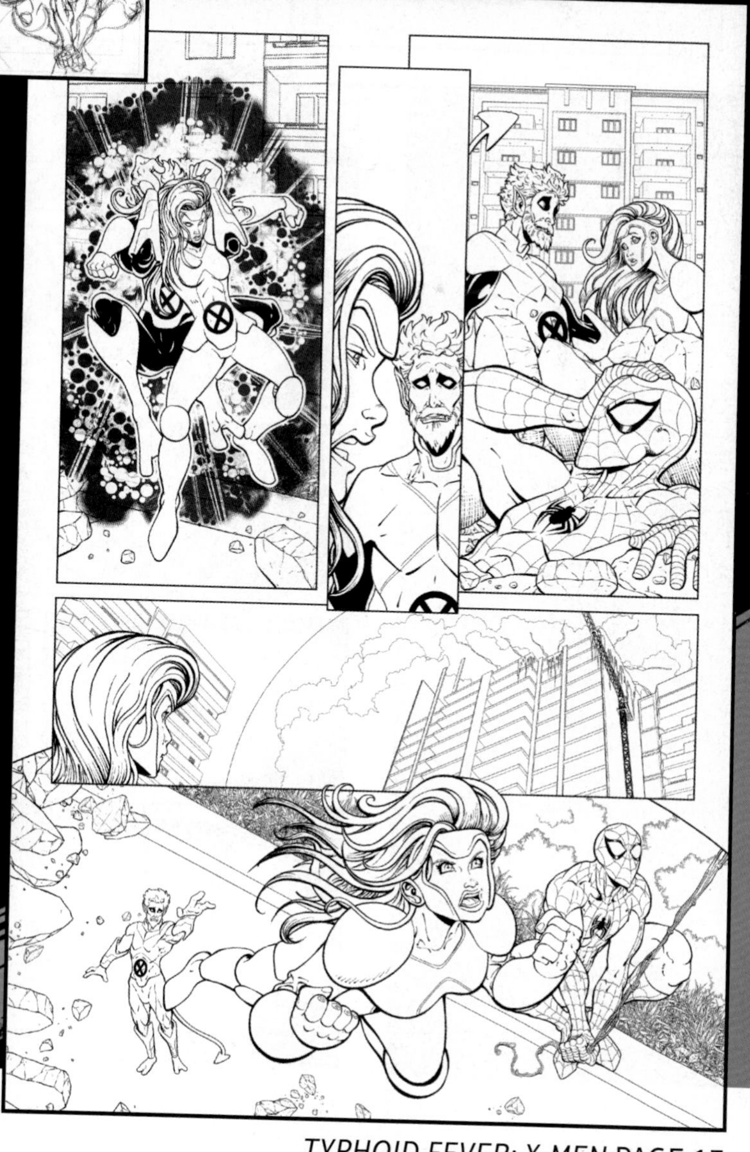

TYPHOID FEVER: X-MEN PAGE 17
ART PROCESS BY **WILL ROBSON**

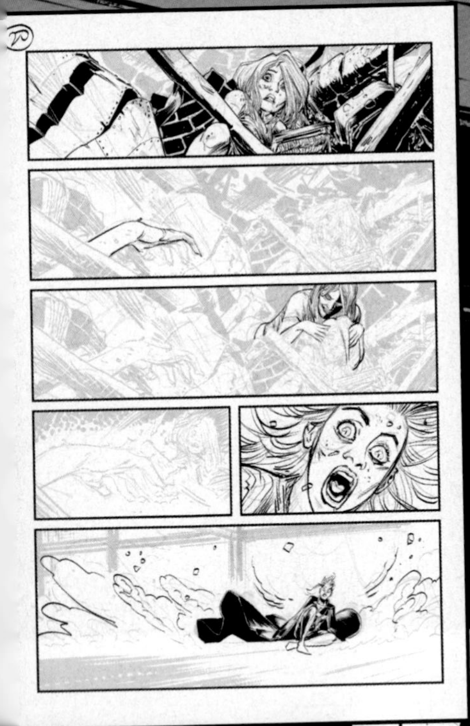

LAYOUTS

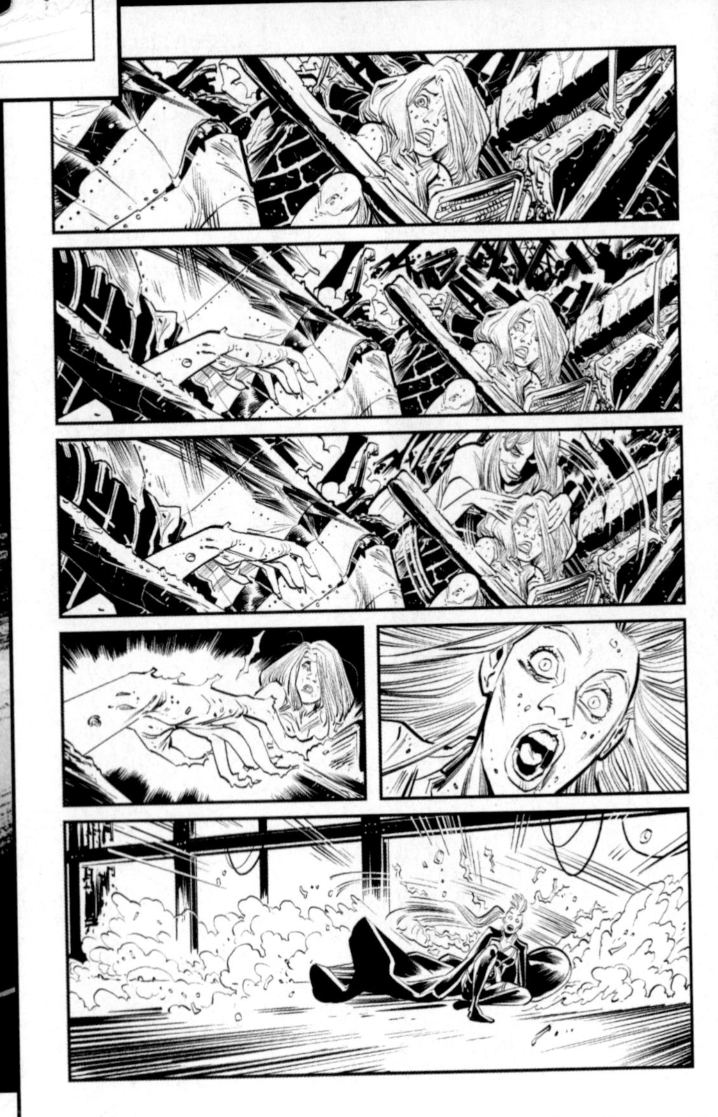

INKS

TYPHOID FEVER: X-MEN PAGE 20
ART PROCESS BY **DANILO S. BEYRUTH**

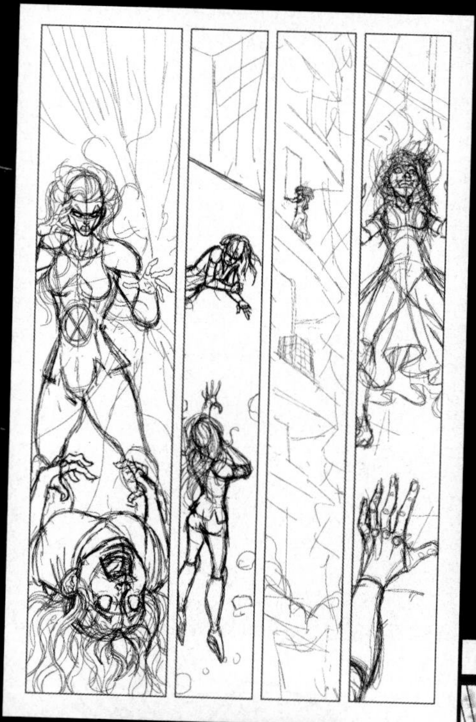

LAYOUTS

INKS

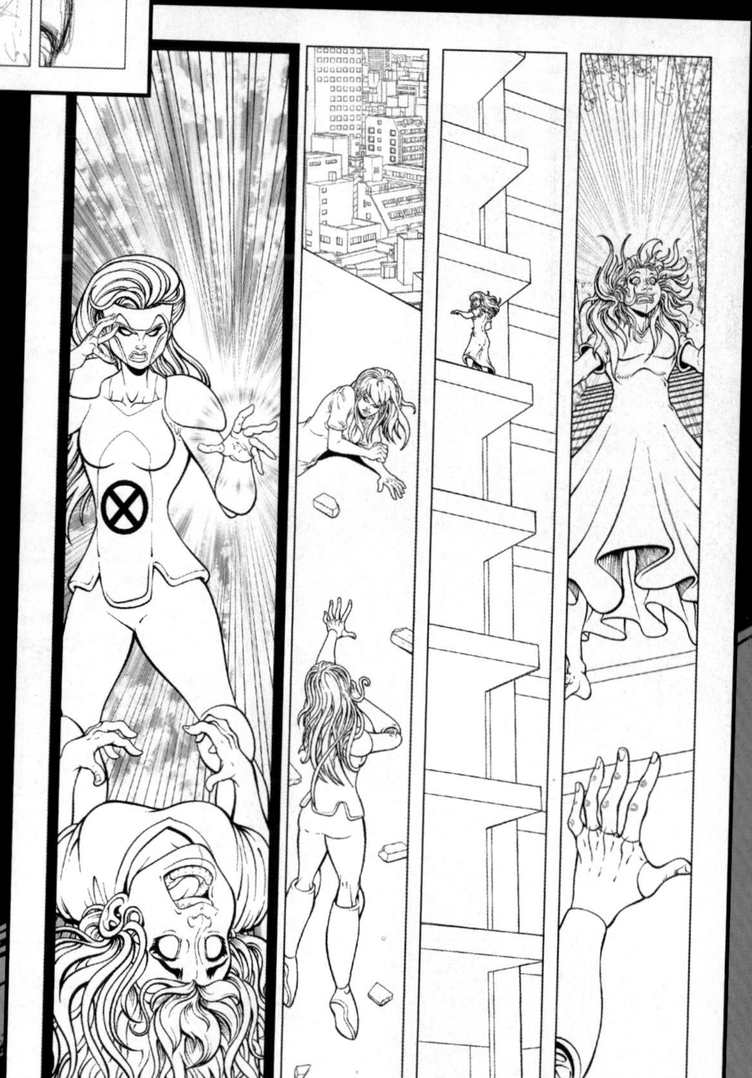

TYPHOID FEVER: X-MEN PAGE 28
ART PROCESS BY **WILL ROBSON**

INKS

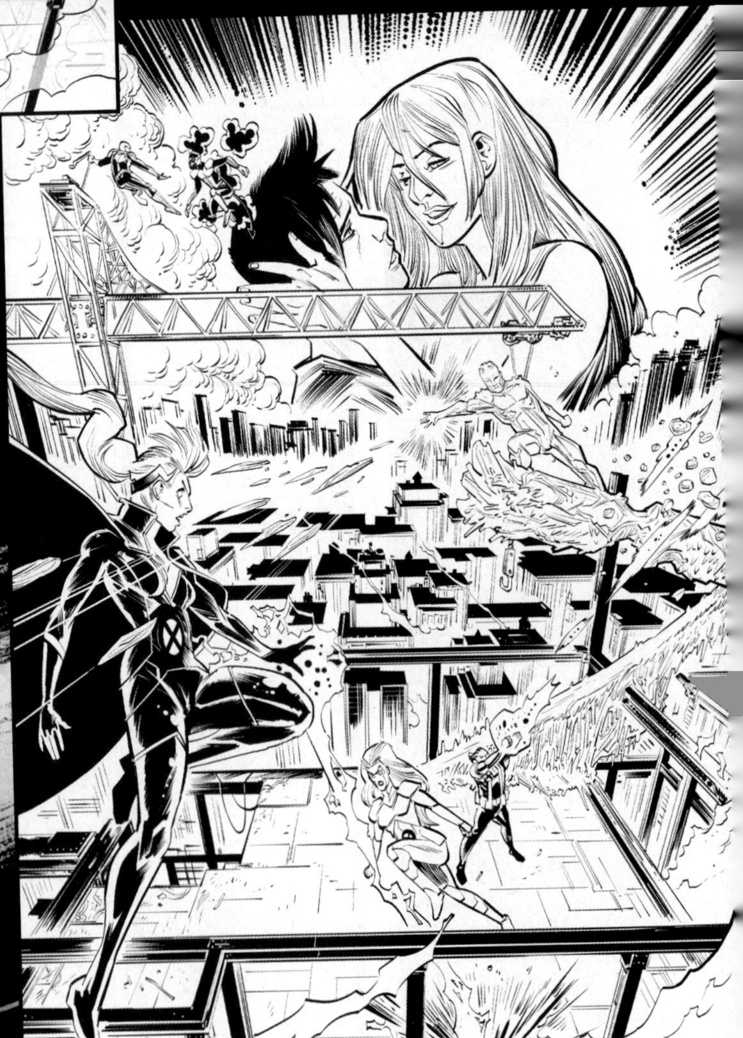

LAYOUTS

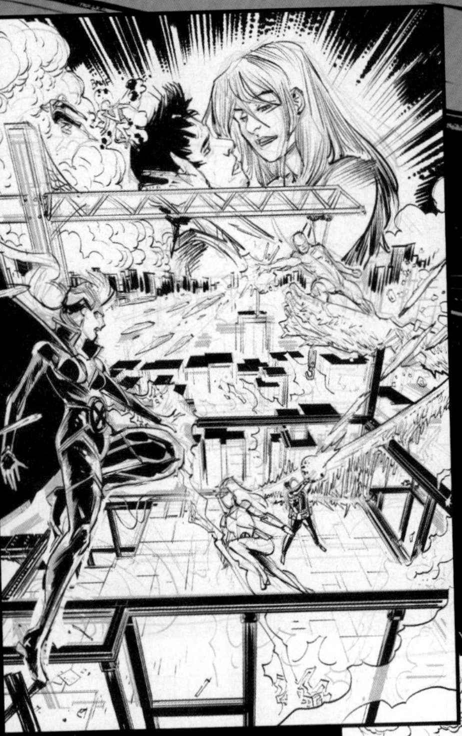

TYPHOID FEVER: X-MEN PAGE 30
ART PROCESS BY **DANILO S. BEYRUTH**